John Yates Beall,
Son of the South

ALSO BY KEN LIZZIO
AND FROM MCFARLAND

*Natchez Eclipse: The Making of French Louisiana
and the Destruction of an Indian Nation* (2026)

John Yates Beall, Son of the South

The Life and Death of a Confederate Privateer

KEN LIZZIO

McFarland & Company, Inc., Publishers
Jefferson, North Carolina

ISBN (print) 978-1-4766-9860-1
ISBN (ebook) 978-1-4766-5736-3

LIBRARY OF CONGRESS CATALOGING DATA ARE AVAILABLE

© 2026 Ken Lizzio. All rights reserved

No part of this book may be reproduced or transmitted in any form or by any means, electronic or mechanical, including photocopying or recording, or by any information storage and retrieval system, without permission in writing from the publisher.

Front cover images: *top*: John Yates Beall between 1861 and 1865. *Bottom left to right*: James T. Brady between 1855 and 1865; Abraham Lincoln, 1863; John Brown printed circa 1898; Stonewall Jackson between 1861 and 1865 (all images Library of Congress).

Printed in the United States of America

*McFarland & Company, Inc., Publishers
Box 611, Jefferson, North Carolina 28640
www.mcfarlandpub.com*

Table of Contents

Preface   1

Introduction   5

1. The Land Where We Were Dreaming   7
2. Dress Rehearsal for War   19
3. Between a Hawk and a Buzzard   28
4. Stonewall's Brigade   43
5. The Battle of the Bread   48
6. As Crazy as a March Hare   55
7. Mosby of the Chesapeake   63
8. Capture   81
9. Strange Peace Party   92
10. The Northwest Goose Egg   100
11. The Johnson's Island Raid   109
12. Last Stop at Dunkirk   127
13. Dix's Show Trial   143
14. Lincoln's Anguish   161
15. The Hanging   183

Postscript   193
Chapter Notes   197
Bibliography   205
Index   207

Preface

IN THE SUMMER OF 2018, I WANDERED into the Special Collections Division of the Washington and Lee University library in Lexington, Virginia, to explore its archives. Having made the Shenandoah Valley my adopted home years earlier, I was hoping to find in the archives an old diary, journal, or text of some kind as the starting point for a biography of an inhabitant of the region. Originally settled by German and Scots Irish farmers in the eighteenth century, the Valley of Virginia is a quiet place. Over the years little of consequence has happened here—apart, that is, from the Civil War. Many battles took place in the valley near the towns of New Market, Winchester, and Kernstown, not to mention Stonewall Jackson's famous Valley campaign in 1862. For this reason, I had a sneaking suspicion that if I found anything of interest, it would probably be a man—or woman—in the Confederacy. The wee town of Lexington today still retains much of its Southern character and identity. Two of its most celebrated individuals happen to be among the Confederacy's greatest generals. Robert E. Lee settled here after the Civil War to run Washington and Lee University (then Washington College) until his death, and Stonewall Jackson taught at adjacent Virginia Military Institute for a decade before the war. That is quite a pedigree for a town of fewer than 3,000 inhabitants in its day.

A few hours of scouring the archives turned up nothing. As I was preparing to leave, one of the librarians, seeing my bereft face, asked if I needed any help. It turned out he was something of a Civil War historian by avocation. When I explained the purpose of my visit, he suggested I look at an obscure Confederate soldier named John Yates Beall. Since Beall was born in the northern neck of the

Preface

valley in what was then Charlestown, Virginia, it seemed like an omen.

As I set out to read about Beall, I was astonished at what I found. Most Confederate soldiers were commoners—farmers, laborers, mechanics, most of whom did not own slaves. John Beall, however, was different. To begin with, he hailed from one of the best families in the state with ancestors who had been landed gentry in England. Surprising, too, was the fact that Beall owned slaves, but that was not the reason he entered the war. Nor, I believe, was it the reason for Stonewall Jackson, in whose brigade Beall served. Likewise, Robert E. Lee. All three and countless others joined the Confederacy out of an abiding loyalty to their beloved state of Virginia. This may be hard to appreciate today, but at the time the state, not the country, was the paramount political entry for many. Had the delegates to the Virginia assembly voted as they were originally instructed—to side with the Union—the war might have followed a much different trajectory than it did.

Another revelation was that Beall abhorred killing. Early in the war, he became repulsed by the bloodshed on both sides. He sought to participate on his own terms by attacking not individuals, but infrastructure. To this end, Beall engaged in privateering on Chesapeake Bay and Lake Erie with varying degrees of success. Wherever he fought, he showed great deference to the enemy; his behavior in battle could even be described as chivalrous. But of all the revelations to be found in his life, the greatest was that President Lincoln refused to commute his bogus death sentence handed down in a mock trial despite a vigorous defense by James Brady, the greatest lawyer of his time. Here certainly were all the elements of a compelling drama.

Because of his relative obscurity, reconstructing Beall's life was difficult, though not impossible. Family and county histories were invaluable for tracing his ancestry and explaining how his forebears came to America and ultimately settled in the Shenandoah Valley. Diaries, journals, newspaper articles, and accounts of specific battles helped flesh out at least some the gaps in his early life. Other segments of his life—such as the Battle of Harpers Ferry and Jackson's

Preface

Brigade—allow us to know where he was and what he was doing *grosso modo*. But as to precisely what he was thinking at the time, one can only hazard a guess. Beall did keep a partial diary of his exploits in the war, which was preserved by his close friend Daniel Bedinger Lucas. Indeed, the best source for Beall's life overall was written by Lucas, who sought to preserve the memory of his lifelong friend.

At the time when I was writing the postscript to this book, statues of Confederate soldiers were being removed everywhere. In the wake of the Charlottesville riots of 2017, the regard for Confederates fell considerably. At Washington and Lee University students were lobbying for the removal of both Lee's recumbent statue in the chapel that bears his name and his very name from the school's diploma. The university administration stood firm, however, on the grounds that Lee was instrumental in making the university the fine liberal college that it is today.

Poor Stonewall was not so lucky. From my office at Virginia Military Institute (VMI), I saw his figure in front of the cadet barracks removed unceremoniously one cold, gray winter day. Not a soul was there to see it save the workmen, as the institute, fearing protests, cordoned off the roads leading to the campus. Likewise, his dictum "You may be whatever you want to be" was erased from the barracks' façade. The acts seemed unbefitting for a man who, for over a hundred years, was synonymous with the institute and whose brilliant military tactics are taught to the school's cadets to this day. When I saw Jackson's stone likeness on its side, cables lowering it gently, it became abundantly clear that this was not an auspicious time to release a book on a Confederate soldier, and I shelved the project.

In the past few years, however, at least two books about Beall have appeared, indicating an abiding interest in Confederates, and in Beall in particular. While these accounts focus largely on his privateering exploits, the current work, *John Yates Beall, Son of the South*, offers a more comprehensive examination of Beall's life and the environment in which he grew up. I hope to demonstrate that while slavery was surely an abomination, the Civil War cannot simply be viewed as a binary struggle between good and evil. The example of

Preface

Beall's conduct in the war, the Union's unjust death sentence, and the courage he showed in his final days before the gallows demonstrate that the war was far more nuanced than that. As war goes, there was much to deplore on both sides—as well as to commend.

Introduction

On a cold, gray February morning in 1864, they began descending on the White House. President Lincoln had just finished breakfast with his wife, Mary, but was already tired, having hosted a state dinner the previous evening for some thirty-three guests. His unannounced visitors that morning came individually and in pairs, sometimes in small groups. The first to arrive were friends who had been schoolmates of the condemned soldier at the University of Virginia: Albert Ritchie, a lawyer who would later become a judge on the Baltimore Supreme Court, and James A.L. McClure, a Maryland politician. They were followed by Francis Wheatley, a prominent Baltimore politician; Congressman Robert Mallory of Kentucky; and a party of genteel, civic-minded ladies from New York. They all had come for the same purpose: to persuade the President to commute the death sentence of Confederate naval officer John Yates Beall, falsely accused of spying and violating the rules of war.

A few days later, Orville H. Browning called in the afternoon. His friendship with Lincoln went back to their days on the Illinois circuit court. After a one-hour discussion that was inconclusive, Browning returned with a petition signed by no fewer than eighty-five congressmen and six senators requesting a commutation of Beall's death sentence. Next to his signature, Ohio Representative and future president James A. Garfield penned a note requesting, at the very least, a temporary reprieve. Missouri Congressman Henry T. Blow also requested more time for the condemned.

Everyone who appeared at the White House that month had good reason to believe Lincoln would pardon the young Virginian. Over the course of the Civil War, he had demonstrated profound

Introduction

compassion for the fate of war prisoners, North and South. Indeed, so compassionate was he that he personally reviewed every death penalty case of soldiers charged with criminal offenses such as desertion, mutiny, or robbery, often going out of his way to find the slightest excuse to commute a death sentence. Usually, the result was a reduction of the sentence to a more lenient punishment. That month alone he had suspended the death sentence of two prisoners of war and paroled another. While he was often easily swayed by appeals for clemency, this time Lincoln was standing firm, unwilling to yield to the unprecedented number of petitioners.

Still, they came. Librarian of Congress Richard S. Spofford called at the White House, as did John W. Garrett, President of the Baltimore and Ohio Railroad, and Massachusetts Governor John Andrew. Even arch-abolitionist Thaddeus Stevens weighed in on Beall's behalf. More than once the Blair brothers, Montgomery and Francis, those quintessential Washington power brokers, turned up. Surely, Francis, one of Lincoln's closest advisers, could prevail, for he had made and broken careers with simply a word to the President's ear. But this time Blair's entreaties fell on deaf ears.

The day before Beall's execution, more supplicants arrived at the White House. On February 23, they included Secretary of the Senate John W. Forney, owner of the *Cincinnati Enquirer* Washington McLean, and Roger A. Pryor. Pryor had been a Confederate brigadier and was fresh from imprisonment in Fort Lafayette, where he had been a cellmate of Beall's, and came to attest to the young man's sterling character. Lincoln was interested in all Pryor had to say about the young Virginian but refused to interfere in the case. Later, priests attempted to get an audience with the President, who was by now exhausted from the whole affair, but they were abruptly turned away.

Why was the President of Compassion, normally so benevolent in matters of life and death, this time so adamant in his refusal to intervene on the young man's behalf? And what was it about John Beall and his trial that had moved so many—most of whom were total strangers—to intercede on his behalf?

This is his tragic story.

1

The Land Where We Were Dreaming

IT WAS A LAND OF SUCH CELESTIAL BEAUTY the Algonquians had called it "Shenandoah," meaning "Daughter of the Stars." Nestled between the gently rolling Blue Ridge Mountains and the towering Alleghenies, the Shenandoah Valley encompassed two hundred glorious miles of pastoral perfection. Green hills rolled in endless waves toward distant ridges swathed in a blueish haze. Quaint clapboard houses dotted the landscape and cows ruminated lazily on the surrounding hills. From their lofty heights the mountains sent down their streamlets to form the valley's two great rivers, the Shenandoah and Potomac. Thomas Jefferson, who once stood on a Harpers Ferry promontory that commanded a magnificent view of the place where the two rivers unite and flow through soaring limestone cliffs, thought it "one of the most stupendous scenes in nature ... worth a voyage across the Atlantic."[1] It was here at the valley's northern neck in Jefferson County that John Yates Beall was born on New Year's Day, 1835.

Unlike most Germans and Scots Irish who had arrived in the eighteenth century to escape persecution and poverty back home, the Bealls were among the wealthiest and most distinguished families in the county. Ironically, the first Beall (pronounced "bell") to set foot on American shores, John's great-great-grandfather Ninian, emigrated as a political prisoner. Born in the village of Largo in Fifeshire, Scotland, Ninian was striking to behold, a towering man with a florid complexion and long, flaming red hair. While serving as Cornet in the Scottish Army raised to resist Oliver Cromwell's claims to the Commonwealth of England, he was captured at the

John Yates Beall, Son of the South

Battle of Dunbar on September 3, 1650. Forced to march south to England in harsh conditions, nearly three-quarters of the five thousand prisoners died from starvation or sickness. Those who survived were condemned to indentured servitude in the British Colonies. Ninian was shipped off to Barbados along with 149 other prisoners to work on Britain's profitable sugar plantations. A few years later he was sent to Calvert County, Maryland, where he was indentured to a carpenter named Richard Hall. After four more years of servitude, Ninian was deemed to have fulfilled his debt to the Crown and released.

John Yates Beall (courtesy of Naval History & Heritage Command Photo Section, Photo NH56 843).

The timing of his release could not have been better. That year Oliver Cromwell died and Prince Charles, the very man for whom he had fought and suffered, was recalled from exile and crowned King. Suddenly Ninian was no longer a pariah. For his selfless service the provincial assembly awarded him fifty acres of land in Calvert County which he named "The Soldier's Fortune."[2]

If it wasn't exactly a fortune, it would soon be the start of one. On his modest tract of land, the enterprising Scotsman began cultivating highly profitable Oronoco tobacco known as "sotweed." With international demand strong and few countries producing the pleasurable substance, Maryland had emerged as one of the world's

1. *The Land Where We Were Dreaming*

leading producers of tobacco. With his profits Ninian began a long and successful career in land speculation. To add to his holdings, he became a surveyor, earning—as was the custom—from a third to half of the land he surveyed as payment. One of his largest acquisitions was a land grant of several hundred acres from the Second Lord Baltimore for having assisted 200 Scots Irish immigrants to settle in the country. By 1676 he had become a land baron, paying 2,860 pounds of tobacco—the mainstay of the Maryland economy—in taxes for at least a dozen farms.[3] At his peak he would hold title to between 13,000 and 25,000 acres of land, some of which he christened after places in Scotland like Largo and Dumbarton, names which endure to this day.[4]

As Ninian's fortunes grew, so did his social standing. He became an active member of the Presbyterian Church and later induced his fellow Scots-Presbyterians to emigrate to today's Georgetown and the District of Columbia—much of which he owned.[5] He served as colonel in the local militia, riding long hours in the saddle to protect Calvert plantations along the Patuxent River against raids by the Susquehannock and Nanticoke Indians. During one raid a party of Susquehannock, having captured several women and cattle, set out for Quaker Pennsylvania, where they expected to receive asylum. Gathering sixty mounted men, Ninian set out in search of them. Upon finding them encamped near the Pennsylvania border, he and his men proceeded to wantonly slaughter the Indians with knives and clubs. Outraged by the savage act, the gentle Quaker William Penn complained to the King, demanding that the Scotsman be hanged. But after reading Penn's report the King instead sanctioned Ninian's bold action.

Shortly after, Beall was commissioned lieutenant on the *Loyal Charles of Maryland*, the war vessel of the third Baron of Baltimore, Charles Calvert. His commander was another militia captain and Protestant, John Coode. In 1689 Coode turned against Calvert over his policy of Catholic and familial preferential treatment in the assignment of public offices.[6] Raising an army of seven hundred Protestants called the Protestant Association, he and Ninian, the oldest at sixty-four years of age, marched on the provincial seat at St.

John Yates Beall, Son of the South

Mary's. There they toppled the government and formed an interim administration with Coode as head and Ninian serving in an advisory capacity. For his role in the rebellion Coode praised Ninian as his "Argyll," a reference to Archibald Campbell of Argyll, Scotland, who had recently fought courageously for the maintenance of Presbyterianism against similar attempts by the monarchy to impose episcopalism in the old country. After a new government was put in place, Coode continued to stir up trouble, but by then, Ninian seemed to have distanced himself from the controversial figure.

When Prince Georges County was created out of Calvert County in 1695, Ninian became the first Burgess elected to represent it in the House of Burgesses, serving five consecutive terms altogether. He was also Commander-in-Chief of the Rangers, Maryland's supreme military command. When the vigorous Scotsman finally retired at seventy-four years of age, in return for his military service the assembly granted him seventy-five pounds sterling to acquire three "serviceable Negro slaves, John, Sarah, and Elizabeth," and any offspring they might produce to assist him on his tobacco plantations.[7] As far as we know, this marked the beginning of the Beall family's relationship with slavery.

Late in life, as Ruling Elder of the Presbyterian Church in Patuxent, Ninian donated a half-acre of land for the building of one of the first Presbyterian churches in America.[8] When the former indentured servant died at his Bacon Hall plantation in Prince Georges County at the age of nine-two, he possessed a vast estate of over 2,100 acres of land, flour mills, and iron works.[9] His son, Colonel George Beall, Sr., inherited the most valuable piece of land—a five-hundred-acre tract Ninian had named the Rock of Dunbarton (later spelled Dumbarton) to commemorate the battle site where he had been captured and where his long journey to fortune in America had begun. George would later sell the land for the creation of Georgetown, thought to be named after him.

Some of the family's considerable wealth trickled down to George's grandson Hezekiah, who, in 1807, used it to purchase land in Jefferson County in the lower Shenandoah Valley. Exactly why Hezekiah chose to resettle in the valley is unclear, though farmers

1. *The Land Where We Were Dreaming*

were typically drawn to the valley's fertile land, abundant water, and lack of native populations, not to mention its serene beauty.

On his mother's side, John Beall hailed from a long line of English landed gentry that traced its ancestry to Walter de Aguillon, a Norman, who stormed England alongside William the Conqueror in the eleventh century. As reward for his military service, Walter was given land in Cumberland County, where he built a large manor house to serve as the family seat he named "Aguilonby." In 1715 Henry Aglionby, a member of Parliament, created a new family seat when he pulled down an old nunnery and erected a mansion in its place which he called "The Nunnery." Henry's granddaughter Mary later married John Orfeur Yates, whose brother Charles had come to America in 1852 and made a killing in importing.[10] Having never married, Charles had no heirs, so he wrote John requesting he send a son to whom Charles could bequeath his vast holdings in Virginia. In reply, John Yates, Jr., was shipped off at the tender age of twelve. Accompanying the boy were his dog Plato, an attendant, and a goat to provide fresh milk while at sea.[11]

Even though his financial future was assured, John Jr. attended Princeton (then known as the College of New Jersey) briefly before transferring to William and Mary to study law. While at school the headstrong youth got into a duel with a fellow student. He was shot in the thigh and expelled. He subsequently floundered about with no direction and no income. Two years later he married Julia Lovell, much to the disapproval of his uncle, who had other plans for his heir. The following year John's first daughter, Janet, was born. With more mouths to feed, he began to cultivate land in Germanna in Virginia's Piedmont region that his father-in law had given him. When Charles's health began to fail, John agreed to manage his uncle's prosperous plantation, Walnut Grove, in Jefferson County. Charles had acquired the 337-acre parcel from an unpaid debt from Lord Fairfax and had stipulated that upon his death John Jr. would inherit it along with the slaves and Charles's plantation in Spotsylvania County.[12]*

---

*The remaining slaves he liberated "for their faithful services and my attachment," and to some of these Charles left annuities for life.

John Yates Beall, Son of the South

In November 1807—the same year Hezekiah Beall moved to Jefferson County—John Yates moved up to Walnut Grove to manage the property. Named for the great number of black walnut trees on the property, Walnut Grove was a thousand-acre tract of wheat, oats, Indian corn, and apples. Herds of cattle, horses, and sheep rounded out the enterprise. Over time John acquired additional land, becoming the largest taxpayer in the county.[13] His wealth allowed him to send his daughters to an elite boarding school in Leesburg.* Upon completion of her studies, the eldest, Janet, returned to Jefferson County and, in October 1826, married one of the wealthiest and largest slaveholders in the county, George Brooke Beall. This union of two of the most affluent and distinguished families in the state would eventually produce seven offspring, of which John Yates Beall was the third.

John Beall's boyhood home in Charles Town, West Virginia, where he lived until the outbreak of the Civil War (Elizabeth Nicholson, courtesy of the Jefferson County Historic Landmarks Commission).

---

*Despite (or perhaps because of) his own failing in school, he was a fervent believer in education and later helped establish public schools near Shepherdstown, making Jefferson one of the first counties in the state to adopt a free education system.

1. *The Land Where We Were Dreaming*

History tells us little of John Beall's early years. He was schooled at home by his mother, there being no public schools in the county at the time.[14] Like rural boys everywhere, he was in the saddle at an early age. By the time he reached his teens he was riding and jousting in the local ring tournaments, a sport adopted from England and popular in Virginia and Maryland at the time. Armed with a lance, he and his mate, Edwin Gray Lee from Shepherdstown, would charge their horses toward small metal rings suspended from branches or arches which they would attempt to spear. The rider who collected the most rings on his lance won the right to select the most fetching lady from among the spectators. John's best friend, Daniel Bedinger Lucas, was unable to partake of these youthful activities, having been crippled in childhood in a tragic fall from the arms of his nurse. Looking back, Daniel would one day celebrate the halcyon, pre–Civil War days in the valley in a poem titled "In the Land Where We Were Dreaming."

When John completed his schooling at sixteen years of age, he accompanied his grandfather and namesake on a voyage across the Atlantic to visit his mother's family at The Nunnery. It had been sixty years since John Sr. had last seen his homeland. Now in declining health, John wished to revisit the land of his youth and settle his affairs. Though ill, he insisted on making the journey, hoping the salubrious salt air would restore him to health. As for

Daniel Bedinger Lucas, Beall's lifelong friend (From *The Land Where We Were Dreaming*, by Daniel B. Lucas [Boston: Richard G. Badger, 1913]; via Wikipedia).

John Yates Beall, Son of the South

"The Nunnery" in Cumberland, England, a manor house built by Beall's great grandfather (courtesy of Nick Kingsley).

young John, he was thrilled at the prospect of meeting real English gentry, and close relatives at that.

The two embarked from Philadelphia on the steamer *City of Glasgow* in May 1851. After a few days at sea the elder John began to recover. On Sunday morning, however, as they were sitting down to breakfast, he was suddenly seized with acute stomach pain. The ship's surgeon, Andrew Alexander, was summoned. Unable to determine the cause of his ailment, he prescribed a tincture of rhubarb and some rest. A few hours later the old man felt better and sauntered up to the deck where he was again stricken, this time with an even sharper stomach pain. John assisted him back to his room and sat by his side, distraught and helpless, as his grandfather tossed and turned in agony. By the time the ship docked at Liverpool, his grandfather was failing fast. He then wrote a precautionary note of instruction to John in the event he might expire before reaching their destination:

Memorandum to John Y. Beall

Whatever of the draft on Brown, Shipley & Co. you do not use get their draft on Alexander Brown and Sons in favour of your father, who will apply it to my estate. If I die, pay all expenses of my funeral, etc.; Mrs. Aglionby will please to select the

1. The Land Where We Were Dreaming

place of interment; if I die at Liverpool, let the corpse be carried by railroad to Penrith. The papers enclosed for Charles Yates are not to be shown to anybody but the Bleaymires. Write, if necessary, to Mrs. Aglionby; see the tombs of my family. I left the key of my writing desk with Mr. S. Elder, in Baltimore; call for it. My other keys are in the black trunk in bank (Charlestown), my will, etc., in the red trunk. All my letters from England are for Charles.

I believe since my attack I have thought of all I hold in regard. I have no ill will against anyone. Tell them to pay all my debts as fast as they can; tell all to favour my wife and my daughter Julia and her children....[15]

So had the trip of a lifetime turned into a nightmare. The two struggled on to Penrith, where they were met by a cousin and the widow of his brother. By the time they reached The Nunnery on June 10, the old man's condition had taken a turn for the worse. This time he remained in a feeble state until he died on July 6. He was buried at the family vault in Ainstable Parish Church, where a plaque memorializes him. Little did the grieving boy know that one day, just below it, would be a commemorative plaque for him as well.

In the fall John returned to America and enrolled at the University of Virginia in Charlottesville. Founded by Thomas Jefferson in 1819 in the rolling hills east of the Blue Ridge Mountains, the university was a quintessentially Southern institution. One of Jefferson's aims in establishing the university was to provide a place of learning where the sons of the South would be insulated from the abolitionist teachings of Northern universities like Harvard and Yale.[16] Despite his own conflicted views on slavery, Jefferson envisioned his university would produce the South's master class by reinforcing slavery as part of the natural social order. In part for this reason, most of the university's students were, like Beall, wealthy scions of Virginia plantation owners, most of whom owned slaves. At over $400 per term, the university tuition was twice that of a Northern university, underscoring its importance to Southern families as a uniquely Southern institution.

The values of Jefferson's South were reinforced at the university in several ways, both subtle and not so subtle. Most professors were pro-slavery and inserted slavery in their courses. Outside the classroom students discussed the subject and wrote about it in student publications. Their pro-slavery sentiments were sometimes expressed in personal attacks on students. In 1855 Catherine Beecher, the sister of Harriet Beecher Stowe, the author of the popular anti-slavery novel *Uncle Tom's Cabin*, was ridiculed for her abolitionist beliefs. Others burned her sister in effigy.[17] The school's prestigious Jefferson Society, where Ralph Waldo Emerson had once been a member, sometimes debated its merits. That the Jefferson Society strongly favored slavery was evidenced in its sending to Preston Brooks a new gold-headed cane to replace the one he had infamously broken while beating abolitionist Charles Sumner on the Senate floor.[18]

Slaves were, of course, the beating heart of the university. Some 125 to 200 slaves worked there, the property of professors and dormitory owners. Their day started around 4 a.m. when they would light the fires in the student rooms and bring them fresh water. Some would then prepare the food while others cleaned student rooms and privies, did laundry, or ran errands for them. The children of slaves also performed tasks such as fetching firewood or milking cows. The social situation thus mirrored the one at home, reinforcing racial disparities as the natural order of things.

In its early years the university was something of a playground for these privileged sons. While some were there to learn, others came simply to make mischief and mayhem. In flagrant disregard of regulations, they drank whiskey and rum, brandished guns and daggers, and gambled on cockfights. They fought with each other, and sometimes with professors. One student was expelled for attempting to bomb his professor.[19] There was at least one documented instance involving the rape of a twelve-year-old slave by three students who were later expelled.[20] Expulsion, however, did not rid the school entirely of troublemakers who continued to prowl the campus and steal into dorms late at night. The nadir came in 1840 when the Chair of the Law Faculty, John Davis, was shot and killed by a drunken Georgia student while Davis was attempting to remove a mask he was wearing. Four years later the militia was called in to put down student riots.[21] While violence was not uncommon at American universities of the time, the raucous Charlottesville campus was a far cry from Jefferson's bold vision of a secular "academical village" where students and professors could live and learn together. Not surprisingly, these incidents did nothing to boost the university's moral

1. The Land Where We Were Dreaming

Thomas Jefferson's "Academical Village" of the University of Virginia (courtesy of Albert and Shirley Small Special Collections Library, University of Virginia).

prestige, and for a time the state general assembly considered withdrawing its annuity of $15,000.

Something of a brooding loner, Beall took little, if any, part in the student hijinks. According to his roommate Daniel Lucas, he was soft-spoken and reserved, had but a few friends, and avoided contact with his professors outside the classroom. "The most undemonstrative of men" concentrated instead on his studies, which in the first year consisted of modern and ancient languages and mathematics.[22] In his third year he took a class in ethics—then called moral philosophy—from the nationally renowned the Rev. William Holmes McGuffey, known as "Old Guff." His own philosophical views had not yet coalesced and vacillated between a "cynical dislike" for religious devotees and the same for hard-nosed skeptics.[23]

Beall's reserve may also be explained by another reason altogether. He had little interest in college and had merely enrolled to satisfy his father's wishes that he become a lawyer.* In his third year

---

*Daniel, by contrast, excelled at his studies. A born orator, he became valedictorian of the Jefferson Debating Society in his senior year and later a celebrated Southern poet.

John Yates Beall, Son of the South

he dutifully matriculated to law but soon after concluded he had no intention of becoming a lawyer. When the school year ended in June 1855, he had had enough. With his older sister Mary, he set out for Dubuque, Iowa, to see his older brother Hezekiah, who had left home a few years earlier on bad terms with his father. Whether their purpose was to persuade him to return home or to join the successful land investment business Hezekiah had started is unclear.[24] In any case, the two siblings had gotten as far as New York when they were urgently recalled home. John arrived in time to be at his father's bedside when the latter died of dysentery on August 2. In his will his father had requested to be buried in a lot in a Georgetown cemetery that had been bequeathed to the family by Ninian.

John was devastated by the premature death of his father. He would later lament, "the loss of a father is one of the greatest a family is called on to endure. It seems impossible to estimate it! In our family, his strong hand would have ruled the children and made all of us more subject—he would have restrained, and restraint was needed."[25] In his grief he turned to religion. He joined the Zion Episcopal Church in Charlestown (which his maternal grandfather had established). He soon became an active member, representing it at the diocese conventions throughout the state.

Any plans John may have had were now abandoned to tend to Walnut Grove and look after his mother, four sisters, and younger brother William.[26] Like his father, he maintained Walnut Grove's high standards and it remained one of the most successful farms in the valley. It appeared as if John would live out his life much as his forebears had—a leader of his community, a man of wealth and privilege, a country squire, a Virginia gentleman—and, yes, a benevolent slave master. Yet unbeknownst to him, dark clouds were gathering on the horizon. Two thousand miles away, war raged in Kansas over whether the territory would emerge as a slave or free state. Some of the most violent parties to that bloody conflict had returned east and were about to shatter the rural tranquility of Jefferson County.

2

Dress Rehearsal for War

In July 1859, an old man using the alias Isaac Smith took up residence with two of his sons and some other men in a rented farmhouse in the Maryland Heights above Jefferson County. He had told locals he was looking to farm in a mild climate because the biting cold of New York had killed off his crops. His real name was John Brown.

The radical abolitionist had good reason to use an alias. A few years earlier he had wantonly slaughtered several slave owners on Pottawatomie Creek in Kansas Territory. Whether he was "a madman," as one Colonel Robert E. Lee believed, or a savior most likely depended on which side of the Mason–Dixon Line you lived on. One thing was certain: John Brown was as dangerous as a wild animal.

Brown had long ago concluded that only violence could bring an end to the evil of slavery. Since his bloody rampage on the Pottawatomie—possibly even before it—he had been mulling a big plan, something so apocalyptic that would strike at the very heart of slavery and ignite a mass uprising of slaves all across the South.[1] By the time he quit Kansas in January of 1859, Brown had a general idea of what that plan looked like. He would raid the federal armory at Harpers Ferry, seize the rifles and munitions, and transport them to a base where slaves in the area would rally, thus forming the nucleus of a great Southern insurrection. He had selected the Harpers Ferry arsenal because of the large number of slaves in the area—some five thousand in Jefferson County alone—and the proximity of the wooded Blue Ridge Mountains where he would be safe from pursuit. The scheme was as bold as it was crazy. When asked to participate, Frederick Douglass declined, warning Brown, "you will never get out alive."[2] Two of Brown's sons also refused to participate, in the belief that he would fail.

John Yates Beall, Son of the South

Brown nevertheless pressed forward. He spent the summer recruiting his force and stockpiling Sharps rifles at his house, which served at once as "barracks, arsenal, supply depot, mess hall, debate club, and home." On Sundays, while families were at church, he sent emissaries to nearby farms to inform slaves of an impending uprising against their masters and to get assurances they would participate.[3] By October 16 everything was in readiness.

John Brown, the fiery abolitionist who led the incendiary raid on Harpers Ferry (courtesy of Library of Congress).

When darkness fell, Brown ordered his tiny force of twenty-two men to shoulder their rifles and proceed to Harpers Ferry.

The raid began smoothly enough for Brown. He was able to take the armory without firing a shot, thanks to a careless guard who, in the darkness, mistook him for the head watchman. Leaving two men to guard the B&O rail bridge, Brown then sent one party to take control of the rifle factory a half mile up the Shenandoah River. Another party was dispatched to the homes of some of Jefferson County's leading citizens and slave owners to bring them in as hostages. William Washington, the great-grandnephew of George Washington, was taken at his 640-acre estate near Halltown.* By dawn some forty hostages had been rounded up and corralled in the armory.

---

*The estate, known as Beall Air, was built in 1797 by John Beall's uncle, Thomas Beall.

2. Dress Rehearsal for War

The next morning, Charlestown residents had scarcely finished breakfast when they were startled by the wild ringing of the courthouse bell and news that a large band of Yankee abolitionists had seized the arsenal. Colonel John T. Gibson immediately called out the local militia, the Jefferson Guard. The Guard was, in the words of one of its members, "one of the most handsomely equipped, if not the best drilled corps in the state."[4] Still, with only sixty men, Gibson believed it was too small to challenge the large number of abolitionists rumored to be at the armory, so he called for additional volunteers to fall in under the capable Captain Lawson Botts, a Charlestown attorney who had completed two years at Virginia Military Institute in Lexington. Among the ninety-two men—and boys—who rallied to the call were twenty-three-year-old John Beall and his younger brother William.

Realizing time was of the essence, Gibson decided not to wait for orders from Richmond and with the men boarded the train for Halltown, a hamlet midway between Charlestown and Harpers Ferry. They arrived around 10 a.m. to a town abuzz with wild rumors of the takeover. One was that the raiders numbered in the hundreds; another, that they had taken over a hundred hostages. Alarmed by what he heard, Gibson called for still more reinforcements from Shepherdstown and Frederick County. After hearing that the rail track ahead was torn up—at least that was true—Gibson marched

Lawson Botts, who led the civilian defense of Harpers Ferry and defended John Brown in court (courtesy of Library of Congress).

his men to a plateau just above the arsenal at Bolivar Heights. By the time they arrived, residents of Harpers Ferry had already been exchanging fire with Brown and his men for nearly three hours.

Located in a deep gorge on a tongue of land between the Potomac and Shenandoah rivers, Harpers Ferry was a scenic setting for an arsenal—and a perfect mouse trap for anyone foolish enough to attack it. Steep bluffs surrounded the town on three sides: Bolivar Heights to the west, Maryland Heights to the north, and Loudoun Heights to the east. There were two bridges that led into town: The B&O rail bridge from Maryland crossed the Potomac, while another bridge led from Loudoun Heights over the Shenandoah River. With rivers and hills on three sides, the only egress was the Shenandoah River flowing northward, which hardly offered an avenue of escape. With Brown thus hemmed in, Gibson decided to seal the bridges and surround him. He sent one detachment across the Potomac above Harpers Ferry to march down the Maryland side and take control of the B&O bridge. Another was ordered to take a position on Loudoun Heights overlooking the rifle factory and the Shenandoah bridge. Leading the rest of his men into town, Gibson sent Captain John Avis to take possession of the houses and shops on Shenandoah Street opposite the arsenal and the Botts Greys to occupy the bridge over the Shenandoah River.[5]

As soon as the Greys reached the bridge, a local rushed up to Lawson Botts saying that he had come from the Gault House, a small tavern on the Shenandoah, where the proprietor was holding several raiders at bay. With but one load left in his gun, the tavernkeeper was in dire need of reinforcement. Botts immediately requested twenty volunteers. Nearly twice that stepped out from the ranks, including John Beall.[6] Botts then attempted to lead his men straight through town, but they were quickly forced to descend to the river after the raiders began raking the streets with bullets. Using the embankment as cover they crept along until reaching the location of the tavern, where they crawled through a basement window just as the owner had fired his last shot.

By now reinforcements from Shepherdstown were arriving, though many were simply B&O employees—and poorly armed at that.

2. Dress Rehearsal for War

Artist David Strother's sketch of the burning of Harpers Ferry arsenal (courtesy of Library of Congress).

They were immediately sent to the rear of the arsenal, where they began firing. Brown's men returned fire, wounding and killing several of them. By 4 p.m., however, heavy fire from the Martinsburg militia finally forced Brown and a few men to flee to the engine house with a handful of hostages.

All this time Brown had been waiting desperately for reinforcements in the form of the slaves he had earlier contacted. But when they failed to show, he very soon realized he was woefully outnumbered and decided to negotiate a surrender. For protection he sent one of his men to the Gault House with a hostage, but the two were promptly seized. Once again Brown tried to surrender, this time sending his son Watson and his aide Aaron Stevens with the acting superintendent of the armory. But no one was in a mood to negotiate and as his emissaries approached, the Botts Greys fired, wounding both Watson and Stevens. Watson managed to drag himself back to the guard house, where he later died. Stevens lay bleeding in the street until two hostages dashed from the engine house and dragged him to Fouke's Hotel, thereby escaping in the process.

John Yates Beall, Son of the South

Harpers Ferry Firehouse where John Brown took refuge just before his capture (courtesy of Library of Congress).

Late in the day the old man sent a message to Colonel R.W. Baylor, who had taken command of the Virginia militia, offering to surrender if he could cross the B&O bridge, where he would then free the hostages. Baylor refused to negotiate and demanded Brown set the hostages free immediately. By now darkness had fallen and the militia began celebrating their imminent victory, circulating in the streets, cheering and shooting in the air. In the Gault House the Greys began toasting shots of liquor to their military victory, all save Beall, who was a teetotaler.

As the pandemonium raged, Colonel Robert E. Lee arrived from Washington with one hundred Federal marines. Taking command, Lee cleared the streets and ordered the disorganized militias to withdraw from the area, including the Botts Greys.[7] At first light he sent his assistant, Lieutenant J.E.B. Stuart, to the front of the engine house to demand Brown's surrender in return for assurances they would not be harmed by the now irate citizens.

"You are Osawatomie Brown, of Kansas?" Stuart asked.

"Well, they call me that sometimes," the old man replied.

Stuart then asked Brown to surrender in return for protection from the drunken mob and the guarantee of a fair trial. Brown

2. Dress Rehearsal for War

refused, insisting that he and his men be given the length of the bridge as a head start in order to escape.

While the two negotiated, Lieutenant Israel Green's men had found some sledgehammers and were awaiting a prearranged signal from Stuart to begin battering the heavy doors of the engine house. When it was clear the old man would not come out, Lieutenant Stuart removed his cap and waved it high over his head. Green's men quickly set upon the doors with their hammers but made little headway, for Brown had reinforced them with ropes and hand brakes from the fire engines. After several minutes of fruitless hammering, Green gave the order to desist. Just then, two dozen marines came racing up with a ladder that had been leaning against one of the shops, to use as a battering-ram. The first two blows had no effect. Falling back, the soldiers made a third run, which produced a splintered hole just big enough to pass through. As Green's men attempted to slip through, Brown fired, wounding two, one mortally. While Brown paused to reload, Green was able to slide safely through. Using the fire engines as cover, Green crept around to the back of the building, where he saw one of Brown's men dead on the floor in a pool of blood and his son Watson lying on a bench bleeding profusely. Standing near the hose cart was hostage Lewis Washington. "Hello, Green," said Washington nonchalantly. Pointing to the kneeling figure next to him he said, "This is Osawatomie." As Brown turned around to see who Washington was speaking to, Green attempted to lower his saber on Brown's head, but the old man wheeled and was struck in the back instead. In the fracas Brown managed to reload his carbine and fired randomly, killing one of Green's men before Green finally stabbed Brown in the left breast.

John Brown's raid was over a day and a half after it began.[8] Only thirty slaves from nearby plantations had responded to his call to revolt. Of the twenty-two men in Brown's band, ten lay dead, seven had escaped, and five were taken prisoner. As it happened, the regular session of Jefferson County court was scheduled to begin on October 20, and within five days Brown was brought to trial on charges of treason. In the case of *Virginia v. John Brown*, the court assigned Lawson Botts to serve as Brown's defense counsel, as his own had been delayed. By a strange coincidence, Botts's grandfather Benjamin had represented Aaron Burr when he was tried on similar charges. On November 2, Brown was found guilty and sentenced to hang.

In the days leading up to the execution, Charlestown was seized with paranoia as residents feared abolitionists would attempt to rescue Brown. With three rail lines passing through town, it would be easy, they imagined, for several hundred radical abolitionists to pose as innocent visitors and infiltrate the town. Rockets seen lighting up the sky at night were interpreted as an attempt to communicate with agents already lurking among them. (The flashing was later discovered to be sparks shooting from distant chimneys.) Vigilance committees were set up to guard against "foreign emissaries plotting outrages."

Governor Wise only added to the anxiety. Fearing a Kansas-style border war with the North was imminent, he hastened to Charlestown with four hundred militia from Richmond and Petersburg. Soon after, he augmented his force with another thousand men from Portsmouth, Wheeling, Charlottesville, Harrisonburg, and Staunton, as well as eighty-five cadets from VMI, including an artillery unit commanded by one Major Thomas Jonathan Jackson. Astonishingly, it was the greatest concentration of troops in the state since Cornwallis surrendered to Washington at Yorktown.

Overnight Charlestown had become a garrison city. Soldiers bivouacked in and around town; others camped out in churches, schools, or homes like Walnut Grove, where they were able to purchase produce from Beall's farm. During the day, volunteers full of patriotism and whiskey paraded through the streets in a show of unity and strength. At night they patrolled Charlestown and Harpers Ferry on the lookout for abolitionists on the prowl. Jittery sentinels sometimes fired at strange movements or sounds in the dark though no one was hurt. As the men waited nervously for the trial to begin, one of the soldiers, a strikingly handsome actor with jet black hair and dark eyes from Company F of the Richmond Greys, eased the tension by reading Shakespeare at the Zion Episcopal Church and other locations. During one of his readings, Beall had an opportunity to meet the talented actor, John Wilkes Booth.[9]

2. Dress Rehearsal for War

On the day before the execution Virginia militias were on high alert. So convinced were they of a last-minute rescue attempt that Northerners who had come down to witness the hanging were barred from entering town. Strangers already in town were arrested. Even four Ohio Congressmen in route to Washington who attempted to stop at Charlestown were denied permission. Though the Governor urged citizens to stay at home and guard their property, John Beall was on duty with the Botts Greys, one of several militias providing security for the execution.

Wise had ordered the gallows erected in a field outside of town. Just before noon Brown was brought up in an open wagon, passively seated on his coffin with his arms pinioned at the elbows by a rope. After he mounted the scaffold, a noose was placed around his neck and a large black linen hood was pulled over his head. The drama was then delayed several minutes as troops assigned to guard the scaffold were still scrambling to reach their positions. During the lull, Brown stood silent and motionless. At last the signal was given and the platform dropped, launching Brown into oblivion. Observers noted that Brown did not struggle, and his body was motionless. A minute passed when his hands twitched briefly; then his body went completely still, save for a slight swaying to and fro in the wind. After Brown was taken down, the Botts Greys accompanied his body back to Charlestown. As he rode down the turnpike, Beall began to look forward to a return to normal in Jefferson County.*

Little did he know that nothing would ever be the same again.

---

*Brown's accomplices were hanged on December 16, 1859.

3

Between a Hawk and a Buzzard

JOHN BROWN MIGHT HAVE BEEN GONE, but fears of further abolitionist attacks continued to haunt residents of Jefferson County. Indeed, slave resistance had been on the rise there for nearly a decade. In some cases, slaves had fled to Pennsylvania to gain freedom or reunite with family, while in others, slaves had attacked their overlords outright. In the wake of Brown's raid, slave resistance had become even bolder. At the moment of the old man's execution, one group of slaves in Halltown had torched their master's house and barn. In the months following, at least a dozen other fires were mysteriously set to local farms. Nearly six hundred of the county's five thousand slaves had escaped outright, seven of whom belonged to Daniel Lucas's father.[1] As far as is known, none of Beall's slaves had attempted to escape.

With four slaves to every ten whites in the county, a general slave insurrection was a prospect too terrifying for owners to contemplate. It was even feared that in the event of further abolitionist attacks, non-slaveholding Virginians in the mountains west of the Blue Ridge might side with abolitionists out of jealousy.[2] In the climate of fear, Wise's militias were kept on. Vigilance committees and slave patrols were formed. When not lawyering Captain Botts drilled his Greys throughout the summer and patrolled the countryside for signs of insurrection. Strangers found loitering were driven out on suspicion of being abolitionist agents.

In the fall came a new concern. Within three months of Lincoln's election, seven Southern states had seceded from the Union. Now the Jefferson County council had to decide where it stood on

3. Between a Hawk and a Buzzard

secession. In the presidential election, fifty-one percent of the county had voted for moderate John Bell (no relation to Beall), who had campaigned on an anti-sectional platform that stressed the Constitution and Union and made no mention of slavery. While some residents favored secession, after a spirited debate, the council handily passed a resolution to remain with the Union.[3] "We say let them go," declared Charlestown's conservative *Virginia Free Press* in a blunt dismissal of the Southern separatists.[4] Despite being a state's rights advocate like his father, John Beall had voted the Unionist platform.

But when still more Southern states seceded, the Virginia Legislature called a special convention to determine to which side it would cast its lot. In keeping with its earlier resolution, Jefferson County selected two Unionists—Alfred M. Barbour, a slave owner and superintendent of the armory at Harpers Ferry, and Logan Osborne, a justice of the peace—over two secessionists to represent it at the convention.* Before embarking, Barbour resigned his position at the armory to avoid any conflict of interest.

The convention kicked off in early February and deliberated for nearly two months. Reports were submitted and impassioned speeches given for and against. Emissaries from several Southern states were on hand to urge Virginia to join the separatist cause. With a diverse economic base and as home to several Presidents, if the South could win her over, Virginia would be the crown jewel in the secessionist cause and tip the balance in the South's favor in the event of a war. But when the vote was finally taken on April 4, nearly two to one decided against secession. The Old Dominion would remain in the Union.

Nevertheless, events on the ground were unfolding so quickly that delegates decided to remain in session instead of returning home. Their instincts proved all too correct. On April 14, after heavy bombardment, Fort Sumter surrendered to the South Carolina militia. Ironically, the first shot of the battle was fired by a Virginian,

---

*One of the secessionists was former Congressman William Lucas, Daniel's father.

John Yates Beall, Son of the South

Edmund Ruffin, who, as a VMI cadet, had been present at Brown's hanging.[5]*

The next day Lincoln issued a call for 75,000 troops from the state militias to put down the rebellion. The new Virginia governor, John Letcher, until now a staunch Unionist, refused to provide his state's quota to fight against his fellow Southerners. "You have chosen to inaugurate civil war," he fumed to Secretary of War Edwin Stanton, "and having done so, we will meet it in a spirit as determined as the Administration has exhibited toward the South."[6] Lincoln's threat of aggression similarly soured convention delegates who overnight were swept up in a tide of secessionist sentiment. On April 17 the legislature held a second vote, sharply overturning the first by a margin of nearly two to one. This time Osborne had voted to secede. As for Barbour, he was already en route to Harpers Ferry with a far more subversive plan in mind.

The prior evening, Barbour was in a smoke-filled room of the Richmond Exchange Hotel hatching a plot to capture the very federal arsenal he had until recently supervised. The meeting had been called by former Virginia governor and arch–Union antagonist Henry Wise to develop a plan to secure the three strategic military sites in the state—the others being the navy yards at Norfolk and Fort Monroe. Among those in attendance were Captain John Imboden and Major John A. Harmon of the Staunton militia, Captains Turner and Richard Ashby of Fauquier County, former state legislator Oliver Funsten from Clarke County, and the editor of the *Richmond Enquirer*, Nat Tyler. Near midnight the conspirators summoned Colonel Edmund Fontaine, president of the Virginia Central Railroad, and John S. Barbour (Alfred's brother), President of the Orange and Manassas Gap railroads, who, upon hearing of the plot, agreed to place their trains at their disposal.

As John Brown had known, the armory at Harpers Ferry was a prize worth the taking. The second of the country's arsenals to be built, it had over one hundred machines and a staff of four hundred.

---

*Ruffin would later become despondent over the Confederacy's defeat in the Civil War and commit suicide.

3. Between a Hawk and a Buzzard

Each year, it produced thousands of percussion rifles and rifled muskets for the army, navy, and marine corps. Seize the arsenal, the Virginians believed, and they would instantly possess 90,000 rifles, not to mention state-of the art machinery for producing the latest long arms.[7] Ironically, it had been Barbour himself who, as superintendent of the Harpers Ferry Armory months earlier, had gotten Washington to dispatch a company of soldiers to protect the armory from an anticipated assault.[8] The very next day, First Lieutenant Roger Jones set out from Carlisle Barracks in Pennsylvania with a garrison of sixty untrained recruits to protect the arsenal. Although only thirty years old, Jones already had ten years of hard battle experience fighting Indians in Texas and New Mexico.

It was well after midnight when Imboden roused Governor Letcher from his sleep to lay out the plan. As soon as the convention voted to secede, Imboden would hasten to Staunton on the Virginia Central to rally his artillery unit. He would then return to connect with the Manassas Gap line, collecting, as he went, many of the local militia as he could rally to the cause. From Strasburg he would march north eighteen miles to Winchester, where he would board the train to Harpers Ferry. There he would rendezvous with Turner Ashby's truculent Mountain Rangers and the Black Horse Cavalry from Fauquier. It was a hastily wrought plan whose success hinged on utter secrecy, and for this reason, in his communications Imboden would refer to their destination as the Portsmouth Navy Yard so as not to disclose their true target. Once in possession of the arsenal's weapons, the Virginians would descend the Potomac valley by rail to attack Washington with troops coming by rail from Norfolk. Just how Imboden thought he could keep secret the movement of 2,500 men across the state was a mystery. Nevertheless, Letcher agreed in principle to the plan, with the caveat that he would take no action against the Federal government without passage of a secession ordinance by the legislature.

With Letcher's provisional backing, the men began to put the elements of their plan into place. Imboden telegraphed captains of the companies along the rail line, instructing them to be in readiness the next day for orders from the governor. Working through the night, he and his confederates shuttled munitions from the Virginia Armory to the railway station. As the train was about to embark, however, their plan was nearly exposed when Barbour made a careless remark that was overheard by a Northern traveler. The traveler hastily scratched out a note of warning, paying a black servant to send the telegram to Washington. Before it could be delivered, however, a member of Imboden's party chased down the servant and, paying him a silver dollar, ripped the dispatch from his hands. Disaster had been averted—or so they thought. What they didn't know was that in tearing the message from the frightened servant's hands, he had failed to notice a second part addressed not to Washington but to the commanding officer at Harpers Ferry, Lieutenant Jones, that read: *Immediate attack planned on troops by militia. Signed, an Unionist.* Though shaken, the servant delivered the truncated message to the telegraph office.

On the afternoon of the 17th Imboden's train pulled into Staunton station to a tumultuous crowd and a small army eager to join him. On hand were the West Augusta Guards under Captain William S.H. Baylor, the 5th Virginia militia commanded by Major General Kenton Harper, and Brigadier General William H. Harman's 13th Brigade. By this time the convention had voted for secession, and Harper, a former newspaper owner who had served in the Mexican War but never seen action, had received word from Letcher conferring command of the entire operation to him. Harper proceeded directly to Winchester by carriage, while Imboden returned east by train, gathering troops as he went. At Charlottesville he rallied the Monticello Guards and the Albemarle Rifles, and the local militia at Culpeper.

By dawn the next day Imboden's trains (he now had multiple trains to accommodate 2,500 men) were approaching Strasburg when an engineer in the lead train grew suspicious and let the engine fires go down. As the train rolled to a standstill, Imboden ran to the forward car to find the engineer beneath the engine with a monkey wrench. He might have succeeded in fooling Imboden had not the engineer of the second train come up to say only the fire was out and nothing else was the matter. Realizing the engineer was attempting

3. Between a Hawk and a Buzzard

to lock the cutoff valves, he denounced him as "a northern man." When the engineer emerged from beneath the engine, Imboden put a cocked Colt to his head and had only to gently persuade him to stoke the fires and proceed. At Strasburg, Imboden ran into yet another hurdle when the farmers refused to lend their horses to haul his artillery to Winchester. Citing the urgent nature of his mission, Imboden abruptly commandeered the horses and proceeded to Winchester, with the bereft farmers following in train in what had become an almost comical procession.

By this time, Lieutenant Jones was already aware of trouble brewing. In addition to the warning from the Unionist, he had received a telegraph from U.S. Army Commander General Winfield Scott warning that three trains of troops had been spotted passing through Manassas Junction on their way to destroy the armory. "Be on your guard," he said.[9]

If there was any doubt in Jones's mind as to the veracity of Scott's report, it was allayed by none other than Alfred Barbour himself. After loading the munitions onto the train in Richmond, Barbour had ridden all night to Harpers Ferry. In the morning he appeared at the arsenal gates, where he announced that the armory would soon be seized by the state militia and urged citizens and his former employees to rise and join Southern interests. Although Barbour had been hoping to protect the armory from destruction, his entreaties fell on deaf ears, for most of the arsenal employees were not Virginians and were indifferent to the Southern cause. In the end only a handful stepped forward, including a gigantic Irishman named Donovan, who shouldered a musket and took his place resolutely at the arsenal gate. Townsfolk, however, had strong opinions on the matter. Some angrily denounced Barbour for betraying his commission, while others cheered it. A brawl soon broke out that, fueled by drinking in the bars, continued into the afternoon in the streets and alleys.

Jones was less concerned about the fistfights outside or the militia seen at Manassas Junction than he was about an entirely new and more immediate threat. Earlier that day a courier from Richmond had arrived in Charlestown with news that the Old Dominion had thrown in its lot with the Confederacy by an overwhelming majority.

John Yates Beall, Son of the South

A proclamation from Governor Letcher accompanying the letter urged Jefferson County's citizens and militia to "rise and protect their honor, their property, and their rights by seizing the national arsenal at Harpers Ferry."[10]

Although Jefferson County had been steadfastly Unionist, in the wake of Lincoln's threat of aggression against the South and the legislature's decision to secede, most now followed Virginia, including John Beall and his younger brother William. Even many county Whigs, hitherto devout supporters of the Union, flipped to secessionist. "He could not," wrote Daniel Lucas of John Beall, "submit to the degradation of assisting in the subjugation of the Cotton States because in the exercise of their undoubted right they had decided to sever the connection between themselves and the other states of the Federal Union."[11]

The issue of states' rights was, of course, the South's standard rallying cry. But Beall's decision to follow Virginia into secession was less about hoary concepts of states' rights or even slavery, even though he owned nearly three dozen slaves. Indeed, as one historian has observed, at the time slavery offered a flimsy basis for secession, as many Southerners were, in fact, ambivalent about a slaveholders' republic.[12] Furthermore, if the war had been solely about slavery, as many historians argue today, then why did four slave states—Kentucky, Missouri, Maryland, and Delaware—each choose to remain in the Union? Not only did each state have its own reasons, but each individual did as well. For Beall, the decision to follow the Old Dominion into secession was driven largely by loyalty to his beloved homeland. Writing from a jail cell in Manhattan three years later, Beall would reaffirm the motives that led to his involvement in the war:

> As long as I am a citizen of Virginia, I shall cling to her destiny and maintain her laws as expressed by a majority of her citizens speaking through their authorized channel, if her voice be for war or peace. I shall go as she says. But I would not go for a minority carrying on war in opposition to the majority, as the innocent will suffer and not the guilty; but I do not justify oppression in the majority. What misery have I seen during these four years, murder, lust, hate, rapine, devastation, war! What hardships suffered, what privations endured! May God grant that I may not see the like again! Nay,

3. Between a Hawk and a Buzzard

that my country may not! Oh, far rather would I welcome Death, come as he might; far rather would I meet him than go through four more such years.[13]

Such reasoning may sound strange today. But in the nineteenth century it was the state, not country, that was regarded as the paramount political entity. Citizens had a much closer relationship to their state than the Federal government, which was perceived largely as an agent for the states and a distant one at that. Before the Civil War, it was "the United States *in* America"; forged in the fire of battle, it would become "the United States *of* America," a true and lasting Union.

In his loyalty to the Old Dominion, Beall was not alone. The day after the Virginian legislature voted to secede, Colonel Robert E. Lee met with Lincoln's personal adviser, Francis Preston Blair, and army commander General Winfield Scott to tender his resignation. Lee had anguished over the decision to break with the Union. The very idea was as repugnant to him as the accusation leveled by Francis Blair, a fellow Virginian, that his real reason was that he objected to parting with his "negroes." To this, Lee responded that if he owned all the negroes in the South, he would gladly yield them up for the sake of maintaining the Union.[14] Hard though it was, Lee was obliged to heed what he called his "Virginia secession duty." At Lincoln's suggestion, Blair offered Lee command of the entire Union army if he would but side with the North, to which Lee responded, "If I owned four million slaves, I would cheerfully sacrifice them to the preservation of the Union, but to lift my hand against my own State and people is impossible." That same day, the fifty-four-year-old Colonel retired from the U.S. army with no other intention "than to pass the remainder of my life as a private citizen."[15] In siding with Virginia he not only had walked away from a promising career in the army but had to abandon his mansion outside Washington overlooking the Potomac.

Returning home, Lee wrote to his sister in Baltimore explaining the reasons for his momentous decision. "With all my devotion to the Union, and the feeling of loyalty and duty of an American citizen, I have not been able to make up my mind to raise my hand against my relatives, my children, my home. I have therefore resigned my commission in the army and, save in the defence of my native State, with the sincere hope that my poor services may never be needed, I hope I may never be called on to draw my sword."[16]

Another Virginian, who had also resigned from the U.S. Army and for the same reason, put it starkly. Referring to his native state, he said, "If I know myself, all that I am and all I have is at the service of my country."[17] His name was Thomas J. Jackson.

By now Beall had grown into manhood. With his dark beard

Brigadier General Stonewall Jackson, in whose brigade Beall served (courtesy of Library of Congress).

and head of hair, elongated face, and sunken eyes, he faintly resembled Abe Lincoln. With the same sense of selfless service, Beall mustered into the Jefferson Guard under the command of Colonel William Allen. As they marched gallantly through the streets of Charlestown, friends and family came out to cheer them on. The mood was festive, more like a parade than a preparation for battle. Observing the high-spirited spectacle was a Virginia resident and celebrated Civil War journalist known by the pen name "Porte Crayon" (David H. Strother), who had observed the raid on Harpers Ferry. Strother described the joyful scene:

> As almost every family in the county had one or more representatives in the ranks, there was a hurrying to and fro of mothers, sisters, sweet-hearts, wives, and children of the Volunteers, showing their excitement in the most

3. Between a Hawk and a Buzzard

varied and opposite forms.... Even the negroes were jubilant in view of the parade and unusual excitement among masters and mistresses.[18]

Beneath all the merriment, however, the mood among some was conflicted. After all, had not Jefferson County passed several resolutions in support of the Union? And had not Barbour and Osborne been sent to vote in *support* of it? Finding themselves "between a hawk and a buzzard," Captain Botts approached Allen, reminding him that Charlestown and most of the surrounding communities had originally been opposed to secession. To discuss their concerns further, Allen repaired to a room with his officers. One officer raised doubt as to the authenticity of the Governor's proclamation. Upon closer examination, it was noticed that it had been signed not by Letcher but the pugnacious Turner Ashby. Allen now became suspicious, fearing that he was being deceived by a small group of secessionists. He then announced that he would not move without orders directly from the state government. When others countered that the original document might well be valid, the former VMI mathematics professor settled on a judicious plan: They would march as far as Halltown, where they would await instructions from Richmond. For his part, Botts was chagrined by his commander's decision to advance farther.

Meanwhile, Lieutenant Jones was in his office at the armory, besieged by panicked couriers rushing

Turner Ashby, the illiterate cavalryman who led Virginians at the Battle of Bolivar where Beall was wounded.

John Yates Beall, Son of the South

in with news that a Charlestown militia was on its way this time to attack the arsenal, not defend it. After seeing what he described as several hundred men advancing down the turnpike, one scout had gone home warning Jones that it would be folly to resist them with their tiny force. On that score Jones, a graduate of the U.S. Military Academy and son of an army major general, needed no convincing. During his interview for the Harpers Ferry assignment, he had told General Winfield Scott that a thousand men would be needed to resist an attack on the armory. Scott replied impassively, "I have no more troops, sir, which I can send you." Jones's response was all too prophetic: "I don't expect to need any more, unless Virginia should pass an ordinance of secession. Then they will be needed."[19]

And needed they were. Informed that the Jefferson Guard was still some distance away, Jones rode out to assess the situation for himself. Near Halltown he encountered a man on horseback who offered details of yet another large militia spotted on the Manassas Line sent by the governor to seize the arsenal. With Allen nearby and Harper's militia but a few hours away, Jones now realized what he needed to do to prevent the armory from falling into enemy hands. He hastened back to the armory and ordered the acting superintendent, Colonel Charles P. Kingsbury, to prepare to set the buildings ablaze.[20]

Blowing up the arsenal would be no mean task, given the number of buildings spread out for a half mile along the Shenandoah. The main building consisted of a massive workshop three hundred yards in length where arms were manufactured. The rifle works was a half mile up the river on Virginius Island. There were several other buildings used to store material such as iron and gun barrels, as well as housing for the staff. To add to the difficulty, the buildings were made of brick and virtually indestructible by fire.

Quietly, so as not to raise suspicion, the men began to hack boards and packing boxes into small chips to help ignite the fire. After mattresses from the barracks were emptied of straw, they were refilled with gunpowder and placed in the various outbuildings of the armory. When darkness fell, a team of soldiers rolled out several kegs of gunpowder. Ironically, because discretion had to be used in moving the powder into the buildings, they drew on smaller kegs

3. Between a Hawk and a Buzzard

that John Brown had hidden in soldiers' chaff bags and that had gone unused in the raid. Once inside, they punctured the kegs and walked from building to building, pouring trains of powder from mattress to mattress, creating an explosive web such that one match would turn the entire complex into an inferno. Because he was afraid local secessionists would attempt to take control of the armory, Jones decided not to destroy the rifle works for fear that his plan would be exposed.

In the early afternoon Allen reached Halltown, where they were met by the Clarke and Nelson Rifles, the Ashbys, the Fauquier cavalry, and future Confederate Secretary of War James A. Seddon. They were now over three hundred strong. While waiting for clarification from Richmond, Allen held a war council among his officers. As the daylight hours waned, there were still no orders from Richmond. Some of the officers became annoyed at Allen's temporizing, particularly Turner Ashby, who was agitating for an immediate attack. Finally, around 8 p.m. an express rider from Winchester raced into camp on a horse spattered with mud and heaving with exhaustion. Opening the rider's dispatch, Allen was relieved to read orders signed by the adjutant-general to immediately seize Harpers Ferry. He sprang from his seat and exclaimed, "Now I can act from a clear conscience."[21]

Others, however, were still uncomfortable with what they considered to be orders to commit a treasonable act against their country. Worse, they were about to engage in battle their own countrymen, some of whom were likely friends. Lawson Botts continued to have deep misgivings about the mission, unsure as to which master to serve, his state or his country. "Great God!" he anguished, "I would willingly give my life to know what course I ought to pursue and where my duty lies."[22] Those who remained staunchly Unionist hoped they could eventually vote against the Secession Ordinance in a state referendum.*

---

*When the referendum was held on May 23, rebel forces were sent to suspected Unionist precincts, with the result that only half of the voters showed up at the polls. A majority favored secession by a vote of 813 to 365. Nor was the Jefferson County militia alone in its dilemma. When the Martinsburg militia was ordered to Harpers Ferry, it marched under a U.S. flag.

John Yates Beall, Son of the South

For now, however, their orders were to march. It was a clear, moonless night. In the darkness the militia made its way down the turnpike in nervous silence, save for the occasional rattling of a saber or a whispered command. Captain Ashby's cavalry was in the rear. Two miles on, a resounding "Halt!" echoed in the darkness. Allen ordered his men to "load at will." Faced with the prospect of shooting at fellow Americans, some of the volunteers vomited and dropped their weapons. Others turned and headed home. Jones's picket quietly retreated, however, allowing Allen to advance without a fight. Further on, another command to halt was followed by yet another Union retreat. When Allen reached Bolivar Heights, he halted on Smallwood's Ridge to await reinforcements.

Down at the armory, Lieutenant Jones was still holding out hope that he would not have to destroy the arsenal he was charged to protect. At 9:30 p.m. he sent a final message to Washington, pleading for reinforcements.

Sir:

Up to the present time no assault or attempt to seize the Government property here has been made, but there is decided evidence that the subject is in contemplation, and has been all day, by a large number of people living in the direction of Charlestown; and at sundown this evening several companies of troops had assembled at Halltown about three or four miles from here on the road to Charlestown, with the intention of seizing the Government property, and the last report is that the attack will be made to-night. I telegraphed this evening to General Scott that I had received information confirming his dispatch of this morning, and later to the Adjutant-General that I expected an attack tonight. I have taken steps which ought to insure my receiving early intelligence of the advance of any forces, and my determination is to destroy what I cannot defend, and if the forces sent against me are clearly overwhelming, my present intention is to retreat into Pennsylvania.

The steps I have taken to destroy the arsenal, which contains nearly 15,000 stand of arms, are so complete that I can conceive of nothing that will prevent their entire destruction. If the Government purposes maintaining its authority here, no time should be lost in sending large bodies of troops to my assistance, and as many of them as possible should be regulars.

A courier has just reported the advance of the troops from Halltown.

Respectfully, I am, I sir, your obedient servant,

R. JONES,
First Lieutenant, Mounted Riflemen, Commanding[23]

No sooner had Jones sent the dispatch than he received confirmation that the Virginia militia had just left Winchester and would

3. Between a Hawk and a Buzzard

arrive within two hours. Any hope of defending the arsenal against Allen's men had now vanished. Shortly after 10 p.m., he ordered the men to torch the arsenal.

On the plateau above town, Allen and his men were suddenly startled by a blinding flash of light accompanied by a booming roar echoing in the gorge immediately below. As they looked on, awestruck, several more explosions followed, shooting sparks into the night sky. Then all went quiet as an orange glow illuminated the hills surrounding the town. At first, they had no idea what had occurred. Some of Allen's men interpreted the flashes to be artillery, while other conjectured the B&O bridge over the Potomac had been blown up. Mounting his horse, Ashby dashed down the hill to ascertain the cause of the mysterious explosions. When Allen learned the armory had been blow up, he immediately ordered the men to march in the hope of salvaging some of its equipment.

By the time they arrived, citizens were already looting the armory. Porte Crayon, who was close behind Ashby, described the scene. "There were women with their arms full of muskets, little girls loaded with sheaves of bayonets, boys dragging cartridge-boxes and cross-belts enough to equip a platoon, men with barrels of pork or flour, kegs of molasses, and boxes of hard bread on their shoulders or trundling in wheelbarrows."[24] When Allen came up, he was dismayed. The 90,000 rifles they had hoped to secure for the Confederacy were not there (they had been shipped out months earlier), and the 15,000 that were had all been destroyed in the fire. At least the weapons-producing machinery was unscathed, thanks to townsfolk who had rushed to extinguish the fire with the arsenal's nearby fire engines.[25]* Secessionists had a noose around poor Donovan and were threatening to hang him, but he was eventually released. "Had he fallen into the hands of the men from the Gulf States," a local volunteer remarked, "he would not have escaped so easily."[26] It wasn't until 4 a.m. that General Harper finally arrived and assumed command.

---

*Eventually the machinery would be shipped to Fayetteville, North Carolina, where it would be used to produce far more weapons than they were hoping to take from Harpers Ferry.

Although he had arrived late for the show, Harper, who had yet to see his first battle, would claim credit for the victory.[27]

Harpers Ferry had been wrested from the Federal government without firing a single shot. To everyone's delight, Virginia's very first action in the war had been a resounding victory. The sons of the South now celebrated, jubilantly, passing whiskey around and shooting into the air. In the following days Harper's officers paraded around town each afternoon pompously attired in epauletted finery that, according to Imboden, "would have done no discredit to the Champs Elysees."[28] Parents and siblings came in from Charlestown with fresh clothing for their boys, as well as "every imaginable delicacy" to eat. Black servants tended to the washing, cleaning, and cooking. Life in Jefferson County seemed to be quickly returning to normal. "Nothing was serious yet," Henry Kyd Douglas of Company B wrote, "everything much like a joke. These were the good easy days."[29]

4

Stonewall's Brigade

THE EASY DAYS CAME TO AN ABRUPT end on April 29, when thirty-seven-year-old Colonel Thomas J. Jackson arrived to replace the inexperienced Harper. Tall with pale-blue eyes and a bushy-beard, Jackson was a little-known professor of natural philosophy and artillery tactics at VMI who had served with distinction in the Mexican War. An obsessively disciplined soldier, Jackson was chagrined to find a ragtag group of raw recruits clad mostly in hunting shirts and armed with obsolete flintlock muskets. In comic contrast, the officers were nattily decked out in "cocked hats and feathers, epaulets, and ceremonial sashes," complete with a retinue of fawning aides all drinking whiskey.[1] "Things presented a most hopeless aspect," he wrote his wife. He quickly jettisoned the liquor and deposed the "featherbed and cornstalk" militia commanders, who puttered home indignant. He replaced them with commissioned officers, most of whom were VMI associates trained in the art of war.[2] Still, the rank and file were mostly raw recruits—farmers, laborers, teachers, and the unemployed—who needed to be whipped into shape, and quickly.[3]

Jackson proceeded to organize the men into a single brigade of five regiments—much to the frustration of the volunteers, who had their own ideas about how to fight. The Botts Greys became Company G under Captain Botts in the 1st Virginia Regiment commanded by Colonel James Allen. Upon mustering into Jackson's Brigade, John Beall was described as "twenty-six years old, a farmer, 5'8", fair complexion, blue eyes, brown hair." At just seventeen years of age, his brother William was the second youngest in the brigade.

Thus organized, Jackson began to hone his ten companies into a single fighting unit. Better equipment and uniforms were brought in, and flintlock muskets were converted into percussion muskets at the Harpers Ferry armory. Each day he marched the troops in formation for seven to ten hours. When they were not marching, he drilled them in increasingly complex maneuvers—first at the company and then at the regimental level—in how to advance and retreat, how to strike camp, and so forth. A lack of resources forced farmers to learn the subtleties of cavalry maneuvers on their plow horses.

Unaccustomed as they were to military life, the volunteers bristled at Jackson's endless marching and drilling, not to mention his irritating obsession with rules and regulations. As if that were not enough, some days Jackson conducted full inspection at 1:30 a.m. Even more off-putting was their commander's icy demeanor. Jackson never smiled and invariably walked about with eyes half closed as if lost in thought. Said one volunteer, "Our senior colonel was a man who never spoke unless spoken to; never seemed to sleep; had his headquarters under a tree ... he walked about alone, the projecting visor of his blue cap concealing his features; a bad-fitting, single-breasted blue coat, and high boots covering the largest feet ever seen, completed the picture."[4]

As time passed, the men became mystified by their new commander's bizarre habits. Each day Jackson went for a walk at precisely the same time, this apparently to harmonize the two halves of his body. On Sundays he would pack himself in wet sheets for an hour, after which he would lead the choir at the Presbyterian Church. Under the same tree where his headquarters sat, he led the choir in nightly prayer and singing. Few of the men attended Jackson's prayer meetings save his staff, who seemed, one private observed, "to have been chosen or elected because they were of his way of life."[5] He ate strange foods such as stale bread and sucked lemons constantly. More mystifying than Jackson's obsession with the sour fruit was his ability to keep a plentiful supply of them on hand. Yet for all of Jackson's idiosyncrasies, the men's alienation would very soon turn to pride in being part of the illustrious "Stonewall Brigade."

To protect against an attack from the north, Jackson sent Companies A and I into Maryland. After struggling up the rugged slopes

4. Stonewall's Brigade

of Maryland Heights, the greenhorns camped without tents or cooking utensils. But they soon devised a way to cook—laying their meat on flat rocks and wrapping their dough around the ramrods of their guns and holding them over the open fire. For protection from the incessant spring rains, however, they had found no solution. When President Jefferson Davis's military advisor, Robert E. Lee, advised him that the presence of his men in Maryland might turn an undecided state against the South, Jackson reluctantly returned to Harpers Ferry.

A few days later, Jackson marched his brigade to Shepherdstown to guard the crossing over the upper Potomac. A long procession of carriages followed in train, filled with weeping mothers and sisters and portly fathers on horseback. When darkness fell, family members returned home, leaving the soldiers to continue marching until well past midnight. "It was our first night-march," D.B. Conrad complained, "and by two o'clock we were 'dead beat!'"[6] When the indefatigable Jackson gave the order to halt, many simply fell asleep by the roadside. The weather soon turned miserable, with a hailstorm so severe it bloodied their faces and tore at their clothing. Nine men deserted. A few days later Jackson marched to Williamsport in heavy rain. So much marching did not endear Jackson to the men, who complained he was killing them. After nearly two weeks on the march with no sign of the enemy he returned to Harpers Ferry, much to the relief of his exhausted men.

In late April, reinforcements came up from Kentucky, Mississippi, Alabama, and Tennessee, bringing Jackson's men to seven thousand strong. Still, they were not entirely battle ready. One local described the Kentucky volunteers as "among the worst specimens of the Confederate army, being composed of rough, Ohio boatmen and low 'bummers' from the purlieus of Louisville and other river towns."[7] Still, Jackson felt he was still three thousand short of the strength needed to guard the critical entrance to the valley, the breadbasket of the Confederacy. "If this valley is lost," he would later say, "Virginia is lost."[8]

In May, General Joseph E. Johnston arrived to replace Jackson. That Jackson's men were still green was evidenced in the General's sneering assessment that he would not give a company of regulars for the whole regiment. Although guards had been posted at the bridges leading to Maryland and Loudoun Heights, Johnston feared that by lingering in low-lying Harpers Ferry he could be trapped, just as John Brown had been. Hearing that General Robert Patterson was approaching from Hagerstown, Maryland, Johnston ordered an evacuation of the town. Prior to departing, he blew up the B&O rail bridge and burned the main armory buildings to prevent key assets from falling into Union hands.

On June 14, Johnston marched to Charlestown, Jackson to Shepherdstown. Upon arrival, Jackson ordered the rail bridge over the Potomac to be destroyed. As private Henry Kyd Douglas of Company B looked on, he could see the glare of the bridge's burning timbers reflected on his father's home on the hill overlooking the river. Aware his father was also a stockholder in the very company that owned the bridge, he awakened to the realization that that war had finally begun in earnest. "I knew that I was severing all connection between me and my family and understood the sensation of one, who sitting aloft on the limb of a tree, cuts its it off between himself and the trunk."[9] Soon after, he saw his father's barn go up in flames as well.

While encamped near Martinsburg, Jackson received word that General Robert Patterson had crossed the Potomac near Falling Waters and was fast approaching. Jackson immediately ordered the men to march, leaving behind, much to their dismay, new tents that had just arrived. Unaware of the size of Patterson's army, he sent the 5th Regiment forward with a cannon with the aim of drawing Patterson's troops out to reveal their size.[10] When Patterson's men opened fire, Jackson sent skirmishers forward who drove them back. After another repulse, the Union army came on, this time in strength. To their wide-eyed astonishment, for the first time the Southern boys could see a long line of blue with the U.S. flag waving at its center. Jackson now realized Patterson's force was much larger than his own and ordered his men to fall back. As they retreated, Union troops advanced through the fields and woods, firing continuously. Despite being outnumbered nearly eight to one, Jackson directed a withdrawal so strategic and disciplined that Johnston would estimate

4. Stonewall's Brigade

his strength at 3,500 men. Falling Waters was the first real action Stonewall's Brigade saw, and for most it was the first time since John Brown's raid that they heard the sobering "whizz of a musket ball and shriek of cannon shot."[11]

After four days in Darkesville waiting in vain for Patterson to appear, Johnston moved to Winchester to be near Beauregard, camped near Manassas Junction. Jackson, who wanted to take on the Blue Coats head on, bristled at another retreat. A week later a courier arrived with news that Union forces had attacked Manassas Junction and that Beauregard was requesting support. At last, a chance to fight! Johnston sounded the call to arms and the men marched toward Berry's Ferry on the Shenandoah, wadeable in mid-summer, crying, with youthful vigor, "On to Manassas!" On the evening of the 18th Johnston's army reached the Piedmont Station (near present-day Delaplane), where the men boarded the B&O. That they were still callow greenheads playing at war was evidenced by an incident on the train. As they were filing into cattle cars, Beall's company spotted a comfortable coach and jumped in and made themselves comfortable. In due course, a member of Johnston's staff, William Pendleton, appeared and ordered them to vacate because it was designated an officers' car. The privates stubbornly refused, and after some empty threats a frustrated Pendleton stormed off.

Soon, the youthful games would be over.

5

The Battle of the Bread

IT MUST HAVE COME AS A CRUSHING disappointment to Beall that when the Botts Greys finally saw their first real action at Manassas (or Bull Run, as the North called it), he was back home on furlough. He had missed not only the first battle of the war but the Confederacy's very first victory as well, news of which was now proudly reverberating throughout the South. Though the battle had been marked by confusion, disorganization, and miscalculation on both sides, the one shining performance had been that of Jackson's Brigade.

On the morning of July 17, Confederate General Bernard E. Bee found himself besieged by Union artillery troops on Henry Hill when Jackson arrived on the scene. Placing his artillery in an unconventional location on sheltered lower ground, he began pounding enemy positions. A series of Union charges failed to dislodge Jackson, who held his position so fearlessly (or stubbornly) that Bee would later liken it to "a stone wall." Whether Bee meant this as a compliment or criticism was unclear. In any case, after Beauregard broke the Union's right flank the Federals had retreated in panic, leaving broken guns, cartridges boxes, canteens, knapsacks, and disabled wagons littering the route all the way back to Washington. For his implacable calm under fire Jackson had received the nickname "Stonewall," with his unit ever after famously known as "the Stonewall Brigade."

In late summer Beall rejoined his now celebrated brigade, keen to see action on the battlefield at last. But much to his frustration, there was none. Three times they marched to Fairfax Courthouse to engage the enemy, but each time it was a false alarm. Most days were spent not in glorious battle but in the monotonous confines of camp. Until they could find Bluecoats to fight, they whiled away the

5. The Battle of the Bread

time playing cards, listening to music, and drinking bootleg whiskey when they could sneak it in.[1] When not idling about camp, they drilled to excess—Jackson's favorite pastime. Colonel Allen, too, drilled his men to make up for losing three company commanders. Morning, noon, and night they drilled, and drilled again, until the men were exhausted.

In October, Jackson, whose strategic acumen on Henry Hill had not gone unnoticed by Lee and Johnston, was promoted to Major General and reassigned to take command of the forces at Winchester. Before departing he paused to give a fond farewell to the men he had honed from scratch.

> You have already gained a brilliant and deservedly high reputation throughout the army and the whole Confederacy ... and I trust in the future ... you will gain more victories.... In the Army of the Shenandoah you were the *First* Brigade, in the Army of the Potomac you were the *First* Brigade, in the 2nd Corps of this army you are the *First* Brigade; you are the *First* Brigade in the affections of your general, and I hope by your future deeds and bearing you will be handed down to posterity as the *First* Brigade in this, our second war of independence.[2]

It was high praise indeed from the man who rarely spoke or smiled. Unfortunately, Beall, who had been absent for the battle, could not share in the accolades.

A few days later Beall was once again separated from the brigade, this time to escort a sick soldier back to Charlestown. Ironically, it would be in his own backyard where he would see his first combat in what might have alternately been dubbed the "Battle of the Bread."

Early in October a Unionist named Abraham Herr, who owned a flour mill on Virginius Island above Harpers Ferry, wished to remove a large store of wheat to prevent it from falling into Confederate hands. At the time, Herr's mill was no longer operating, having been crippled by Patterson's Union forces during his brief occupation of the town that summer. Patterson had ostensibly overlooked nearly 20,000 bushels of unmilled wheat remaining in Herr's storehouse. Whether out of Union sympathy or a desire to spare his mill further damage should it be found, Herr approached Major Jacob Parker Gould, commander of the 13th Massachusetts Volunteers, stationed three miles downriver at Sandy Hook. With the B&O bridge destroyed by Johnston a few months earlier, Herr suggested Gould transport the wheat to Maryland by boat. Gould passed along the idea to his commander at Darnestown, Major General Nathaniel Banks, who ordered him to seize the wheat immediately and transport it to Washington, where it would be used to make bread for the soldiers. To assist Gould, Banks dispatched three companies of Wisconsin Volunteers and a section of the Rhode Island Battery.

On the morning of October 8, Gould proceeded to the storehouse, informing no one of his mission, not even his officers. Upon arrival at Harpers Ferry, he set up camp on the north side of the Potomac on Maryland Heights before proceeding to the island. Near the mill he found a large deck boat and in the B&O canal two large scows, which he lashed together to form a single barge. He then ran tow ropes six hundred feet across the Shenandoah to ferry the grain across to the canal. To prevent news of his activities from reaching Charlestown, Gould dispatched one company to form a two-mile-long picket on Bolivar Heights stretching from the Potomac to the Shenandoah. The next morning Gould ordered another company to form an advance picket on a ridge west of Bolivar Heights. It had rained heavily overnight and as the men were struggling across the raging Potomac gunfire could be heard on the plateau above. A small party of rebel cavalry scouts had spotted the picket and skirmished briefly before riding off with a wounded soldier.

By now, Gould's soldiers had begun the backbreaking job of bagging and loading the wheat—along with several citizens impressed for the task but never paid. Each day they began at 7 a.m., bagging it and then ferrying the heavy sacks across the Shenandoah to the canal. Now that they had been spotted by rebel scouts, Gould insisted the men work flat out until midnight. Some company commanders, though, refused to work after dark, insisting their men needed rest from the grueling work.

Five days into the mission, Gould received word that rebel forces were concentrating in the area. He immediately sent a telegram requesting assistance from Colonel John W. Geary commanding

5. The Battle of the Bread

the upper Potomac with the 28th Pennsylvania Infantry. A towering six-foot-six-inch Pennsylvanian weighing 260 pounds, Geary had served in the Mexican War and been an able governor of "Bleeding Kansas" for several months. Within days Geary was at Harpers Ferry with no fewer than six hundred men and four cannons of the Rhode Island and New York batteries. To protect Harpers Ferry, Geary placed two of the cannons on Maryland Heights and another on the B&O raid line opposite the town. The fourth he placed in Virginia, commanding the southern approach to the town. He then ran a long picket line across the Bolivar plateau—much as Lieutenant Jones had—stretching from the Potomac to the Shenandoah. To protect against an attack from the north he left one company of the 13th Massachusetts on Maryland Heights.

The Confederate forces gathering in the area were those of Lieutenant Colonel Turner Ashby, who had been posted just north of Charlestown to prevent Union forces from advancing down the Shenandoah Valley. The thirty-seven-year-old, nearly illiterate Ashby possessed a sneering disregard for military rules and regulations. Though his cavalier attitude irked the fastidious Jackson to no end, what he lacked in military discipline was compensated with dazzling equestrian skills and reckless daring in battle.

The war had already become deeply personal for Ashby. Four months earlier, his brother Richard had been butchered in a clash with Union forces along the Potomac. After being struck in the head by a saber, Richard lay wounded on the ground when his attacker savagely ran a bayonet through his abdomen and fled with his spurs and horse. Ashby had since harbored a deep hatred for Northerners and was obsessed with revenge. When his scouts reported that Geary of Kansas notoriety was at Harpers Ferry, he set out with three hundred militia and two companies of the 7th Virginia Cavalry to put a stop to their work—and exact retribution for his brother's death. Joining Ashby was a motley mix of Jefferson County farmers, mechanics, and other civilians. When Beall heard Ashby was in Bolivar preparing to attack Geary, he hastened to Halltown to join the fight.[3]

A little after daybreak on October 16—two years to the day of Brown's raid—Ashby's men rushed from the woods west of Bolivar and opened fire on the Union picket. Intending to catch Gould in a crossfire, Ashby had placed three cannons on Bolivar Heights—one of which was a massive thirty-two-pounder mounted precariously on common wagon wheels—and four smaller ones in Geary's rear on Loudoun Heights along with several snipers. Behind Ashby's infantry the cannonier began alternately throwing solid and grape shot while the smaller guns threw fuse shells with astonishing precision. Caught off guard by the barrage, Geary's men were thrown into disarray and retreated. When Geary summoned troops from Maryland Heights to protect his rear, Ashby's guns on Loudoun Heights—which had been placed too low on the hillside to reach Bolivar—turned to shelling the soldiers attempting to ferry across the Potomac. Meanwhile, snipers on Loudoun Heights were taking pot shots at Herr's mill, greatly frustrating Gould's work.

With Geary on the defensive, Ashby ordered his left and right flanks to advance pincer-like as he pressed from the center. As Geary fell back into Bolivar town, Ashby's men advanced, assuming positions in some of the outlying houses. Ashby now attempted a bold, direct assault on Geary's position. Seated gallantly on his snow-white mare and backed by a long line of rear infantry firing continuously, Ashby charged Geary's line. On the right flank leading one company of militia was John Beall.[4] As the rebels advanced, they let out an eerie, demoniacal cry that spooked the enemy, a sound that would soon become famously known as "the rebel yell." Despite having the tactical advantage, Ashby was nonetheless woefully outnumbered and outgunned.

The Battle of Bolivar was a microcosm of the Civil War writ large. Three hundred Confederates, nearly all armed with smoothbore flintlock muskets, were attempting to defeat four hundred fifty Federals with lighter and more accurate Enfield rifles. As the fighting raged, Beall noticed several Federals had taken cover behind an abandoned brick house from which they were pouring heavy fire on Ashby's men. Seeking to dislodge them from the house, Beall called upon several militia to follow him in a charge. As he and his men rushed forward, the Federals scattered, firing as they retreated. Beall had gotten off two shots with his musket when, as he paused to

5. The Battle of the Bread

reload, a ball struck him obliquely in his right chest, passing through his body. He fell instantly, discharging his gun as he went down. The fighting continued as Beall lay bleeding and unconscious. When he came to, he was dismayed to see his men had absconded, leaving him alone on the battlefield. Grabbing his musket, he hobbled back to safety, gasping for air. When he reached Ashby's line he collapsed and passed out. It happened that Judge Andrew H. Hunter, the Charlestown attorney who had prosecuted John Brown, had come down to Bolivar in his horse-drawn wagon to collect the wounded from the battlefield. Upon seeing Beall, Hunter lifted him into the wagon and carried him back to Walnut Grove.

By this time the momentum of the battle had begun to turn in Geary's favor after a Union shell had shattered the axle of Ashby's heavy cannon and it had to be abandoned, though not before it was spiked.[5] A little before noon Lieutenant J.W. Martin of the 9th New York, who had managed to dodge the heavy fire from the Loudoun Heights, came up with a rifled cannon. As Martin took aim at Ashby's remaining guns, Geary ordered two of his Pennsylvania companies to conduct a right flank maneuver, which succeeded in gaining the high ground near the Potomac. Seeing he had weakened the Confederate line, Geary now thrust his center forward, causing the rebels to break and scatter into the woods near Halltown. While in full retreat, Ashby courageously attempted to fire his only remaining cannon. But when Union shells struck his ammo caisson, causing a terrific explosion, he finally withdrew. As he rode off, Ashby was shot from his horse but managed to remount and escape. Once in control of the battlefield, the Federals began collecting their dead. To their horror they found that the bodies had been stripped naked and repeatedly bayoneted, evidence of Ashby's vengeful wrath. One body was gruesomely laid out in the form of a crucifixion, with arms outstretched and palms lacerated with a dull knife.[6]

In his report of the battle, Geary, who had a reputation for shameless self-promotion, claimed a resounding victory for the Union, wildly exaggerating the rebel force at 3,000 and the number of rebel losses at one hundred fifty.[7] For his part, Ashby falsely claimed to have killed twenty-five Bluecoats while losing only one man with nine wounded.[8] The reality was that each side had lost only a handful of men, and while the outcome wasn't a draw, it was far from the resounding victory Geary had claimed. Still, Geary had staved off Ashby's attack, allowing Gould to harvest 15,000 pounds of wheat. In the evening both sides went their way like two stray dogs in a street scrap, Geary to Maryland Heights and Ashby to Halltown.

The wounded Confederates were carted off to Charlestown courthouse, where local women had set up a makeshift infirmary. On his way back to camp that night, Ashby stopped by the courthouse to visit them. At each pallet he stopped to inquire as to the nature of the man's injury and say a few encouraging words. One wounded man he did not visit was John Beall, who was at Walnut Grove being looked after by his mother and sister. The ball that had struck him had shattered four ribs, one of which had pierced his lung.

With only one good lung, Beall was now unable keep up with Jackson's interminable drilling, let alone the grueling marches, and he was given a temporary medical discharge from the army.

It appeared Beall's participation in the war was over as soon as it had begun.

6

As Crazy as a March Hare

BEALL SPENT SEVERAL WEEKS RECUPERATING at Walnut Grove. When he was well enough to travel, his doctor advised him to go south for the winter. He set out in December, visiting relatives along the way in Richmond, North Carolina, and Georgia, finally alighting in Tallahassee, Florida. There he made the acquaintance of a General Robert W. Williams and his wife Susan. The childless couple took a liking to the wounded veteran and invited him to stay at their plantation on Pascagoula Island, Louisiana, while he recovered. Beall remained a guest of the Williamses for several months, all the while contemplating how, with his disability, he could continue to serve the cause of the Confederacy. It happened that during his stay, two cousins of Susan's, Fanny and Martha O'Bryan, arrived at the Williams home, seeking refuge from the heavy fighting around Nashville. Beall soon became smitten with twenty-five-year-old Martha, a schoolteacher, and within months the two were secretly engaged.

By spring Beall was feeling well enough to return to active duty—or so he thought. Bidding farewell to his Louisiana hosts, he returned to Virginia, leaving his betrothed in their care. After a few weeks in Richmond visiting friends and getting updated on the latest developments in the war, he traveled to Madison County, where he stayed with an aunt and uncle. His intention, it seemed, was to locate Jackson's army so that he could rejoin his unit. He had been there but a few days when he received exciting news: Jackson was back in the Shenandoah Valley. Indeed, his old commander was in the early stages of a campaign that would seal his reputation as one of the most brilliant military strategists in American history. Known as the "Valley Campaign," it involved a series of rapid, unpredictable, and wide-ranging maneuvers aimed at tying down General Nathaniel Banks's vast army in the valley and preventing him from moving east to join McClellan's attack on Richmond.

Jackson had opened his campaign at Kernstown on March 23. Despite suffering a minor tactical defeat there (the only one in his career) against Colonel Nathan Kimball's numerically superior 5th Corps, he had nonetheless won a major strategic victory. Having seen how dangerous Jackson could be when outnumbered, Lincoln ordered Banks to remain in the valley, and the Union forces were unable to take Richmond.

Two days after Kernstown, Jackson headed south with Banks in full, if desultory, pursuit. Hearing that Jackson was now marching down the Valley Turnpike, Beall borrowed a horse and dashed off to find his old unit. Little did he know that finding the unpredictable and peripatetic Jackson would be like chasing a jackrabbit. The first day he rode the entire day, covering about sixty miles. In his eagerness to find Jackson, he blundered headlong into Union troops near Newtown. Unable to reverse course without raising suspicion, he casually rode into a barnyard, pretending to be busy with the cattle inside. When passing soldiers entered to question him, Beall pretended to be the proprietor, gruffly instructing them to close the gate behind them when they entered so as not to allow his cattle to stray. When the soldiers departed Beall sought out the owner and, finding him loyal to the South, gave him his personal papers to mail to his mother lest he be caught with them.

In the morning he resumed his search. Heavy rain overnight had washed out the wooden bridges and made rivers impassable, forcing him to trace a circuitous route in search of his regiment. He rode and rode but there was no sign of Jackson. Where in the world could he be, Beall wondered. By this time the unpredictable Jackson wasn't even in the valley. Upon reaching New Market, Jackson had veered sharply east, pushing his exhausted men over Blue Ridge to Swift Run Gap to deceive Banks into thinking he was heading to Richmond. A few weeks later Jackson marched south to Charlottesville, where he boarded a train to Staunton. From there he marched thirty-five miles west into the rugged, densely forested Alleghenies. At the village

6. As Crazy as a March Hare

of McDowell, he engaged forces commanded by General Robert C. Schenk, driving them back into West Virginia.

By the time Beall reached the Alleghenies, Jackson was already gone. Having ridden the entire day in pouring rain, Beall halted at nightfall to rest and dry his soaked clothing. "I completely broke down," he said, "and was unable to keep up with the army."[1] Weak and exhausted, he finally abandoned his search—and his quest to rejoin Jackson's Brigade. He passed the night at the Six-Mile House, where his mood was lifted somewhat by news of the Battle of Fair Oaks in which McClellan had marched up the Virginia peninsula only to fail in taking Richmond. As for the indefatigable Jackson, he was already a hundred miles away, about to hand the Federals another loss, this time at Front Royal. In all, Jackson would log over six hundred miles in forty-eight days.

With Bluecoats swarming over Jefferson County, Beall thought better than to return to Walnut Farm. Detouring to Uniontown, Maryland, he sold his horse and bought a train ticket to Dubuque, Iowa, to see his older brother. With Hezekiah's help, he found work running a flour mill in nearby Cascade under the name John Yates.[2] He took an upstairs room in the home of the mill's owners, Thomas Chew and his wife Margaret, who were sympathetic to the Southern cause and privy to Beall's true identity. For two months he worked at the mill, keeping a low profile, reading, and mulling over how he could participate in a war in his debilitated condition. Though safely ensconced in the heartland a thousand miles from the battlelines, he continued to follow each development of the war with rapt interest—"Genl. Geary had his arm broken by a minie ball, and Genl. Price is a prisoner," he entered in his diary.[3] He began to accept the possibility that, in his condition, he might have to sit out the war and go into partnership with his brother.

Events soon dictated otherwise. Late one night in September, Margaret woke him with news that his identity as a rebel soldier in hiding had been exposed through the "imprudence of his friends."[4] Beall immediately packed his bags and bolted. After stopping in Dubuque to bid farewell to Hezekiah, with $1,620 in gold he set out for Canada. At the time, Canada was still a British subject,

John Yates Beall, Son of the South

and although Britain had officially declared its neutrality in the war, Canadians sympathized deeply with the South as a weaker power whose interests were being trampled on by the North.

After a journey marked by delays necessary to maintain his cover and obtain more funds, he arrived November 19 in Dundas on the western tip of Lake Ontario. (It was here he conceived of a plan to rescue Confederate prisoners being held along the lakes, though it would be a year before he would implement it.) Settling in Riley's Hotel, he now prepared to execute a plan he had first conceived while in Louisiana: He would sail to Great Britain and sign on with one of the Confederate raiding ships being secretly built there. Prior to his departure, however, came another setback: After his wound re-opened, a Canadian doctor warned that he was still too weak to withstand the rigors of service at sea. Indeed, with a photo of himself sent the same week to his cousin, Elizabeth Aglionby, he described himself as "prematurely old. Exposure, hardship, suffering, the drain of an unhealed wound, anxiety, hope deferred have done the work of time on the body."[5] Many a night he lay awake, tortured by the memory of that fateful moment at Bolivar, from which the wound he sustained seemed to have closed every door to participation in the war he so desperately sought. To add to his sense of weariness, he received a letter from his sister Mary informing him that in August his beloved commander Lawson Botts had been killed at Manassas, shot through the mouth.

Out of commission, perhaps, but he was not without soulmates. Dundas was seething with rebels, as were other Canadian cities on the border. Describing Confederates in Montreal, Canadian historian Barry Sheehy wrote:

> From 1861 until the end of the war in 1865, clandestine activities in Montreal closely resembled what occurred in places such as spy-riddled Casablanca, Lisbon, or Geneva during the Second World War. The city was alive with refugees, soldiers of fortune, blockade runners, U.S. army recruiters, and spies; all of them afloat on a sea of illicit money flowing from Confederate bank accounts, cotton trading, blockade running, and the sale of arms, food, and equipment to Richmond.[6]

Some, like Beall, had been wounded and had come to Canada to sit out the war; others were escapees from Northern prisons who had

6. As Crazy as a March Hare

come to regroup and find a new entry point back into it. One of Beall's comrades, twenty-three-year-old Oliver Lee Bradley, a Kentuckian from Breckenridge's Brigade, was waiting for his father's consent to rejoin his unit. Still others were already conducting cross border raids against Northern states. In his association with them, Beall found not only companionship. He came up with several ideas for renewing the fight, one of which was freeing the nearly three thousand Confederate prisoners living in deplorable conditions on Johnson's Island in Lake Erie.

While in Dundas, Beall began keeping a diary, as much to record his own exploits as to chronicle a conflict he regarded as nothing short of apocalyptic. In impassioned language, he commented on virtually every noteworthy event of the war, the movement of every army—Union and Rebel—the advance and retreat of every general, and every battle, tallying the number of dead and wounded, hoping to decipher in them portents of a Confederate victory.

> In Kentucky, Morgan has been cutting up on a grand scale, having captured cities, towns, thousands of prisoners, and arms, and millions of stores—threatening Cincinnati, Louisville, and Frankfort. In Missouri several battles, or rather skirmishes, have been fought, and many thousands have been enlisted for Price, who is moving on Rolla and Springfield. So much for military affairs. We must conclude that, during the last month, the Confederates have been successful in a high degree—defeating choice armies, capturing immense stores, and many thousands of arms and ammunition in proportion.[7]

To add to his optimism, several rebels had just returned from England, where, to everyone's excitement, Confederate vessels were being built in Clyde.

In early January, Beall checked out of Riley's Hotel and boarded a southbound train. His destination was unclear, though he may have been hoping to see Martha before returning to the war in some capacity. Whatever his intention, he got as far as Kentucky when his way forward was stymied. The previous summer, Kentuckian John Hunt Morgan, the "Thunderbolt of the Confederacy," had swept through the state like a vicious tornado, destroying railroad and telegraph lines, seizing supplies, taking prisoners, and wreaking havoc in the Union rear. With rail lines impassable, Beall mulled returning to

John Yates Beall, Son of the South

western Virginia by way of the Ohio River, but all passenger steamboats had been commandeered to resupply General William Rosecrans's army in Tullahoma, which had just defeated General Braxton Bragg in Murfreesboro. With so many routes closed, Beall rode a rail car to Baltimore and from there sailed south on one of the many rebel oyster boats called "pungies," being used to blockade Union ships.[8] On board he befriended a Confederate soldier from Missouri named Schluter who had recently escaped from a Union prison. The two continued up Virginia's northern neck, reaching Richmond in late February 1863. Beall went directly to Dan Lucas, now successfully ensconced in a law partnership on Main Street.

As luck would have it, his other childhood friend, Edwin Gray Lee, was there. "Ned," as he was known, had served as an aide to Stonewall Jackson and fought at the First Battle of Bull Run and in the Shenandoah Valley Campaign. Like Beall, he had recently been released from the army for an unknown lung condition that had similarly prevented him from keeping up with Jackson's marches.[9]* With Ned and Beall disabled, it must have been a bittersweet reunion for the three farm boys from Jefferson County. But with the war raging there was little time for self-pity. Beall had come to Richmond to seek funding for his scheme, and Ned was just the man he needed to get it in motion—he was a second cousin of General Robert E. Lee. And Ned was able to arrange an audience for Beall with President Jefferson Davis.

A few days on, Beall and Ned were in President Davis's office in what was called "the Confederate White House" (it was actually gray) on 12th and Clay streets in the stately Court End neighborhood of Richmond. They met in Davis's dark office, with the only light being a few gas lamps and logs burning in the fireplace.

The ideas Beall planned to present had germinated while he was in Dundas fraternizing with escaped rebels. He offered for the President's consideration a couple of options, all of which involved some form of irregular warfare designed to harass and undermine

---

*Ned would later learn his lung condition was tuberculosis, which would eventually kill him.

6. As Crazy as a March Hare

the enemy. The first was capturing the USS *Michigan* and using it to rescue the Confederate prisoners on Johnson's Island. A heavily armed and properly manned ship on Lake Erie like the *Michigan* could then lay waste to virtually every city along its shores from Buffalo to Toledo, or exact tribute from cities in return for a guarantee of nonaggression. Another idea was to conduct privateering on Chesapeake Bay. Privateering on the Chesapeake and adjacent waters, conducted in small craft, could disrupt Union shipping and obtain valuable supplies for the Confederacy.

Edwin Gray Lee, Beall's boyhood mate who ran the Union blockade to Canada (courtesy of Washington and Lee University Special Collections).

Privateering had been a successful strategy used against larger, more powerful ships since the Revolutionary War. But of late the Confederacy had deemphasized the practice, as the Union's successful blockade of Southern waters effectively prevented access to ports by Confederate ships.[10] Nevertheless, during the hour-long meeting Davis had become sufficiently impressed with Beall's ideas as well as his maturity to refer him to his Navy Secretary, Stephen R. Mallory.

Smart, self-confident, and audacious, the fifty-year-old Mallory had been one of Davis's first Cabinet picks. He had spent much of his career as a customs collector and maritime lawyer in Pensacola and Key West, and knew much about warfare on the water. Though hampered by limited resources, Mallory had developed the first ironclad

John Yates Beall, Son of the South

vessel of the war, the *Virginia*, which had revolutionized naval warfare. He would eventually develop a formidable fleet of ironclad warships that became the bane of Union seafaring. In Mallory, Beall could find no more sympathetic ear, as the Navy Secretary was always open to new ways to confound the enemy. After listening to Beall's proposals, Mallory gave the go-ahead for his Lake Erie plan.

At last Beall had found a place in the war, one worthy of the great drama he believed it to be.

7

Mosby of the Chesapeake

WITHIN DAYS OF ITS APPROVAL, the cabinet released $100,000 for Beall's operation. It was February, and everything needed to start by the middle of April, when Lake Erie would be free of ice.

A few days later, Davis began to get cold feet. While Beall's plan was sound enough, any ship would have to be launched from Canada and thus risked jeopardizing relations with Great Britain. It could even prompt Britain to retaliate and side with the North. Although he continued to feel Beall's plan had merit, Davis decided to shelve it for the moment. Instead, he ordered Beall to proceed with his second option: privateering on Chesapeake Bay. Such an operation could be conducted with no messy political ramifications. Despite Beall's lack of maritime experience, Mallory gave him the go-ahead.

From the moment the first shot of the war was fired, Chesapeake Bay became a hotly contested piece of real estate. Over one hundred fifty streams and rivers from Delaware, Maryland, and Virginia flowed into this vast estuary, highways of water that meant the ability to transport troops and supplies and to strike deep into the heart of enemy territory. Up the James led to Richmond, up the Potomac to Washington. Whoever controlled the 5,000 square miles of this inland sea—and its 12,000 miles of shoreline—could control the direction of the war.

With its naval superiority, it was the Union that placed greater strategic importance on the bay. (The Confederacy focused its military might on protecting its breadbasket in the Shenandoah Valley.) A month after the outbreak of the war, Washington had created a "flying flotilla" of light ships to patrol the bay and its rivers. Initially only a few boats were procured, and the flotilla increased in strength steadily over the course of the war. Beall was well aware of Union naval superiority in the bay, remarking to President Davis that "the tide waters of Eastern Virginia are entirely in the Federal power, if not actual possession; this enabling them at any time to bring an army to the White House—Fredericksburg, City Point, or Bermuda, hundreds."[1] Yet with only five ships, the Union would be hard pressed to check smugglers or raiders like Beall. It was a largely virgin theater of the war, ripe for the kind of mischief-making Beall had in mind.

Of especial concern to the Union were the loyalties of those living along the Chesapeake. Two thousand rebels lived on Virginia's eastern shore, "many armed with good muskets and rifles and serviceable cannon."[2] Not only did these planter populations represent a military threat, but Northerners feared they might win over Maryland and Delaware—states already ambivalent about their place in the war—to the Confederacy. As early as 1861, Major General John Adams Dix, the head of the Maryland Department, had warned Lincoln of the dangers posed by Virginia's eastern shore where secessionist activity in Accomack and Northampton counties was rife. Dix was able to get Federal troops to break up rebel camps there. But when he lobbied for assistance in disrupting illicit trade between the two shores to check secessionist influence in Maryland, he was ignored. Southern sympathizers by the thousands were able to cross the bay from the North unfettered to join Confederates in Virginia or further south. Still others dodged Union blockades at night in small boats laden with goods for the Confederacy.

On March 5, Beall went before an examining board and received a final medical discharge from the army before being commissioned acting master in the navy by Secretary Mallory. Ned Lee, who had already received a medical discharge, joined the Chesapeake venture. Having served as an officer in the army, Lee was given a captain's commission and placed in overall command of the operation. Apart from childhood larks on the docile rivers of the Shenandoah Valley, neither of them had any seafaring experience whatever.

With their commissions in hand, the two set about to organize the mission. Mallory agreed to provide uniforms, weapons, and

7. Mosby of the Chesapeake

ammunition, Beall and Lee boats, food, and supplies. As was the government's practice with privateers, neither would draw a salary, but instead would be compensated with a share of the booty they seized. Had not the two ample personal means at their disposal, the mission likely would never have gotten off the ground.

Two small boats were procured, named for their colors, the *Raven* and the *Swan*, which Beall affectionately referred to as "the birds." The *Raven* was a two-masted, fore-and-aft-rigged sailboat, the *Swan* a river cargo boat that had been doing flag-of-truce time for the Confederacy in Mobile, Alabama. Next, the men began to recruit twenty volunteers to form a combat unit. There was one catch, however: Recruits had to be nonconscriptable. In the first two years of the war the Confederacy had lost so many men that it had recently instituted a compulsory draft of all white males between the ages of eighteen and forty-five, which it was now rigorously enforcing. Their challenge was thus to find men possessing the trustworthiness, fitness, daring, and resourcefulness for the dangerous mission, but who were otherwise ineligible for military duty.

Ironically, the first to pass muster were not Southerners but two Scotsmen, Bennet G. Burley and John Maxwell. A more odd-looking pair the two could not have been. Twenty-two-year-old Burley was a short, stout Lowlander, and Maxwell a tall, lanky Highlander with broad shoulders and a moustache. The two had been toiling away as clerks for a Scottish shipping company when the war between the states broke out. Seeing an opportunity to trade their humdrum existence for swashbuckling adventure, they quit their jobs and sailed to New York. After slipping through the Union line, they appeared at the War Department in Richmond. There Burley attempted to ingratiate himself by displaying blueprints for a complicated explosive submarine device that, once attached to a wooden ship, could be detonated from a distance. The device was the invention of his father, a Glasgow mechanic who had served in the British military. Officials, however, were unimpressed with Burley's invention and threw the Scotsmen into Richmond's Castle Thunder prison on suspicion of being spies.

It wasn't as if the Confederacy wasn't interested in explosive devices. Since the outset of the war, it had sought ways to protect its vulnerable harbors from incursion by Union ships. The first attempt was by General Gabriel Rains, a West Point grad who developed a bomb that could be used on land as well as water. Called the Rains Patent, it was made of sheet iron and had a fuse protected by a thin brass cap covered with beeswax.[3] So effective had the bomb been against Union troops in the Peninsula Campaign that Northerners denounced it as inhumane. Perhaps his most ingenious naval ordnance was the "coal torpedo," a deadly blob of cast iron filled with explosives and made to look like a lump of coal. When the Confederacy established the Torpedo Bureau to develop and improve various explosive devices such as land and naval mines, not surprisingly, Rains became its head. Although hampered by lack of materials and funds, he managed to establish torpedo manufacturing plants throughout the South. Despite Rains's achievements, perfecting a device that was successful underwater had proved elusive. Many simply floated away; others corroded if left too long in water. With the Union dominating the seas and waterways, the War Department was forever on the lookout for new ideas.

Thus, when Burley blew the manacles off his wrists shortly after being thrown into prison, his pyrotechnic prowess caught the attention of Lieutenant John Mercer Brooke, Chief of Ordnance and Hydrography at the War Department. A graduate of the U.S. Naval Academy and an inventor in the arts of war as well, Brooke had been involved in the conversion of the steam frigate *Merrimack* into the formidable ironclad CSS *Virginia*, as well as in the design of the heavy, rifled, eponymous Brooke Gun. Interested to learn more about how Burley's novel "torpedo" worked, he summoned the inmates to the war department.

In Brooke's office, Burley explained that his device could only be attached at night. Using a small skiff, two men would row to within close distance of an enemy vessel. One would swim the rest of the way and, taking care not to get the detonator wet, screw the device to its hull and return to the skiff, laying out the lanyard as he swam. Rowing a safe distance away, he would then yank on the lanyard and, bam! Brooke, however, was skeptical that such an intricate device

7. Mosby of the Chesapeake

would work in practice; he wanted to see a real-life demonstration. Since the only Union ship at anchor was in Union territory, he suggested the Scotsmen prove the merits of their device by blowing up a vessel in New York harbor. Crazy as it sounded, it was precisely the kind of adventure the two Scotsman were seeking, and they accepted the challenge.

The next day, Burley and Maxwell slipped back into Union territory and boarded a train to New York. Once at the wharf they selected, from among the many ships at anchor, a frigate near the pier. At dusk they returned and rented a small boat from a fisherman, saying they wanted to do a few hours of night fishing. After rowing to within several meters of the frigate, the lanky Maxwell slipped into the harbor with the bomb. Holding the device high above the water with one arm, he side-swam over and attached it to the hull. Twice he had to stop work when he heard a sentry pacing on the deck above but he managed to attach it, all the while treading water. Once Maxwell was back in the skiff, the men rowed a short distance away and then pulled on the lanyard. Alas, no spectacular explosion followed, only silence. Assuming the detonator had gotten wet, the two high-tailed it back to Richmond.

Despite the flub, their attempt had not gone unnoticed. The next day the *New York Herald* ran an alarming headline: *Curious Infernal Machine Found Attached to the Bottom of War Steamer in the Hudson River!* Even though they had failed to blow up the ship, the two Scotsmen had at least proven they were not spies and were immediately commissioned acting masters in Beall's operation.

Among other recruits to the mission were newspapermen who were exempt from the draft. It happened that when Beall approached the *Richmond Enquirer*, two of its employees had long been contemplating enlisting in the war. When the war broke out, W.W. Baker, a thirty-two-year-old printer at the paper, had gone to one of the editors, George C. Stedman, and sought his advice on joining a branch of the military. Stedman told him he, too, was thinking about signing up but advised Baker to wait until he had decided on a course of action, as he wanted Baker to accompany him. When Stedman heard of the Chesapeake mission, it seemed the perfect opportunity, one

John Yates Beall, Son of the South

unencumbered by the dull routines of conventional military life, yet filled with the promise of excitement, adventure, even loot.[4]

As the weeks passed, Beall and Lee were able to find only a few more men suitable for the mission. Not surprisingly, few candidates fit the bill, and most were rejected for health reasons. Three others at least—all Virginians—had naval experience: Edward McGuire, who had been an acting navy master, Roy MacDonald, and Thomas McFarland, editor of the *Richmond Whig*. With valuable time being lost, Beall and Lee agreed that they would depart for the Chesapeake with the crew they had thus far cobbled together and seek more later.

On April 2, 1863, the rebel party set out for Mathews Courthouse, Virginia. Although officially part of the Confederate Navy as the Volunteer Coast Guard, the crew called themselves "Beall's Party." Tucked deep on an inlet of the East River between the York and Rappahannock rivers, Mathews Courthouse was an ideal base from which to launch attacks on Union ships. Another reason for selecting Mathews was that it was near the home of Sands Smith, Sr., and his brother Thomas, who offered to put the rebels up on their six-hundred-acre farm at Horn Harbor. Now retired, the Smiths had known Beall and Lee since accompanying John Brown to his execution as part of the fierce Black Horse Cavalry of Fauquier County. Such were the Southern sympathies of other locals that they welcomed the privateers into their homes and treated them like family.

Once settled in, Lee and Beall began laying in supplies and surveying the backwaters and inlets of the bay. On one exploratory outing on the Back River, they chanced upon a camp of "contrabands"—runaway slaves—not ten miles from Fort Monroe. In the ensuing skirmish the rebels killed one, captured another, and put the rest to flight. During another outing a few weeks later, the entire operation nearly came to a crashing halt when marines coming ashore from a gunboat caught them by surprise at the mouth of the East River near Mobjack. Lee's men killed an officer and an enlisted man. In retaliation, the Union soldiers captured and hanged one of theirs and burned the houses of eight locals believed to be Southern sympathizers.

Despite the discouraging setbacks and slow start, the privateers

7. Mosby of the Chesapeake

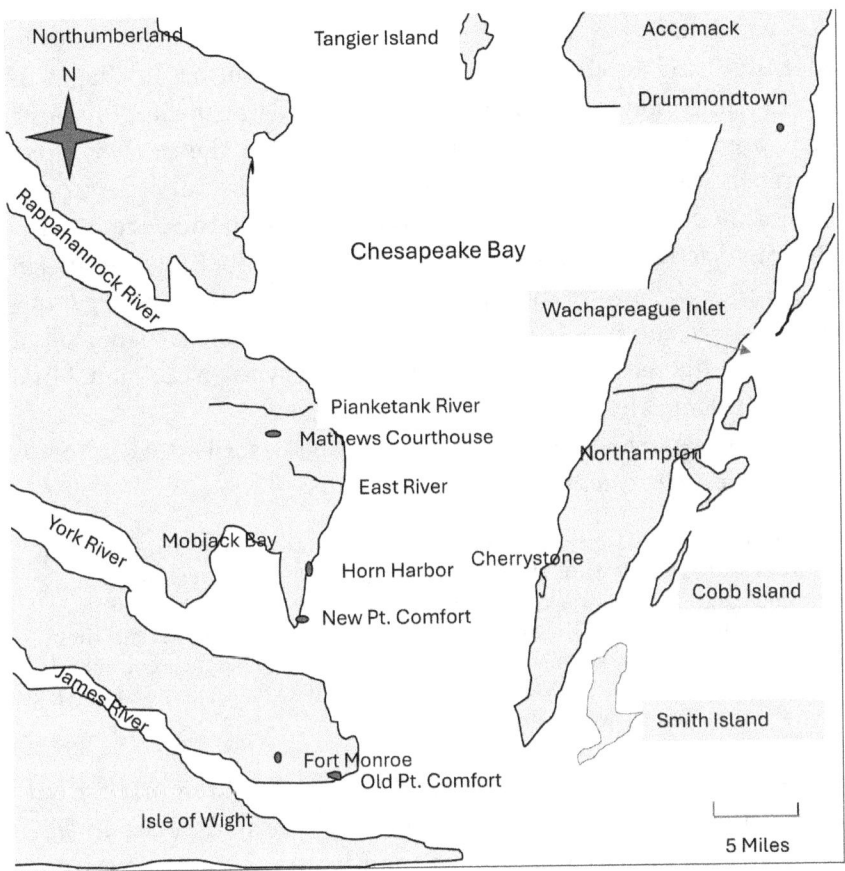

Places related to Beall's privateering activities on the Chesapeake Bay (map by the author).

remained determined to wreak havoc on the bay. In mid–June Beall returned to Richmond to procure additional weapons, maps, and supplies while Lee went to Lexington, Virginia, to visit his sister for a few days. During his furlough, Lee's mother-in-law heard of his raiding plans on the bay and, fearing for his safety, approached her husband, General Pendleton, to find a secure office job for him.

Her fears were well founded. As soon as Lee and Beall returned to the coast, they were nearly captured in a close brush with Union soldiers. While standing along Pepper Creek, they suddenly noticed two Federal barges churning upstream. Taking cover in the brush

John Yates Beall, Son of the South

they watched as two dozen Yankees came ashore and went door to door inquiring about rebels suspected to be in the area. When residents denied having seen any rebels, the Federals began to search their premises. At one point they came near to the thicket where the rebels were hiding when one of the rebels, without orders, carelessly announced their presence by opening fire on the Federals. The Federals hastened back to their ship and began shelling the thicket where the rebels were hiding. When the dust settled, the Federals came ashore again, this time torching several homes suspected of harboring the rebels. One of the homeowners was an old man, blind and bedridden, and another a solitary old widow.

In his report to Secretary Seddon, Lee described with horror their pitiless treatment of innocent civilians:

> I have never witnessed so contemptible an exhibition of cowardice or such unwarranted vandalism. The excuse they gave the defenceless old men, women and children was that we had killed an officer and a man for them and wounded several! They knew we were soldiers, and not citizens; they came to capture us, and because they were resisted, the officer commanding the vessel retaliated upon those who had never aided, sheltered or fed us, and with whom we were utterly unacquainted.[5]

At this point Lee had enough. Whether out of remorse for putting civilians in harm's way or due to the repeated delays in their mission, he resigned and returned to Richmond to look for a government job. In the meantime, he continued to purchase supplies for Beall. Ned's unexpected departure became a stroke of good fortune for Beall, who was given command of the operation. He now aspired to be to the eastern shore what fellow Virginian John Singleton Mosby had been to Virginia, conducting lighting-fast raids on Union targets—cutting communications, disrupting supply ships, burning lighthouses, seizing cargo—all the while gallantly eluding capture, the Mosby of the Chesapeake.

As Beall was preparing to launch his maritime war, news reached him of something earthshattering back home. On June 20, 1863, western Virginia had seceded from Virginia and joined the Union as the new state of West Virginia. A mountainous region with an economy that rested more on mining than on slave-based

7. Mosby of the Chesapeake

agriculture, it had been against rebellion from the start. Included in the new state were Jefferson and other counties of the panhandle. Charlestown's name had changed to Charles Town. As Beall's family biographer notes, the rupture with the state must have come as "a bitter shock to Beall's psyche."[6] Even though he continued to think of himself as a Virginian, the loss of a good portion of his beloved state to the Union—not to mention his own county—was a grave personal loss. That Jefferson County was now part of the Union meant that as long as the war continued, he could no longer return home.

In early July Beall began operations in earnest. His first target: the USS *George W. Rodgers*, a steamer plying the waters between Cherrystone and the mainland at Old Point Comfort (today Hampton). To capture the vessel, he dispatched a squad under Roy McDonald's command, but he arrived at Cherrystone just minutes after the *Rodgers* had departed. All was not lost, however, for before returning McDonald severed the twenty-five-mile-long submarine telegraph cable between Cherrystone and Old Point. In his report of the incident to Mallory, Beall included a snippet of the cable as proof.

On the first of August the privateers set sail for their next target on Smith's Island—Cape Charles lighthouse, an installation essential for navigation of Union ships to Fort Monroe. The island had once been owned by General Robert E. Lee's father-in-law, George Washington Parke Custis, who years earlier had sold a portion of the land to the Federal government for the construction of the lighthouse. By the time of the Civil War most of the island was owned by Robert E. Lee and his wife Mary.

Departing at dawn, Beall crossed the Chesapeake, stopping briefly at Devil's Ditch Inlet before arriving at the island. The crew took cover in the brush, while Beall and MacDonald casually sauntered into the lighthouse on the pretext of being visitors. The operator, a Northern sympathizer named William Stakes, received them rudely. You're loafers, he said, who should be out fighting rebels instead of sightseeing. Stakes nevertheless gave his ne'er-do-wells a tour of the facility. Afterward, Beall, a twinge of irony in his voice, announced, "My friend, I am highly pleased with the lighthouse, and your management of it, and I have a party of friends belonging to the

John Yates Beall, Son of the South

Confederate States Navy who would like to look at it!"[7] With a whistle, Beall summoned his crew. He informed Stakes that they were with the Confederate Navy, and that if he did not interfere in their operations he would not be molested. Over the next several hours the rebels proceeded to destroy the lighthouse, including its valuable lens and machinery, as well as ongoing construction designed to raise its height. While Beall's men ransacked the place, he ordered the keeper's wife to prepare them a mid-day supper. In parting he confiscated the keeper's boat, warning him not to leave the lighthouse for twenty-four hours or he would destroy the lighthouses at Hog Island and Cherrystone as well. The privateers had made off with a trove of equipment as well as three hundred gallons of valuable whale oil worth $7,400, which Beall sent by wagon to Richmond.

Two days later, Stakes commandeered a local boat and travelled to Eastville, where he reported the attack to the Union navy as well as Beall's threat to destroy more lighthouses.

In one fell stroke, Beall had become the most wanted man on the eastern shore.

On August 5, U.S. Navy Secretary Gideon Wells ordered Captain Geert Gansevoort, commander of the USS *Roanoke* based in Hampton Roads, to hunt down the privateers and destroy their boats. A first cousin of Herman Melville, Gansevoort had intelligence that the Confederates had taken refuge on Hog Island on Northampton County's eastern shore. But Gansevoort had been unable to find the boats there, for after each outing Beall cleverly hid the sails and oars in the bushes and temporarily submerged the boats with sandbags. Gansevoort did, however, manage to capture one of Beall's men as he was returning from Richmond.

The Union believed that Beall could not have succeeded in his attack had he not been aided by residents of Northampton County. War Secretary Edwin Stanton wanted to make locals pay for the destruction. He dispatched to the area several infantrymen who forced one resident, Anne Parker Thom, to pay a hefty $90 in reparations. The men stayed the night *chez* Thom, eating and taking what they pleased. In the morning, they forced her to take an oath of allegiance to the Union, then left, taking several of her slaves for good

7. Mosby of the Chesapeake

measure. Later a tax was levied on all 221 residents of the county, with soldiers going door-to-door to collect payments. Such treatment could hardly have endeared fence sitters in the war to the Union cause.

In the weeks that followed, a half dozen more privateers arrived at Mathews, bringing the number of Beall's crew to eighteen. In mid–September they set out in the boats for Cape Charles with no apparent aim in mind other than to make mayhem where they could. Dividing the crew, Beall took half with himself in the *Swan*, and the remainder went with MacDonald in the *Raven*. A few days later they passed Smith's Island, now protected by a three-gun battery erected in response to Beall's attack. At Racoon Island near Cape Charles, they found a Yankee sloop, the *Mary Anne*, and two fishing scows, which they promptly seized. The scows were laden with fishing tackle, which Beall allowed his men to confiscate. Satisfied with their accomplishments, they spent the remainder of the day fishing contentedly in the shoals near Cobb's Island.

Brimming with hubris from his latest conquests, Beall now swung out into the Atlantic in search of bigger quarry. On the third day out, rough weather came up, forcing him to take shelter in Wachapreague Inlet on the northern neck of Maryland's eastern shore. As luck would have it, anchored there was a large sloop, the *Alliance*, bound from Philadelphia for the Union-controlled Island of Port Royal, South Carolina. Beall reasoned that to ride out the storm might give the *Alliance* an opportunity to depart, so he decided to attack that very night. At 11 p.m. the *Alliance*'s crew turned in while the captain and his mate played dominoes in the cabin. Beall ordered MacDonald to attack from the starboard side while he would attack from port side. But as MacDonald drew up alongside the sloop, the *Raven* was thrown violently against her, breaking her tiller and sending MacDonald lunging headfirst into the water. He managed to scramble back into the boat, which, in the strong current, had drifted to the port side. All the men now rushed aboard starboard, armed with revolvers and sabers. Beall and his men dashed to the forecastle and seized the crew, while MacDonald raced to the cabin. There he found the captain, David Ireland, and his mate still engrossed in their game. As soon as Ireland saw MacDonald, he started for the stateroom to get his sidearm. Pointing a cocked pistol at him, MacDonald shouted for him to halt. Ireland obliged.

Having secured his prisoners, Beall came up and ordered his men to go below and bring up samples of everything they found. To their delight, there was a pirate's treasure: $200,000 in sutler's goods, including a cornucopia of delicacies. After the men had indulged in "a veritable feast of good things," Beall ordered that under no circumstances were they to go below deck again and disturb the supplies.[8] If they wanted something, they need only let him know and he would see to it that their needs were met. Curiosity soon got the better of some of them. They began wandering below, tearing open boxes of cigars and food, greedily trying to find something better than what they had been served. When Beall heard men were below deck rooting around the supplies, he became apoplectic with rage. Summoning them to the deck, he lined them up along the vessel's gunwales and sternly admonished them for blatantly disobeying his orders. He then announced that they would be searched and if any cigars or other items were found in their possession, he would shoot the offender on the spot. Now some of the men had their pockets stuffed with prime Havana cigars. "Realizing that we were in a tight place," Baker recalled, "we crowded back to the rail and as close together as we could get, and with our hands behind us, emptied every pocket into the sea. I have thought that Captain Beall knew what we were doing, although he could not see our hands at work. At any rate when the search was made, we all were found to be innocent, and Captain Beall dismissed us with a fatherly caution not to again disobey him, and I can say that I am sure that in all the months after he never found real cause to complain."[9]

A few days on, more trophies were gathered. At dawn on the 21st near the mouth of an inlet, they encountered the schooner *J.J. Houseman*, which they seized. The following night they captured two more schooners, the *Alexander* and the *Samuel Pearsall*. After taking their crews prisoner, Beall stripped the boats of their cargo. After scuttling them he sent all three adrift into the Atlantic.

Returning to the *Alliance*, he decided that instead of destroying

7. Mosby of the Chesapeake

her he would deliver the ship to Richmond. To reenter the shoal-ridden bay, however, he would need a reliable navigator. Calling Captain Ireland on deck, Beall asked whether he was thoroughly acquainted with the channel leading from the Atlantic. Ireland proudly replied that he knew every nook and cranny of the coastline and every channel in between. "Very well, Captain Ireland," Beall replied, "this is a fine vessel with a most valuable cargo, of which our people in the South are sadly in need, therefore your crew will be placed under your command, and you will please run us as soon as possible out into Atlantic. I shall stand by you, and if you should allow us to run aground, I shall be under the disagreeable necessity of shooting you. I am sure, however, that you realize the gravity of the situation and will not play us false."[10] So advised, Ireland summoned his crew aft and in a short time the vessel was cruising along in the Atlantic. When they reached Cobb's Island, Beall went ashore and located a pilot who was familiar with the Piankatank River—less guarded than the James River—where he had decided to run the *Alliance*. While there he released all the prisoners who agreed not to disclose the pirates' whereabouts for three days, save Ireland, his mate, and ten of his crew who refused. The recalcitrant prisoners were taken to Cape Charles and transferred to Beall's boats, with a pilot and two guards to each. At nightfall Beall set out westward in the *Alliance*, with the "birds" trailing close behind. During the night high winds came up, which began to throw foamy sea caps into Beall's smaller boats. Mid-way across the bay McGuire, who was piloting the *Swan*, shouted out to Beall that if the wind got any stronger their schooners would soon be sunk. The two boats were lashed together for safety, while the prisoners frantically bailed water. All night long they bailed, until dawn, when the storm subsided. Ireland later remarked that in all the years he had spent at sea he had never come as close to drowning as he had that night.

At the Cherrystone Lighthouse the *Raven* and *Swan*, still with their captives, turned for Horn Harbor while Beall continued toward the Piankatank in the *Alliance*. As the *Alliance* pilot approached the mouth of the river, a Union gunboat suddenly appeared, causing him to panic and run aground. To salvage the ship's valuable cargo,

John Yates Beall, Son of the South

Beall ordered his men to transfer the contents to wagons onshore. But when the gunboat began shelling, he set the *Alliance* ablaze along with most of her contents. Fearing ground troops would soon appear, he ordered his men to submerge the *Raven* and *Swan* in the cove at Sand Smith's. Meanwhile, MacDonald was to take a few men and escort the prisoners to Richmond, while he would depart alone for the capital. After they rendezvoused in Richmond, the cargo was sold, and every man received a handsome dividend from their share of the booty. All in all, the Chesapeake venture had been a resounding success. They had destroyed several ships and acquired valuable cargo for themselves and the Confederacy, all without the loss of a single man.

After several days of R&R, the privateers returned to Mathews, where a rude reception was awaiting. In their absence the *Alliance* prisoners they had released had made their way back to Drummondtown, where they reported the incident to Federal authorities, who in turn alerted the Atlantic Blockading Squadron.

Based in Hampton Roads, Virginia, the Atlantic Squadron had the gargantuan task of blockading Confederate ports from the Chesapeake to Key West. Its flagship gunboat, the *Commodore Jones*, a heavily armed, flat bottomed, side-wheel ferry, guarded Yorktown, while the schooners *Samuel Rotan* and *General Putnam* intercepted blockade runners at Mobjack Bay and the York River. With only three steamers and a schooner to supplement the Potomac Flotilla in the Chesapeake Bay, the squadron was finding it hard enough to intercept blockade runners in the bay, let alone hunt down privateers lurking in its countless coves and inlets.

After the burning of Smith's Lighthouse, the commander of the *Commodore Jones*, Lieutenant J.H. Gillis, had tried to mount a naval expedition to capture Beall, but his call to arms was met with indifference. Frustrated, he turned for help to army Brigadier General Isaac Wistar, commander of the District of Eastern Virginia in Yorktown. Because Wistar was ill, Gillis was fobbed off on an assistant adjutant general "who seemed to think that his acquainting himself with the contents of the last number of *Harper's Magazine* was of more importance than his public duties."[11]

7. Mosby of the Chesapeake

Such was the cavalier attitude of superiors when Gillis learned the *Alliance* had been captured. He immediately sailed to Cherrystone to obtain details of the incident and to confirm the existence of a rebel steamer seen near Sand Shoals. At the wharf he encountered Captain J. Bush of the *J.J. Houseman* and the steward of the *Alliance*, who recounted the details of their capture, adding that Beall was headed to Richmond with his booty. If Beall's group was captured, the two said they would be able to identify the privateers, "who appeared to have no organization, and were not dressed in uniform."[12]

With renewed urgency Gillis once again pressed squadron headquarters to act, requesting 250 men, two twelve-pound howitzers, and two vessels to scour the inlets between Fort Monroe and the Piankatank River. By now Beall had wrought so much damage on the bay that Gillis's entreaties were finally heard. To capture the nettlesome guerrillas, a joint military exercise would be undertaken under the command of General Wistar.

A lawyer with a Ph.D. in science from the University of Pennsylvania, Wistar had been wounded at Ball's Bluff and Antietam but otherwise had failed to distinguish himself as a field commander. Under the impression that Beall commanded a large band of privateers, Wistar marshaled a small army for the mission: the 4th Colored Infantry, detachments from the 11th Pennsylvania Cavalry and 1st New York Mounted Rifles, and two sections of artillery. His troops would be accompanied by no less than five gunboats requisitioned from the army and three navy schooners. His plan of attack was to march north from Gloucester and seal off the northern neck of Mathews while two regiments of infantry attacked Mathews from below. While they swept the mainland, the army's five gunboats would patrol the extensive jagged coastline between the Rappahannock and York Rivers, with the *General Putnam* at Mobjack Bay, the *Samuel Rotan* at the mouth of Horn Harbor, and the *Young Rover* at the mouth of Milford Haven. While the gunboats scoured the inlets, Gillis would run the *Commodore Jones* up the Piankatank and the East River. It was a net so vast and all-encompassing that even a lizard could not slip through.

John Yates Beall, Son of the South

On October 5 Wistar set out with a thousand men, intending to sweep the area all the way to the Rappahannock. When he reached Mathews, he began a house-to-house search for the privateers, much to the annoyance of many of the residents. During his search, Wistar's men were briefly diverted when a black man said that the owner of the country store had poisoned a barrel of whiskey for the benefit of the soldiers. When questioned, the owner indignantly denied it, accusing the local blacks of fabricating the baseless yarn to appear in a favorable light to the Yankees. To prove it, the owner quaffed a tumbler-full of the whiskey to no effect save for some slight inebriety. Requiring no further proof, the cavalrymen proceeded to empty the entire barrel.

As the search continued, the rebels, who were hiding in the brush, received word from Sands Smith that soldiers had found in the house of Colonel Tabb three compasses, which they presumed Beall had pilfered from the Union schooners. To confirm the report, Beall dispatched Gabriel Edmundson to Tabb's house. Using the tall bay brush as cover, Edmundson made his way stealthily. Halting a safe distance away, he peered through the foliage to the front of Tabb's house but saw nothing suspicious. As time passed, he became drowsy. Removing his coat, he spread it out on the ground and lay down. Soon he was fast asleep. A short while later he was awakened by the clattering of horses' hooves and soldiers' voices. He hastened back to Beall with the disturbing news, inadvertently leaving his coat behind. Concerned by what would happen to Smith if soldiers discovered the boats, Beall at once ordered they be sunk, which they were able to do without being detected. By now Union troops had set up pickets at the gate of Smith's brother Thomas, while all along the road between Mobjack Bay and the Piankatank River, troops in three impenetrable lines were closing in on Mathews.

Despite being overwhelmingly outnumbered, the privateers did have one advantage: They were intimately familiar with every path and every secret passage through the dense brush. So well were they able to elude their pursuers that even as Union pickets stood on alert outside Smith's gate, Beall and his crew attended a supper given by his daughter Lizzie in Smith's very house. Not everyone

7. Mosby of the Chesapeake

dined as comfortably as Beall, however. According to William Baker, "I remember that a part of the supper consisted of sweet potatoes and shall never forget how hard they were to swallow as I thought of those Yankees at the gate."[13]

When darkness fell, Beall asked McFarland, who had been an Indian scout, if he could locate all the Union pickets in town. When McFarland assured him that he could, Beall ordered his men to follow McFarland single file from Smith's property and not to so much as whisper. As they wended their way through the brush, McFarland would go a little distance ahead to ascertain the location of the pickets, which he found about a hundred yards apart—and then led them in a safe direction. Right after they crossed the first picket, Edmundson stubbornly insisted on retrieving the coat he had left behind that afternoon at Tabb's house. According to Baker,

> Captain Beall consenting, we all laid down about five feet from the road, by the side of a ditch, and in a minute or two a Yankee relief guard came tramping by. I thought that my heart would punch a hole in the ground, it beat so fiercely as the Yankees moved up so quietly that it was impossible for us to move without being seen by them. We had to stay there and quietly hope that they would not see us.[14]

In due course Edmundson returned with his coat, and they resumed their stealthy march. By dawn McFarland had deftly guided them though all three pickets and they rested at Dragon Run, a tributary of the Piankatank.

Meanwhile, things had gone terribly wrong at Sands Smith's. After a cavalryman made some lewd remarks about his daughters, the old man had become so enraged that he went into his house, grabbed his double-barrel shotgun, and emptied both barrels on the offender, killing him on the spot. Before he could reload, he was struck down with a saber but was not seriously hurt. Smith was then bound and thrown into his buggy while the incident was referred to the entire command for summary judgment. Several of Smith's daughters came running out of the house in tears, begging the Yankees to spare their father, but were coldly pushed aside. Smith was tried in a drumhead court and found guilty. He was tied to his buggy and dragged for several miles while soldiers hurled epithets at the suffering man. They came to a halt at an old persimmon tree, where Colonel Samuel Spear ordered him to be hanged. After the drop failed to kill him, the entire squad emptied their muskets into the old man. His body was buried in a shallow grave head-first with his feet sticking out of the ground. Above the grave was the threatening inscription:

> *Warning to damn bushwhackers. Every damn man we catch with arms in the woods, we will hang so high that the birds will build nests in them.*
> *So take warning, such will be your fate, you damn cowards. Here lies the body of an old bushwhacker.*[15]

When Beall heard of the gruesome fate of his friend, he was overcome with grief.

After three days Wistar terminated the operation, painfully aware of his failure and incensed at locals for refusing to cooperate in the manhunt.[16*] That, however, did not stop the feckless general from declaring the mission a resounding success.

> Pretty much the whole of the [Confederate] Coast Guard besides a small regiment of cavalry and other prisoners were captured, many small vessels brought off or destroyed, and a considerable number of arms, cattle and horses taken and brought in. The success was so complete that it received honorable mention in the Annual Report of the General-in-Chief of the Army and was transmitted to Congress by the Secretary of War.[17]

It was not uncommon for officers on both sides of the war to exaggerate their achievements on the battlefield, but Wistar's version was so far from the truth as to be pure fiction. In fact, he had captured only two of Beall's men, Burley and McFarland. Nor were the boats they had seized Beall's, as those had been safely submerged beneath the bay waters.

When they learned that Wistar had returned to Yorktown and the coast was clear, the rebels emerged from their lair at Dragon Run. Deeming the peninsula now too hot to resume activities, Beall temporarily dispersed his men and returned to Richmond, vowing to fight another day.

---

*Fortunately, Beall's brother William, who had been detailed by Special Order of Mallory to report to Beall on October 4, had not yet arrived.

8

Capture

Beall lingered a month in Richmond, visiting friends, getting caught up on the latest developments in the war, and waiting for things in the Chesapeake to calm down. On November 10, he summoned his merry band of privateers and proceeded to the bay. Once in Mathews, they raised their boats from their watery lairs and set out east, Beall in the *Raven* and McGuire in the *Swan*. This time, Beall was fighting for more than the South's independence: He intended to make the Yankees feel the full force of his wrath over the brutal murder of Sands Smith.

Late on a blustery afternoon they cruised into Tangier Inlet on the coast of Accomack County. After capturing a schooner being used as a tender boat, they held in place for the night. When dawn approached, Beall proposed that several men take the *Swan* to a deep cove and hide while he remained in the *Raven* with the captured schooner. They were to return at dark, when they would attack a gunboat spotted lying at anchor a few miles upstream at Chesconessex. After McGuire pointed out that the *Raven*, being much larger than the tender-schooners in the area, might attract attention, it was decided that Edmundson would take several men and hide the birds in a nearby cove, to return at eight the next night. Taking Baker, Fitzgerald, Thomas, and Crouch, Edmundson sailed off with the birds. After finding a suitable inlet, he left Baker and Fitzgerald with the boats while the rest went ashore to sleep. At daylight, Baker and Fitzgerald were distressed to see that the cove was not as secluded as it had appeared in the dark, but it was now too late to move them without running the risk of capture.

A few nervous hours passed when, just as they feared, a

John Yates Beall, Son of the South

fisherman passing by the mouth of the inlet sailed up and asked Fitzgerald and Baker what they were up to. Trying his best to appear at ease, Fitzgerald replied that they had come down from Baltimore to do a little hunting and were waiting for the tide to rise so they could move up to Chesconessex. Apparently satisfied with their response, the fisherman wished them luck and sailed off. Fitzgerald and Baker went back to sleep in the boats, assuming they had seen the last of him. What they didn't know was that the fisherman had sailed straight to Chesconessex and alerted the gunboat commander. Around 5 p.m. the two awoke to see two large Union vessels approaching hard from the mouth of the inlet, bristling with soldiers armed to the teeth. Turning to his partner, Fitzgerald said, "Baker, this is a hot thing ain't it?"[1]

As the boats drew up alongside the birds, the Union commander cried out, "Surrender! What command do you belong to?" Intimidated by the arsenal of weapons trained on them, Baker blurted out, "Captain Beall's command!" No sooner had he uttered the words than the soldiers dashed ashore and began firing indiscriminately into the brush, hoping to flush out the rest of the pirates. When no one appeared, Lieutenant John W. Conner and Sergeant Robert W. Christopher of Company B of the First Eastern Shore of Maryland Volunteers commandeered every pungy and skiff they could find and began to scour the coves for the other pirates.

All this time Beall had been waiting for Edmundson, but by now he had concluded something was amiss. His men now urged him to abscond, but Beall refused, out of concern for his absent men. He insisted they search for the others. The next morning they were idling in an inlet when they were startled by a great rushing sound in the bushes. They turned to see hundreds of Union troops pouring from the woods just as enemy boats were moving up the inlet toward them. Realizing he was hopelessly surrounded, Beall surrendered, though not before throwing everything of value overboard to prevent it from falling into enemy hands.

Beall's capture was heralded throughout the North as a major coup. Wistar publicly expressed his delight that "the notorious Captain Beall" had been caught at last. The rebels were taken to the

8. Capture

headquarters of the First Separate Brigade of the 8th Army Corps in Drummondtown. Under interrogation Beall made no attempt to hide the fact they were privateers. He confessed to capturing several Union vessels as well as destroying the Smith Island lighthouse. A search of his boats turned up incriminating documents indicating they were receiving no pay from the Confederacy but drew their remuneration from the sale of the booty they captured. On top of this, they were without official orders and not in uniform. District commander Brigadier General Henry H. Lockwood therefore recommended to Secretary Stanton that they be treated as pirates, not prisoners of war.

> They are unable to show anything which, in my judgment, would entitle them to be considered or treated as prisoners of war.... They are without orders and many of them without uniform.... [T]hey are but partisans, receiving no pay from the so-called Confederate States, and trusting entirely for remuneration for their services to the possession of such property, public or private, as they may chance to capture.... I would respectfully suggest that they be tried either by military commission or that they be sent back here [Drummondtown] for trial by the civil authorities.[2]

Wistar, too, called for "economical" (viz., summary) justice to be meted out. Lockwood further recommended that the prisoners be tried in civil—as opposed to military—court in Accomack or Northampton County to appease residents' anger and to discourage other pirates from committing similar depredations in the bay. "I think twelve men at least in the county of Accomack," Lockwood wrote, "can be procured who will be disposed to deal with these fellows as their outrages deserve."[3] Conviction for piracy spelled certain death for the Confederates.

The next day the rebels were put on a gunboat to Baltimore—the very one they had set out to capture days earlier—and secured in a large cabin on the main deck. Peering through the door, Beall noticed the cabin door opened out to the forward deck where two sentinels were posted. Near them was a stack of muskets that had been carelessly laid out for the relief guard. Turning to the men he whispered that if they would overcome the two sentinels at the door, he and the others could then seize the muskets before the other guards could be under arms. Stedman and McGuire immediately agreed to go along, but the others insisted that the plan was too risky as they had no idea how many armed men were on the upper deck. Enraged by their refusal, Beall blasted them as "a set of dastardly cowards."[4] A short time later their fears were vindicated when he realized that what had looked like an opportunity was in fact a trap set in the hope that they would do just that, for on the upper deck was a full company of infantry waiting for the rebels to rush out so that they could shoot down every one of them, thus sparing the bother of trial.

Late in the evening the ship docked at Fort McHenry on Baltimore's inner harbor. Built in 1798, the fort was a bastioned pentagon encircled by a dry moat. During the War of 1812, it had famously withstood heavy bombardment and thwarted British penetration of the harbor. When the Civil War broke out it was converted to a prison for Confederates and Yankee deserters, as well as Marylanders suspected of being Confederate sympathizers. Escape from McHenry, they concluded, was not going to be easy.

After being registered by name and rank, the rebels were placed in chains and herded into an old stable near the provost marshal's office. Beall and the other officers—McFarland, Stedman, and McGuire—were confined separately in the attic above. As the crew was being led to their cells below, a Union deserter approached Baker and greeted him with a congenial slap on the back. After his mates had been similarly greeted, Baker noticed that the welcoming hand had been chalked. He soon found out why. Once in his cell, one of the prisoners approached Baker, saying as a newcomer he would have to be "initiated into the mysteries of the prison." Somewhat nervously Baker followed him downstairs. "Don't make any resistance," the deserter warned, "or they will go through you and take that ring off, but if you don't resist, they will have no excuse to rob you." Upon reaching the lower level Baker found two dozen Yankees holding an outstretched blanket into which he was instructed to jump. At once Baker complied and, with a "Hip, Hip Hurray! Hip, Hip, Hurray!" the men proceed to launch him into the air three times, each time "as high as a church steeple." He later learned those who refused to go along with this harmless bonding ritual were relieved of all their valuables.[5]

8. Capture

On the second day of their incarceration the sergeant of the guard came into the cell and called Baker's name. Upon answering, he was handed a large willow basket containing various fruits, cakes, jellies, and tobacco—gifts of a generous lady. The greeting card having been torn off, Baker never learned the identity of his benefactress. Later, still more baskets arrived from the mysterious woman, though General Lockwood refused to allow them into the prison.

The next day the provost marshal summoned the Confederates to his office to inform them that Lockwood had ordered that they be kept in irons. Beall protested vigorously, but the marshal replied impassively that he was simply following orders from Lockwood, who in turn had been directed by Major General Robert Schenck. All were shackled save Baker, Thomas, and Crouch, who were exempted only because their heavy boots were too large for the irons to lock over. Their momentary elation quickly evaporated, however, when the officer in charge said, "Sergeant, take these three men up to the blacksmith shop and have a ball and chain riveted upon each." Leading the men into yard the sergeant turned to Baker and, pointing to a sixty-pound cannon ball attached to a two-foot chain, said, "Take up that ball and chain and come on." Heaving the massive ball to his shoulder, Baker followed him to the blacksmith shop, nearly breaking down along the way from the crushing weight. When the sergeant wasn't looking, Baker slipped the ball under a work bench and pulled out a much smaller ball with a longer, six-foot chain. After Crouch was ironed with a forty-pound ball, the blacksmith turned to Baker, who smiled and said, "Put this one on me." Aware that Baker had switched balls, the sergeant conceded, "Well, as you appear to be the smallest of the lot, I'll give it to you." He then pulled out a bigger ball with short chain, and riveted it on Thomas, who, ever after, had to drag it along on the floor, while Baker could sling his across his shoulder and walk with ease.[6]

From time to time the guards would remove the manacles from the men and allow them to circulate in the yard for exercise. The prisoners eagerly availed themselves of the opportunity because after the Battle of Gettysburg the prison population had grown to nearly seven thousand. Only Beall refused to leave his cell, to protest the

John Yates Beall, Son of the South

policy of manacles as inhumane. When the guards first attempted to remove them, Beall shouted angrily, "No! Let them alone! Until your *government* sees fit to remove them."[7] Edmundson soon learned from a Union prisoner how to make a wooden key that they used to unlock the manacles at night and put them back on before the morning inspection. Yet Beall stubbornly refused to avail himself of even this momentary relief, insisting on remaining in shackles until his protests were heard.

Forty-two days later, the irons were finally removed, thanks to Edmundson's resourcefulness. From the day he was first locked up, he had studied the movement of the guards in the hope of finding an opening to escape. After several days, he noticed that during the daytime the guard of the exercise yard often allowed the regular Yankee prisoners to enter his cell to converse with deserters, returning to their own cells at night. One night, as the guard was ushering the Yankees back to their cells, Edmundson, still in his civilian clothes, had approached the gate and barked, "Well, let me out!" "Who are you?" the guards asked to which Edmundson haughtily replied, "I am a member of the 27th New York, and you let me in a while ago to see one of my regiment who is confined here in irons, and if you don't let me out in a hurry I will report you to the provost marshal for letting me in." With this, the guards opened the door and pushed him into the yard, admonishing, "Don't you come in here again!"[8] Edmundson had casually made his way across the yard and slipped into a cell containing Yankee prisoners. No one noticed him enter, not even the guards, for they were too busy looking on as the others sang and danced. Unnoticed, Edmundson ascended to the first floor and jumped out of a window to the ground below. On his hands and knees, he crawled toward Baltimore Bay, intending to swim to Canton a mile away. As he reached the water's edge, a sentinel spotted him. "Who comes there?" he shouted. As it was a moonless night, Edmundson, resourceful as ever, began to root about and grunt like a pig while slowly backing out of sight of the sentinel, who by now assumed he was one of the many hogs that were kept in the fort. Edmundson quietly made his way to the exterior wall of the fort, where he paused to study the movement of the sentinels on top. Two

8. Capture

sentinels would walk toward each other and, after a word, would then turn back-to-back and march to the end of their respective posts. The precise moment the sentinels turned to march back, Edmundson grabbed the top of the wall and hoisted himself to freedom.

The morning after his escape the sergeant came in at 9 a.m. to conduct the inspection. When he called "G. Edmundson," Baker answered, "Here." Not seeing Edmundson, the sergeant walked over and, looking Baker full in the face, once again called Edmundson's name. This time Baker was mum. Realizing Edmundson had escaped, the sergeant became apoplectic. He marched the Confederates to the provost marshal's office, where each was questioned separately. All feigned ignorance of their comrade's whereabouts. But when the sergeant got to Crouch and Annan, the only two men Edmundson had confided his escape plan to, they refused to utter so much as a single word. Convinced they were privy to Edmundson's whereabouts, the sergeant had them gagged and bound to a chair. Wielding a large wooden club, he proceeded to beat them nearly senseless, but each blow to the head or body only hardened their resolve to protect their comrade.

When General Lockwood learned of the escape, he ordered all the men, the officers included, crammed like sardines into a dark, closet-sized room with a single door and window. Soon after, he visited the prison to inform Beall that a trial would soon be convened, and the rebels would "get their just deserts." Beall retorted that he was quite confident the Confederacy would protect them and needed no favors from the Federal government.

His comment was prophetic, for Edmundson was now in Richmond, where he informed Ed McGuire's brother Hunter—whom he knew to be close to Stonewall Jackson—that Beall and his men were being held in chains and would soon be tried on charges of piracy. When Jackson learned of the plight of his former private, he told Hunter to send a message to Secretary Mallory saying that for every one of the men that went to the gallows Jackson would hang five Union captives.

Mallory might well have already been aware of Beall's dire situation, for when first incarcerated Beall had been allowed to write a letter that had gone straight to Confederate Commissioner of Prisoner Exchange Robert Ould. Subsequently, Ould dashed off a letter to his federal counterpart to the effect that nineteen Union marines had been placed in chains in retaliation, including one Ben Porter. In singling out Porter, Ould had raised the ante considerably, for he was a nephew of Colonel Peter A. Porter, the commander at Fort McHenry.

The gambit worked. In mid–December Lieutenant Starr entered their cramped quarters and handed Beall a copy of the *Baltimore Sun*. In it was an article copied from the *Richmond Whig* titled "Retaliation," which Beall proceeded to read with delight to his men:

> Information having been received by the government that Acting Master John Y. Beall and Edward McGuire, of the Confederate Navy, with sixteen men, are now confined in irons in Fort McHenry, to be treated as pirates. Commissioner of [Prisoner] Exchange Robert Ould has directed that Lieutenant Commander [Benjamin H.] Porter and Ensign [Edward P.] Williams, with sixteen marines, be confined in irons in Charleston, S. C, to be held as hostages for the good treatment of Captain Beall and his command.[9]

When he finished, Baker turned to Lieutenant Starr and said with a grin, "Now Lieutenant, you all fellows can hang us, but those Yankees will surely swing in Charleston."[10] A few days later, General Benjamin F. Butler instructed Starr to remove the manacles and to henceforth treat the Confederates as prisoners of war. On January 11, the pirates were marched to the harbor, where they boarded a steamer for Fort Monroe. A few days later they were transferred to Fort Norfolk, where they were required to sign a statement certifying that their irons had been removed and that they were now being treated as prisoners of war.

For two months Beall and his mates remained imprisoned at Fort Norfolk. During that time, they mulled over various plans for escape, some of which were inspired by a Norfolk man named Andrew Coffin who had been thrown in with them for merely having expressed his sympathies for the South. A few days after Coffin's arrival they were informed that in the morning they would be transferred to Point Lookout, Maryland, eighty miles north. That night

8. Capture

Fort Norfolk, where Beall was imprisoned after his capture on the Chesapeake (courtesy of Library of Congress).

Beall worked on a plan to escape, assigning each man a role. Knowing intimately, as he did, the many islands and inlets of the bay, he chose the waters near Newport Lighthouse as the opportune place to overpower their guards and take command of the ship.

In the morning, the guards entered and removed Coffin. When Beall asked where he was being taken, the guards replied that he was going to Baltimore to stand trial. A few hours later the Confederates boarded a steamer for Point Lookout. All were in high spirits, fully expecting to be free by evening. But as it sailed north, the ship suddenly made an unexpected stop at Fort Monroe, where it took on a company of regulars to augment the tiny force on board. Within seconds the soldiers affixed bayonets and ordered the prisoners into the main cabin. It was then that Beall realized how naive they had been to trust Coffin, for he was a federal informant placed in their midst by the wily General Butler.

Around midnight the steamer arrived at Point Lookout on the southern tip of St. Mary's County. Established after the Battle of Gettysburg to house the burgeoning number of rebel prisoners, the facility was little more than a hastily assembled collection of tents and shacks that offered scant protection from the winter cold or coastal storms. Chronic shortages of food and firewood led to a high rate of diseases such as dysentery and typhoid fever. Rats were so prevalent that catching them was a pastime among prisoners. To make matters worse, most of the four hundred guards were black and harbored such a deep hatred for their charges that murders were not uncommon. Indeed, over the course of the war more than three thousand Confederates would perish during their incarceration there.

There was one bright side to the dismal conditions. Two months, on the Confederates learned that five hundred sick prisoners were to be sent south in a prisoner exchange. Anxious to see a certain romantic interest of his, Baker decided to feign sickness. Approaching Dr. Emmet Stratton, a prisoner who had been assigned as a physician in the tent-hospital, he asked to be placed on the sick list. Scrutinizing Baker head to foot, Stratton said he doubted the chief surgeon would approve as he looked perfectly hale and healthy. Baker stepped aside to see what he could do about that. During his time in irons at Fort McHenry, he had developed festering sores on his ankles. Rubbing the sores for greater effect and spreading the blood around, he rolled up his pants and hastened back to the chief surgeon crying, "Doctor, I don't know what is the matter with me, and if I stay here I will never get well; please let me go." "What's the matter with you, sir?" the doctor asked. To which Baker replied, "Doctor, I don't know, but I'll never get well while here." Unmoved by Baker's pining or the sores, the doctor pointed to the line of healthy men and brusquely said, "Get in that line." Undeterred, Baker took his place in the sick line, which the good doctor failed to note. Eventually he was put aboard the flag-of-truce steamer *New York* and landed safely in Richmond, a free man.[11]

Days after Baker's escape, Beall and the other officers were transferred to a Union base at City Point at the confluence of the James and the Appomattox Rivers. On May 5, they were released in a prisoner exchange, though most of Beall's crew and his brother

8. Capture

Will would not be released until October. As commander, Beall was reluctant to leave them behind, but during his time at Point Lookout his health had markedly deteriorated.

He was also no good to the Confederacy behind bars.

9

Strange Peace Party

In May 1864 the war came to Richmond's doorstep. On the day that Beall was exchanged, General Ulysses S. Grant had initiated his Virginia Overland Campaign, aimed at maneuvering Lee's Army of Northern Virginia into a final, decisive battle of the war.

After his bitter defeat at Gettysburg, Lee had led his beleaguered army on a tortuous retreat to Virginia, where the campaign began. With an army twice the size of Lee's, Grant crossed the Rapidan River and attacked Lee in a dense thicket near Spotsylvania known as the Wilderness. Despite suffering massive casualties, Grant pressed on to the southeast, hellbent on grinding Lee down in a bloody war of attrition. Near Spotsylvania Court House the two armies again clashed in a battle that lasted a fortnight. A few days into the fighting, Major General Philip Sheridan moved his entire 10,000-man cavalry south toward Richmond in a bid to draw out General Jeb Stuart's cavalry where he hoped to defeat it, while simultaneously cutting off supply lines from the capital and threatening its residents. When Stuart saw Sheridan moving toward the capital, he took the bait, dispatching 3,000 of his men to intercept him. Six miles from Richmond the two cavalries collided near an abandoned inn. While leading a countercharge, Stuart, Lee's most valuable cavalry commander, was felled by a bullet.

The next morning Richmond's residents were making their way to church when they were startled by a thunderous barrage coming from Sheridan's cannons on the Mechanicsville Road. Even though

9. Strange Peace Party

still weak from his prison ordeal, Beall shouldered a musket and set out to join in the repulse of Sheridan. On his way out of town he was disheartened to pass the litter bearing the wounded Stuart, who would die that evening.

Upon reaching the Chickahominy River, Beall fell in with the celebrated Texas Hood's Brigade and fought the entire day. When the brigade moved out the next morning, Beall, too weak to march, decided to return to the city. Outside Mechanicsville he happened upon an old friend from Charlestown, Lieutenant David Henderson of the Topographical Corps. To regain his strength, Beall decided to remain with the corps for several days and partake of its rations.

After a week in Richmond visiting friends, Beall set out by rail to visit Martha. The journey took nearly a week due to the destruction of tracks in some areas and the need to avoid Union troops in others. Martha was staying at the home of Colonel Chambers and his wife in Columbus, Georgia, as she had been unable to return to Union-controlled Nashville. Beall had not seen her in nearly two years, though they had stayed in touch via correspondence. During the two weeks they spent together John urged her to marry him and move to England. Martha could stay with his cousins in Aglionby where she would be safer, and he could sign on with a Confederate warship. But she declined, feeling that to leave the Confederacy at such a dire time would be unpatriotic. It was a decision she would live to regret. In parting she gave John a small, leather-bound notebook into which he would henceforth make regular diary entries of his exploits in the war. The fortnight he spent with Martha he would later describe as "the happiest of my life."[1]*

Since his prison exchange Beall had been mulling his next operation. By the time he returned to Richmond in late May, he had decided he wanted to reprise his plan for privateering on the Great Lakes. In the capital he sought out his former district Congressman, Alexander Boteler—now serving as a military judge—to arrange an

---

*Beall could not go back to Walnut Grove, not only because it was no longer in the Confederacy but because the Union army had reduced his farm to a barren waste. The timber had been cut down, the fences torn up for firewood, and the outbuildings destroyed.

John Yates Beall, Son of the South

audience with Navy Secretary Mallory. Before the tall, bespectacled Mallory, Beall once again laid out his old ideas—seizing control of the waters, raiding Union ships, and exacting tribute from the towns along the shores. But the centerpiece of his plan—and the one likely of greatest interest to Mallory—was the rescue of the prisoners on Johnson's Island in Lake Erie. Of course, the previous year Mallory and Seddon had hoped to do precisely that, but their plot—flawed to being with—was scrapped at the last minute by President Davis, who was still concerned about blowback from Great Britain. A few months later a second attempt had sputtered out when one of the conspirators, fearing personal reprisal, tipped off Canadian authorities.

When Mallory first rejected Beall's proposal for freeing the Johnson's Island prisoners, he said he would be willing to reconsider it in the future if circumstances changed. And they had. Substantially. By 1864 the outlook for the Confederacy had become bleak. Vicksburg had fallen. Tennessee had been abandoned, and the states west of the Mississippi had been severed from the main body of the Confederacy. Union forces now occupied a great portion of the Southern territory, which prevented the Confederacy from furnishing supplies to its armies. Conscription had forced nearly the whole male population of the South into the military, yet there was still a dire shortage of men to fight. The only hope seemed to be in instigating an uprising in the North that would force Union troops to turn back for the protection of their own territory, thus leading to the release of the Confederate prisoners.

At that very moment, Lee's dwindling army was struggling to hold off Grant's bluecoats along the North Anna River. What was more, the North possessed more men, machinery, and weapons and could easily outlast an already exhausted Confederacy. Even the hoped-for diplomatic recognition from Great Britain and France had failed to materialize. By late winter Davis had begun to grope desperately for some way out of the war, either through diplomacy or—improbable though it seemed—outright military victory. And the place he intended to pursue both ends was not in the South or the North but an entirely new theater—the Great Lakes region.

9. Strange Peace Party

Davis's strategy for turning the war around was two-pronged: one aimed at peace, the other at opening a new front in the war. His peace plan aimed to tap into the North's growing disenchantment with the war and unseat Lincoln in the upcoming elections. With a new, more pro-peace administration in place, Davis hoped to negotiate a truce favorable to the Confederacy. The idea of stirring up anti-war sentiment in the North was probably first tendered by Robert E. Lee as early as June 1863 in a letter to Davis:

> We should neglect no honorable means of dividing and weakening our enemies, that they may FEEL SOME OF THE DIFFICULTIES experienced by ourselves. It seems to me that the most effectual mode of accomplishing this object, now within our reach, is to give all the encouragement we can, consistently with truth, to the rising peace party of the North.[2]

One faction of the Democratic Party in particular—known derisively as "Copperheads" for their treacherous infidelity—had long been opposed to the war. They were also deeply critical of Lincoln's management of it, his misguided crusade in abolishing slavery, and his curtailment of civic freedoms. Lincoln had drawn even further criticism when, just weeks after Gettysburg, he called for the drafting of an additional 500,000 men. As the war entered its fourth year, even Northerners who had once supported it believed that an outright military victory was now unachievable. With U.S. elections scheduled for November, Davis believed he could spur anti-war voters to unseat Lincoln.

To accelerate this process, Davis planned to send a "peace party" to Washington while simultaneously inciting a broad uprising in the Great Lakes region—where anti-war sentiment was the strongest. In Illinois, Indiana, Ohio, and Michigan, fathers and brothers were being drafted to fight and die for a cause with which they felt little connection. They neither owned slaves nor found a common aim in trying to free them. In addition, the disruption of traditional trade and transportation routes along the Mississippi for corn, cattle, and lumber was wreaking economic ruin all along the upper reaches of the river. The opposition to the war was so strong that numerous secret societies had sprung up in the Midwest numbering in the thousands and ready to rise in rebellion. Or so Davis wanted to believe.

John Yates Beall, Son of the South

To fund his wild schemes, the Confederate Congress appropriated $5 million, a staggering amount for a nation on the brink of bankruptcy. In March 1864, Davis formed a commission consisting of three prominent Southerners with, in his words, "a view to negotiation with such persons in the North as might be relied upon to aid the attainment of peace."[3] The three commissioners were Senator Clement C. Clay, James P. Holcombe, and Jacob Thompson.

On the surface at least, the résumés of the three emissaries read like a *Who's Who* of the South. Clay, a former lawyer trained at the University of Virginia, had served two terms as an Alabama legislator and U.S. Senator. When the war broke out, he resigned his Senate seat to become a senator in the First Confederate Congress before being named to the peace commission.

A graduate of Yale and the University of Virginia law school, the bespectacled Holcombe was an eminent legal scholar who had authored several legal treatises, including one on creditor law in Canada. Considered the finest international affairs lawyer in the Confederacy, he had earlier been sent to Halifax to exploit tensions between England and the United States over Canada's seizure of the U.S. steamer *Chesapeake*. He had then been directed to remain in Canada to locate Confederate soldiers who had escaped from Northern prisons and assist them to return to the South to resume active service.

The head of the commission, fifty-four-year-old North Carolinian Jacob Thompson, was a self-made aristocrat. He had studied and later taught law at the University of North Carolina. In the 1830s he moved to practice law in the Natchez area of Mississippi, where he amassed a fortune speculating in land ceded by the removal of the Chickasaw Indians. He subsequently moved to Oxford, Mississippi, where he married Catherine Jones, the daughter of the wealthiest landowner in Lafayette County (the novelist William Faulkner would base some of his fictional characters on Thompson). Beginning in 1839, Thompson embarked on a successful political career, serving several terms in Congress before becoming Secretary of Interior in the administration of James Buchanan. After Lincoln's election, while still serving as Interior Secretary, he was appointed

9. Strange Peace Party

by Mississippi to persuade North Carolina to secede from the Union. Brushing aside administration complaints of a conflict of interest, in an open letter to the state legislature Thompson warned that emancipation would lead to the destruction of the South's institutions and subjugation of its people. When the war broke out, he resigned to become Inspector General of the Confederate Army. A year later he left the cabinet to become aide to General P.T. Beauregard at the Battle of Shiloh, chiefly, it seemed, to garner the laurels of the battlefield. Two years later, Thompson was residing comfortably at his plantation in Oxford, Mississippi, tending to his business affairs, when he received a telegram from President Jefferson Davis: "If your engagements permit you to accept service abroad for the next six months, please come here immediately."[4]

The distinguished pedigree of the commissioners made them well suited for a peace mission—difficult though it was—but none possessed the gritty street smarts required for its second task should it fail in the first: to foment war.

Thompson's instructions from Davis were as ambitious as they were unrealistic. First, he was to contact "influential" businessmen, politicians, and anti-war activists in the North to broker peace discussions with Lincoln.

Jacob Thompson, leader of President Davis's secret delegation to Canada (courtesy of Library of Congress).

John Yates Beall, Son of the South

(Lincoln had spurned previous attempts by Davis to negotiate directly.) If peace overtures failed, Thompson was to then subvert the Union war effort employing various means, including sinking ships plying the Great Lakes, inciting insurrection in the Northwest, and freeing the desperately needed Confederate prisoners being held in camps around the Great Lakes. Miraculously, Thompson was to accomplish all this while somehow respecting the neutrality of Canada.

On the morning of May 6, Thompson and Clay boarded the *Thistle*, a lightning-fast blockade runner built in Scotland. In Thompson's briefcase was a million dollars in Confederate notes convertible in gold. The ship lay low in the water with baled cotton, barrels of turpentine, tobacco, rice, and sugar, staples that the Confederate States would trade for European guns and manufactured goods at a layover in Bermuda. She steamed down the Cape Fear River, reaching Fort Fisher in late afternoon. To avoid the gauntlet of thirteen U.S. cruisers stationed at the mouth of the harbor, the crew waited until dark to proceed, for the *Thistle* was painted a colorless sea-gray, making it virtually invisible at night. To further avoid being detected, they burned anthracite coal—which produced little smoke—and placed a hood over the furnace. When she was finally spotted at dawn, the USS *Connecticut* pursued her for five hours before the *Thistle* finally outran it.[5]

Things went wrong from the start. During the voyage Thompson and Clay, who was never entirely comfortable with the assignment to begin with, had a falling out over disagreement as to who was leading the commission.[6] When they arrived in Montreal another argument broke out. Disturbed by the number of Federal agents lurking in the city, Thompson ordered them to move to Toronto. Clay, whose frail health had been aggravated by the voyage, balked, saying he had had enough of traveling and would go no further. Clay then petulantly demanded, and received, a $93,000 advance for expenses to be placed in his personal account in the Bank of Montreal.[7] Surprisingly, Thompson acquiesced, glad to be rid of the troublesome Alabaman, and then set out for Toronto with Holcombe.

In Toronto Thompson took up several suites in the elegant

9. Strange Peace Party

Queen's Hotel overlooking the bay. Not only did the luxurious hotel meet the Southern aristocrat's requirements for sumptuous dining and fine wines, but the telegraph office on the main floor allowed for instant communication with allies and emissaries. It was also a Mecca for Confederates of one sort or another: spies, wealthy Southern families waiting out the war in safety, and escaped prisoners, individuals who could be of use to Thompson. There was no mistaking the escapees:

> They hung around the lobby and bar of the Queen's, trying to appear respectable in torn gray coats and cracked jackboots or in castoff clothes they had robbed from some clothesline after climbing the board fences of Camps Chase, Morton, or Johnson's Island. They were gaunt, hollow-eyed men, with faces lined and tanned the color of old leather by the relentless sun which had scorched the treeless prison yards that rainless summer.[8]

Through intermediaries, Thompson first approached several influential Northerners in the hope they might broker a peace deal with Washington. Within a fortnight, however, he concluded that the men in a position to influence Washington were unlikely to support ending a war that they were growing rich on. Indeed, in a meeting with Washington Hunt in Niagara Falls, the ex-governor of New York had told him that the businessmen Thompson was seeking were on the alert to scuttle any attempts at peace.[9] Desperate for results, Thompson tried inducing various New York dailies to publish editorials urging a cessation of hostilities. He sent the *New York Daily News*—owned by two Copperheads—$25,000 to "trumpet peace," but the costly endeavor failed to produce any results.

It was time for more war.

10

The Northwest Goose Egg

From the moment Beall had reappeared in Mallory's office peddling his old ideas for privateering on the Great Lakes, the Secretary had seen a role for him in Davis's grand plan for war in the Northwest. Since activities on the Great Lakes were conducted by the Confederacy's loosely organized clandestine service, the Signal Corps, Mallory referred Beall to its director, Major William Norris. A Yale graduate, the Baltimore-born Norris had abandoned a career in law to join the Confederacy. While serving in General John B. Magruder's Army of the Peninsula in Yorktown, he pioneered the use of secret communications in the navy. When the Signal Corps was organized in 1862, Norris became an obvious choice to head it.[1] An elite body, the Corps consisted of over 1,500 officers and agents in a network that extended from the deep South and across eastern Canada.

In Norris's office, cluttered with decoding machines, Beall described his success in raiding on the Chesapeake, his capture and eventual release, and his long-simmering plan for raiding on the Great Lakes. Although impressed with Beall's experience as well as his ideas, Norris had neither funding nor authorization to sanction his activities. He referred him to Seddon, with his stamp of approval. Seddon immediately offered Beall a lieutenant's commission in the Secret Service, an offer that Beall promptly rejected. Not only was he uninterested in espionage, he also did not want a superior directing his every move. Having seen the atrocities of the war and been repulsed by them, he did not want to be directed to commit an act he found morally objectionable. In short, he wanted to do his own thing, an honorable thing, not espionage or soldiering, but being a

10. The Northwest Goose Egg

John Yates Beall in civilian disguise in Canada (from Daniel Bedinger Lucas, *Memoir of John Yates Beall: His Life, Trial, Correspondence, Diary and private manuscript found among his papers, including his own account of the raid on Lake Erie* [Montreal: John Lovell, 1865]).

spoiler, making the war as intolerable as he could for the North while minimizing the unnecessary loss of life.

Even though Beall's own plans dovetailed perfectly with Thompson's mission in Canada, Seddon doubted Beall could raise enough men on his own for such a hazardous mission. Beall insisted he had more than two dozen men ready and willing to serve, several of whom, like Baker, Stedman, and Fitzgerald, had ably served under him on the Eastern Shore.[2] To convince Seddon, he sought out senior officials who could vouch for his word. He dashed off a letter to Colonel William Mackay Holliday, commander of Company D of the 33rd Virginia Infantry in Stonewall's Brigade. He also wrote to his old friend Andrew Hunter, who had collected him from the battlefield at Bolivar Heights and was a former Confederate state senator from Union-occupied Charles Town District, where he also advised Robert E. Lee on civil and military affairs. Hunter responded the same day with a letter of endorsement:

Hon. J.A. Seddon, May 23, 1864

Dear Sir: I have known Mr. Beall, the writer of the within, from his earliest infancy, and have observed closely his bearing and conduct since the very beginning of the present war, and I beg leave to say to the Secretary, in the first place, that he may rely with the most implicit confidence, not only on assurance given within of his ability to raise the company of men referred to, but upon any and every other statement that Mr. B. makes on the subject or on any other subject. I consider Mr. B. one of the most gallant and patriotic young gentlemen that Virginia has produced during the war, and that he is not less noted for intelligence and his loyalty to truth and honor. I have the best reasons for speaking thus emphatically of Mr. B. and I do not hesitate to pledge my own reputation for the correctness of what I here avouch.

Respectfully, Andrew Hunter[3]

Hunter's word was all the convincing Seddon needed, and he gave Beall the full authorization.

Whether for reasons of secrecy or sheer enthusiasm, Beall bolted from Richmond without informing anyone, not even Dan Lucas. "His friends in the South had lost sight of him," Lucas wrote, and "no one knew whither he had gone, or on what errand."[4] Indeed, so quickly had he departed that only William Baker, his old mate from Chesapeake raiding days, was ready to accompany him. Upon arrival in Canada, he was to report to Commissioner Thompson.

10. The Northwest Goose Egg

Thompson, meanwhile, was already desperately grasping at any hare-brained scheme to open Davis's new front in the war, with the latest and greatest being a massive uprising of anti-war activists in the Great Lakes region dubbed "the Northwest Conspiracy." His co-conspirator in this far-fetched enterprise was a vain and pompous forty-three-year-old peacemaker turned warmonger named Clement L. Vallandigham.

During his two terms as Congressional representative from Ohio, Vallandigham had been a vociferous opponent of the war. In one speech on the House floor he declared:

> Twenty months have elapsed, but the rebellion is not crushed out; its military power has not been broken; the insurgents have not dispersed. The Union is not restored; nor the Constitution maintained; nor the laws enforced.... Six hundred days have passed; a thousand millions been expended; and three hundred thousand lives lost or bodies mangled; and today the Confederate flag is still near the Potomac and the Ohio, and the Confederate Government stronger, many times, than at the beginning.[5]

As opposition to the war grew, Vallandigham turned his criticism toward Lincoln. Addressing the closing session of the 37th Congress in March 1863, he denounced the President for infringing on civil liberties, suspending the writ of habeas corpus, closing opposition newspapers, and arresting anti-war politicians and editors. The Lincoln administration, he said, had produced "one of the worst despotisms on earth," adding that the war had brought nothing but "Defeat, debt, taxation, sepulchres, these are your trophies."[6]

In 1863 Vallandigham lost his seat in Congress after his Dayton district was gerrymandered in favor of Republican voters. By then, he didn't need to hurl invective at Lincoln as the Northwestern states of Ohio, Iowa, Indiana, and Illinois were awash in anti-war sentiment. They had felt deceived by Lincoln's issuance of the Emancipation Proclamation on January 1, 1863. All along, the Northwest states had believed the war had been about preserving the Union and the Constitution when, in fact, it was an "armed crusade about slavery," according to Democratic congressman from Ohio George H. Pendleton.[7]

Nevertheless, Vallandigham continued to fan the flames of discontent. He was eventually arrested on vague charges of treason. Worried that Vallandigham might be perceived as a martyr by opponents of the war, Lincoln had him exiled to the South in May 1863.

Bored in exile, Vallandigham made his way to Windsor, Canada, from where he had made an unsuccessful bid to become Governor of Ohio. He subsequently became "Supreme Commander" of the Order of the Sons of Liberty, a quasi-military organization composed mainly of Democrats who opposed both the war and the draft.[8] At first Vallandigham was lukewarm to the idea of more violence. He had never espoused the Southern cause and preferred to reach some accommodation with Lincoln. But he rallied to the South after realizing he was becoming a marginal player among anti-war activists.

In late June, Vallandigham met with Thompson in an old boarding house in St. Catherine to flesh out details of the Northwest Conspiracy. Vallandigham boasted that his Sons Order claimed over 300,000 members spread throughout Missouri, Kentucky, Illinois, Indiana, and Ohio, an exaggeration that Thompson, in his eagerness to make something happen, swallowed whole. These imaginary legions were to revolt, overthrow the existing governments of Ohio, Illinois, and Indiana, seize the federal arsenals, and establish a Northwest Confederacy all in one perfectly synchronized and magical act of defiance.[9] Because the Union would then be split into three parts, the North would be forced to end its contest with the South. It was a perfectly fanciful plan, long on grand ideas and short on detail, hatched not by military strategists but by politicians.

As historian Stephen Starr wrote:

> [The] plans of a Copperhead uprising as they were understood in Richmond, seemed attractive indeed. Even if the [up]rising failed to bring about the creation of a Northwest Confederacy, a widespread insurrection in the heartland of the Union and the withdrawal from the field of the military forces needed to deal with it, would paralyze the Northern war effort and would render impossible the prosecution of the war for months and perhaps forever; at the very least, the Confederacy would gain a desperately needed breathing space. Moreover, any such insurrection, even if ultimately unsuccessful, would dishearten and demoralize the troops from the northwestern states, the only component of the Union armies that the South believed had done any real fighting in the war. And if there were a second secession, one which did not carry the stigma of being based on a desire to perpetuate

10. The Northwest Goose Egg

slavery, the moral advantage which the North enjoyed in the eyes of the world would be utterly destroyed. The greatly wished-for recognition of the Confederacy by the European powers and the irretrievable collapse of the Northern effort to reconstitute the Union by force of arms would then inevitably follow.[10]

Thompson chose twenty-five-year-old Colonel Thomas H. Hines to implement the plan. Slender and effeminate-looking with pale blue eyes and a drooping mustache, Hines had demonstrated a Houdini-like ability to elude the enemy. After being captured in Ohio with General John Hunt Morgan, he was placed in Johnson's Island prison before being transferred to the Ohio Penitentiary. While there, Hines discovered a way for them to escape by tunneling beneath the prison grounds, an idea inspired by his reading of *Les Misérables*, in which the protagonist, Jean Valjean, had similarly escaped through the underground passages of Paris. After leading Morgan back to Confederate lines, Hines was captured in Tennessee and sentenced to hang but escaped once again. He subsequently spent most of his time dressed in civilian clothes, conducting espionage in Kentucky.

Although Hines had no experience operating as a subversive agent in a foreign country, Davis gave Hines full authority to collect and organize the Confederate soldiers residing in Canada and to assist them to return to the Confederacy from Canada.[11] Like him, most were escaped prisoners. So broke was the Confederacy at this point that Seddon forwarded him 200 bales of cotton from Mississippi to be converted into operating expenses. When the commissioners arrived, Hines was given a bigger role in the Midwest revolt: Once the uprising was in full swing, he was to lead two regiments from Chicago to free the prisoners at Camp Morton in Indianapolis. With the freed prisoners he was to seize the governments of Ohio, Illinois, and Indiana, after which he would march south and take Nashville.

Meanwhile, left to his own devices in Montreal, Clay had come under the spell of Kentuckian George N. Sanders, a political schemer who had been involved in wild attempts to assassinate heads of state while serving as consul in London. Unbeknownst to Thompson, in early July Sanders, who had virtually no authority to act on behalf of the Confederacy, approached William "Colorado" Jewett, a shady New York merchant, to pass word to Horace Greeley that the South was interested in discussing peace with the North. As the owner/editor of the influential *New York Tribune*, Greeley enjoyed the President's confidence, though they rarely saw eye to eye. Differences notwithstanding, Greeley urged Lincoln to listen to what the two commissioners—Holcombe had since come under Sanders's thrall as well—had to offer. Lincoln was skeptical, believing Sanders and Clay were acting on their own. Nevertheless, he agreed to at least hear the commissioners out. So little faith did Lincoln place in the meeting that he insisted Greeley meet on his behalf. The President's suspicions were confirmed the next day when Clay informed Greeley of a minor detail he had neglected to mention: The commissioners were not authorized by Richmond to negotiate a peace deal. If, however, Washington were to inform Richmond of its willingness to provide safe passage for the commissioners to Washington, then "we would at once be invested with the authority to which your letter refers." Hearing this, Lincoln abruptly washed his hands of the two freelancers.[12] Crazily, Sanders now urged the two commissioners to rob banks in Niagara Falls and Buffalo as a way of diverting troops from the frontlines, an idea that the even the feckless commissioners dismissed as foolhardy for it would jeopardize their relationship with Canada.

As Clay and Holcombe blundered along, so, too, did Thompson. Thus far, his grand uprising had been a flop. July 22 had come and gone with no action from the Sons of Liberty. They refused to take action unless Southern troops moved against Kentucky and Missouri, an action entirely beyond Thompson's authority. With the Confederacy in meltdown, Thompson began throwing money at virtually every scheme that came his way. He handed out thousands in gold to "every scoundrel who dreamed up a wild tale of how he was preparing to spread havoc among the Federals by burning army transports or military installations."[13] To a Mr. Minor Major he paid $2,000 to burn steamboats on the Mississippi. When he subsequently learned a few boats were burned near St. Louis, he concluded

10. The Northwest Goose Egg

he had gotten value for his money and proceeded to finance another interloper, a Mr. Churchill, to burn Cincinnati. Nothing came of it. On another occasion a Dr. K.I. Stewart turned up from Richmond claiming he had secret orders from President Davis for which he needed $25,000. When asked to produce his orders, he could not, but told Thompson that for $500 he would return to Richmond and retrieve them. Thompson naively forked over the advance and the raider was never seen again. He next tried to create a financial panic in the North by buying up gold and smuggling it out of the country to weaken the Union greenback. For once the costly scheme was showing promise, until the gold-buying agent was arrested and thrown into prison.

There was still the Midwest insurrection to bank on. But August came and the Sons were still asking for more time to organize the various groups on the ground. Little did they know that by this point they had been infiltrated by a double agent, a Kentuckian named Felix Stidger, who was communicating their every move to the military commander in Indianapolis.[14] Though aware that the plan had now been compromised, Thompson ignored this and agreed to move the date to August 16. But when Thompson met with Midwest representatives a few days later, they once again pleaded for more time. Once again, he postponed the uprising, this time to August 29, the day of the National Democratic Convention in Chicago. So many attendees would be on hand that the Sons could blend easily into the crowd. To facilitate transportation of the Sons to Chicago, Thompson gave $12,000 to Amos Green, a Copperhead leader in Illinois. Another $2,500 went to Hines, who distributed the money to sixty-two Copperheads, along with weapons and ammunition. When at last the time to revolt arrived, most of the Sons failed to show, largely because at the last minute the Indiana Copperheads refused to take part in the uprising. The few Ohio and Illinois men who did show up lost their nerve when they learned the Union army had sent reinforcements to Camp Douglas. With the end of the Convention, the Confederates felt it no longer safe to linger there and left, having accomplished nothing apart from arousing the suspicions of Federal agents. Later, it was learned that many of the Confederate agents hired to distribute funds for arms had simply pocketed the money.

In desperation, Hines and Castleman now proposed that the Sons of Liberty organize 500 men to break out prisoners at Rock Island, a proposal for which Thompson readily advanced him $18,450 in greenbacks. By this point, Clay had grown skeptical of doing anything but advanced Hines another $4,100 in gold, followed by $30,000 in greenbacks a few days later, for arms and expenses. In return, Copperheads promised to act on election day. The day before the planned attack, however, a Douglas commander arrested over 100 Confederates at various hideouts in the city and seized the weapons. After eluding capture by hiding in a box spring, Hines fled to Richmond, still flush with travel advances.

Despite all the false starts and extravagant waste of money, Thompson refused to concede defeat. In fact, by the time Hines had arrived in Richmond, he was well into a new scheme, this time with John Beall.

11

The Johnson's Island Raid

Beall had arrived back at Riley's Hotel on August 14. As instructed by Seddon, he reported straightaway to Thompson, who was delighted to see him. He had been waiting for someone like Beall to execute a scheme he had been contemplating since he first set foot in Canada—seizing the man-of-war USS *Michigan* patrolling Lake Erie. Possession of this, the U.S. Navy's first iron ship and sole gunboat on the Great Lakes, would confer mastery of the entire network of lakes to the Confederates, allowing rebels to strike terror into the very heart of the North. It would also be used to facilitate the liberation from Johnson's Island of Confederate officers whose leadership was sorely needed on the frontlines.

Thompson had conferred overall command of the mission to a confidence man named Charles Henry Cole. A shadowy figure with an uncertain past, Cole may have served by turns in the Confederate and Northern armies—and deserted from both. He claimed to have been captured while serving in the cavalry of General Nathan Bedford Forrest, though it is more likely he had deserted from the Union at that time. A few days after he was imprisoned in Johnson's Island in September 1863, his captors sent him and several other prisoners into a steamer hold to collect straw for their bunks. After the other men had collected the straw and left the ship, Cole hid in the straw, betting the guards had lost count of the prisoners. When the ship stopped in Sandusky for the night, Cole slipped off the ship. Posing as a civilian worker, he fled to Canada, where he offered his services to Thompson.

At Thompson's behest, Cole conducted a scouting mission along the lakes. What he found were towns ripe for the taking. Buffalo,

John Yates Beall, Son of the South

Prison at Johnson's Island, site of Beall's failed attempt to free Confederate soldiers (courtesy of Johnson's Island Preservation Society).

which contained a large arsenal with cannon, mortar, and small arms, was poorly protected. Detroit and Milwaukee were sitting ducks. In Cleveland he toured the large weapons factory that was about to ship cannons and ammunition to several towns along the lake.

Johnson's Island, however, would be no easy mark. The three-hundred-acre site was the first facility built during the Civil War expressly to house military prisoners.[1] Lieutenant Colonel William Hoffman, who was charged with building the prison, had selected the island precisely because it was easily defensible and close to rail lines in Sandusky. Hoffman, who had extensive experience designing military outposts around the country, used a unique approach to the design of the Johnson's Island prison. To prevent escape, the entire facility faced inward. Blockhouses on two of the opposite corners allowed guards to look down simultaneously on the barracks as well as the exterior of the prison. The prison was also surrounded by a twelve-foot-high fence. Guarding the island overall were one hundred soldiers of the 128th Ohio Volunteers, backed by the massive fourteen guns of the USS *Michigan* anchored in nearby Sandusky Bay.

As an architect, "Old Hoffy," as he was known to his subordinates, was a stickler for detail. But there was one thing he had grossly underestimated—the size of the prison. Even before the first batch of two hundred prisoners arrived on April 11, 1862, Hoffman realized his error and had begun to expand the facility to accommodate up to 5,000 men "by crowding."[2]

11. The Johnson's Island Raid

USS *Michigan*, the Union gunboat Confederates plotted to seize (courtesy of Library of Congress).

Just two days after the first prisoners arrived, Secretary of War Edwin M. Stanton had instructed Hoffman—with no explanation—that Johnson's Island would be reserved solely for officers. This became an important factor in Beall's decision to attack Johnson's Island. Many of the prisoners were officers and essential to the waning Confederate war machine. Some, such as Brigadier General M. Jeff Thompson from Jefferson County, Virginia, and Colonel Richard Henry Lee of Stonewall's Brigade, were almost certainly known to Beall.

The prisoners were languishing in insufferable conditions. Initially, the prison wasn't crowded and provided greater access to food and health care than other prisons.[3] But as the war wound on and the North learned of the severe conditions in Southern prisons, daily rations were reduced to a small loaf of bread and piece of meat with no coffee or sugar, and no longer any packages from home. Three shallow pits furnished the prisoners with muddy but potable water. Inmates were also denied the chance to supplement their diets with food purchased from Sandusky stores. Hunger became especially acute during the winter months when Lake Erie froze over. By 1864 a breakdown in the prisoner exchange cartel had caused the prison population to swell to over 2,600 prisoners. What was more, its location on the lake assured winters would be bitter cold, especially as Southern prisoners were invariably thinly clad. Summer provided little relief. It became damp and humid, and heavy lake rains often turned the prison yard to knee-deep mud.

John Yates Beall, Son of the South

Several yards from the main prison were the dungeons, each somewhat larger than a coffin, in which officers condemned to death by court-martial were chained hand and foot. When allowed to move about the yard, some were forced to drag an iron ball of sixty pounds weight.

When Cole returned to the island—this time as a curious visitor—he had found guards on heightened alert. Since the opening of the prison in 1862, Union officials had periodically received warnings from Canadian authorities that Confederates were planning to raid the prison. While General Henry Halleck had long thought these rumors to be unfounded, exposure of a plot that February confirmed their fears. The 128th Ohio Volunteers were subsequently reinforced with regiments from the Army of the Potomac.[4]

Upon Cole's return to Toronto, Thompson sent him to Sandusky to begin working on infiltrating the *Michigan*. Cole intended to ingratiate himself with the officers of the ship with a view to bribing several of the crew on board and drugging others to sleep. Ironically, it was his predilection for duplicity and self-presentation that made him the perfect man for the job. With a hefty advance in American currency from Thompson, he took up residence in Sandusky's posh, five-story hotel, the West House, near the waterfront. Posing as the secretary of the fictitious Mount Hope Oil Company of Titusville, Pennsylvania—of which ex-president Millard Filmore was director—he soon ingratiated himself with some of the ship's officers, feting them with sumptuous meals at his hotel, complete with fine wines. On at least two occasions he sent cases of wine aboard the *Michigan*, once to Ensign William Pavey, with whom he became particularly close, and another time to the officers generally. So extravagantly did he entertain that one observer was prompted to cynically remark, "The conspirator's service at Sandusky to the Confederacy, large as it looms in the newspaper stories inspired by himself, seems actually to have been confined to the expenditure of a considerable portion of its revenue over the bar at West House."[5] Cole was often seen with a woman there he claimed was his wife Annie, but whom the men of the ship recognized as a woman of easy virtue, elsewhere known as a Buffalo-based prostitute named "Irish Liz." Her real name may have

11. The Johnson's Island Raid

been Annie Davis or Annie Brown, though she also went by Belle Brandon. Whatever her name, the alluring Englishwoman with coal black eyes framed by a bob of shimmering black hair was inexplicably enthusiastic about the Southern cause. Several times she had approached Thompson seeking an appointment in the Confederate Secret Service. After repeated rejections, Thompson finally relented and sent her to Cole. For her sleuthing, he would later laud her as one of the most marvelous women he ever met.

In return for his generosity, Cole and Annie had been guests on board the *Michigan* on several occasions. During one of his visits Cole succeeded in bribing the engineer for his future cooperation in disabling the ship's machinery. As for the ship's commander, Captain John C. Carter, Cole concluded, "I do not think he can be bought."[6] In time, Cole was even given access to the Johnson's Island prison, where he mixed freely with the inmates. On one occasion Cole met with several of the Confederate officers and divulged the plan to seize the gunboat and free them. In preparation for the breakout, the prisoners organized into companies and armed themselves with crude clubs fashioned from stove wood. Archibald S. McKennon, of the 16th Arkansas Infantry, was elected to lead the revolt, though he was deeply skeptical of its success.

> We were organized into companies and regiments and had armed ourselves with clubs, which were made of stove wood and other materials at hand with which to fight. We were in constant expectation of orders, which never came, to make the fight. It would have been a pitiable affair, for the undertaking was wholly impractical.[7]

While Cole was schmoozing in Sandusky, Beall came down to meet with him and work out the final details of their ambitious plan. This was it in a nutshell: In several days Cole would extend an invitation to the officers of the *Michigan* to a champagne dinner at his hotel "to honor their service to the nation." While most of the officers were reveling onshore with Cole, the boat's engineer, whose loyalty he had bought, would disable the engines. Meanwhile, Beall was to seize the 220-ton mail steamer *Philo Parsons* lying at wharf near Detroit. Putting the passengers and crew ashore, he would then proceed along the mail route to Sandusky, making the usual mail stops along the way. In this way he expected to obtain possession of the *Parsons* without a conflict or loss of life, something that was always important to him. By the time Beall arrived in Sandusky Bay, the officers dining with Cole would be fast asleep, Cole having drugged the dinner wine. Cole would then fire a rocket, signaling an all-clear for Beall to attack the nearly empty *Michigan* and for the prisoners to revolt. Once in control of the ship, Beall would train the ship's massive guns on the camp and demand the prisoners be released. They would then steam to Johnson's Island, where Cole would have placed ten Confederate soldiers among the guards.[8] Once freed, the prisoners were to attack Sandusky, steal horses, and make for Cleveland, backed by the boats. From there they were to strike across Ohio, which was largely unprotected, for West Virginia. If the plan seemed too good to be true, it was.

Once briefed by Cole, Beall returned to Windsor to put together a crew and obtain supplies. One day, while walking down the streets of Toronto, he chanced to run into none other than Bennett Burley. The irrepressible Burley had escaped shortly after being taken prisoner by Wistar. Returning to the navy as acting master, he served in several privateering expeditions on the James River and Chesapeake Bay. During one outing, he captured the entire guard at Cherrystone as well as two steamers, a schooner, and a large supply of stores. A few months later he was captured near the mouth of the Rappahannock by a sergeant of a "colored infantry" looking for torpedoes near the river's mouth. A search of his person turned up documents

The merchant steamer *Philo Parsons*, which Beall seized on Lake Erie (courtesy of Naval History & Heritage Command Photo Section, Photo NH67016).

11. The Johnson's Island Raid

authorizing him to go beyond Confederate lines. Burley was charged with spying and imprisoned in Fort Delaware, forty miles south of Philadelphia. Once again he escaped, this time by tying canteens to his waist and swimming over three miles through the fort's drain duct down to and across the Delaware River. Mid-river he was picked up by a schooner but managed to convince the captain that he was a British subject returning to Canada who had fallen overboard from his ship. From Philadelphia, Burley had made his way to Toronto. His unquenchable thirst for adventure still intact, he accepted Beall's offer to be second-in-command in the expedition.

By mid–September the supplies were in hand and the crew, most of whom had apparently been recruited from the toughs lounging at the Queen's Hotel Bar, were assembled and they were ready to put their plan into play. Invitations to dinner went out to the *Michigan*'s officers for dinner on September 19.

On the morning of September 18, Burley and a few of his mates boarded the *Philo Parsons* at Detroit. On board were forty passengers. As the steamer made its way down the Detroit River, the ship's captain, Sylvester F. Atwood, made an irregular stop at Sandwich on the Canadian side to pick up three of Burley's "friends," something he had arranged with the captain the previous day. As the boat drifted by the wharf—still in motion—three rebels hopped aboard. Burley had told the captain that they were taking a "pleasure trip" and would likely get off at Kelley's Island. One of the three who boarded at Sandwich, distinctly Southern in appearance in gray pants and a black cloth sack coat, was John Beall. Near the mouth of the river, they stopped at Amherstburg, where fifteen more of Beall's crew—all roughly dressed—silently boarded. Neither Beall nor Burley acknowledged them. They carried no baggage save an old trunk fastened with a rope and filled with revolvers, hatchets, swords, coils of rope, and grappling hooks. Judging from their ragged appearance the ship's part owner, Walter O. Ashley, took them to be "skedaddlers," Northerners crossing into Canada to evade Lincoln's unpopular draft.

Once out in the open waters of Lake Erie, Burley began to mix freely with the passengers. The adventure-seeking Scotsman clearly relished his latest role. After chatting amiably with the passengers on

John Yates Beall, Son of the South

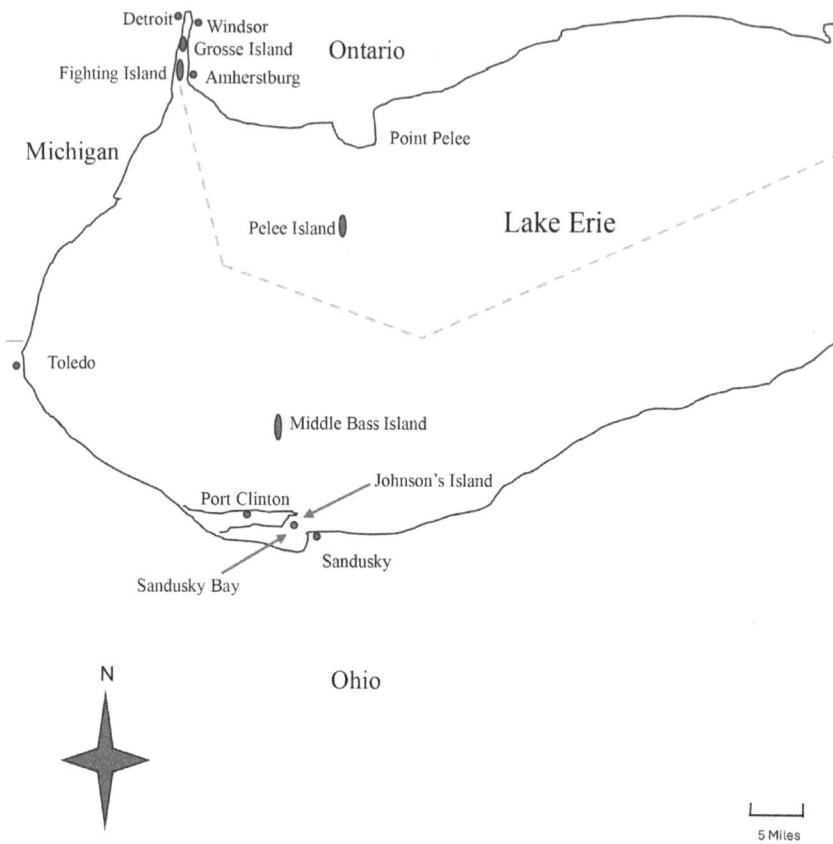

Western Lake Erie, showing Johnson's Island and major coastal cities (map by the author).

deck, he wandered into the cabin and sat at the piano, where he gaily turned the music pages for ladies who were taking turns playing. As the *Parsons* plied southward, it made its routine stops. At Middle Bass Island Captain Atwood went ashore to spend the evening with his family, as he often did, leaving the ship in the command of his mate, De Witt Clinton Nichols, and its clerk and part-owner, Ashley. Around 4 p.m. Nichols touched on Kelley's Island, the last stop before Sandusky.

As soon as the ship embarked, Beall casually sauntered up to the wheelhouse and engaged Nichols in conversation. A few

11. The Johnson's Island Raid

minutes passed when Beall walked down the hurricane deck and beckoned Nichols to the smokestack. When Nicholas came over, Beall announced he was a Confederate naval officer and was commandeering the ship in the name of the Confederacy. "You must pilot the boat as I direct," Beall said, "and here are the tools to make you."[9] With that he pulled out his revolver and ordered Nichols to cruise down and lie off the harbor at Sandusky. Meanwhile the wheelsman, Michael Campbell, was running from one of the rebels to the upper deck when he saw the passengers being forced into the cabin at gunpoint and surrendered. Ashley was standing on the main deck front of his office when three of the rebels approached and ordered him into the ladies' cabin. When he refused, Burley rushed forward and, leveling his pistol at him, barked, "Get into that cabin, or you are a dead man."[10] Ashley continued to hold his ground until Burley began to count—one, two, three—before Ashley was inside the door and two armed guards were placed on either side. The rest of the passengers were put in the fire-hold and the hatch was weighed down with pig-iron.

Through the cabin's window, Ashley watched the action as the takeover of his ship on the main deck began. One of the raiders brought up the old chest and the men armed themselves with revolvers and hatchets. Burley ordered several men to clear the decks to lighten her for her new mission. Thrown overboard were a sulky and the rest of the pig iron. In an orgy of rage Burley then took his hatchet and began smashing everything in sight—the doors to the luggage room and saloon and the trotting sulky—"I don't know what for," Ashley later testified.[11]

Beall, by contrast, was the courteous Southern gentleman. When a woman with a sick baby pleaded with him that her baby needed to remain on deck and breathe fresh air or it would die, Beall consented. Another passenger with nearly $80,000 in his possession timidly approached Beall and asked to know how much of it he would be permitted to retain on condition of surrendering the remainder. Beall assured him that none of his or any of the passengers' personal effects would be disturbed.

An hour passed when Beall came into the office to secure the boat's papers from Ashley. As he held out the documents, Ashley begged Beall not to destroy his boat. After a brief silence, Beall responded with perfect logic that if he, Ashley, were a U.S. soldier and he captured a Confederate vessel would he not destroy it?

The takeover, which took thirty minutes, had gone like clockwork. All the boat's crew were stowed away save the engineer, James Denison, Campbell, who was ordered to take the wheel, and the fireman in charge of stoking the engines. The Confederate flag was hoisted over the ship—the only time it would fly over the Great Lakes during the war—and they set out for Middle Bass Island. There Beall released all the passengers save Ashley and the engineer, telling them not to report the incident for at least twenty-four hours.

No sooner had they embarked, when Denison told Beall the *Parsons* had just enough wood for her boiler to reach Sandusky and customarily refueled at Middle Bass on her return. Intending to run her seven or eight hours, Beall decided to return to Middle Bass. The reappearance of the *Parsons* naturally raised suspicions at the shipyard. When Burley called out for wood, the owner refused and was shot at, as were two other dock workers. Upon hearing the shots, the wood owner's son raced to Atwood's house crying that someone was trying to kill his father. Within minutes Atwood was at the dock yelling "What the hell's up?" He was greeted by four of Beall's men, who ordered him onto the *Parsons*. By this time, all the commotion had drawn a crowd of onlookers to the dock. To disperse it, one of the rebels fired indiscriminately into it, seriously wounding a local resident; such was the nature of the Confederate ruffians Beall had thrown together for the mission, one of the passengers describing them as "a mean, low-lived set."[12]

No sooner had Beall gotten the situation under control than another complication unexpectedly emerged. With a whistle, the *Island Queen*, a large sidewheel ferry steamer, drew up at her usual berth to take on fuel. When deckhands failed to appear to take her lines, Captain Orr realized something was amiss. He tried to speed forward, but it was too late. Beall and his men were already aboard, brandishing their weapons, ordering the crew to surrender.

It so happened that the *Queen* was carrying a group of forty

11. The Johnson's Island Raid

Union soldiers from the 130th Ohio regiment at Johnson's Island who were on their way to Toledo to be mustered out of service. Taken completely by surprise by the rebels, they and the crew were led onto the *Parsons*, where they were squeezed into the hold. But the *Queen*'s engineer, Henry Haines, refused to come out of the engine room. Someone shouted, "Shoot the son of a bitch!" One of the ruffians shot through the door, striking Haines in the cheek. Though he sustained simply a flesh wound, he surrendered. One of the rebels then called for a key to the baggage hold. Without asking the clerk, Burley announced, "I will make a key."[13] With that he took one of the axes and smashed the door open.

Realizing he could not spare men to guard both the passengers and soldiers, Beall decided to put the passengers and most of the crew ashore on the condition that they agreed not take up arms against the Confederacy until they were officially exchanged. What this meant in practice is unclear, since once released on the island they were on Ohio soil and free to go where they pleased.

Ever honorable in warfare, Beall then went to the office, where two ladies and a young man stood quivering with fear. "Ladies you will have to go ashore now," Beall said politely, "as we are going to use this boat."[14] Ashley asked if Beall was going to put him ashore as well. Beall replied he would, though Ashley would not be allowed to take the ship's books or his personal property. The Union soldiers were also paroled on the condition that they never again take up arms against the Confederacy, while the passengers were made to promise they would say nothing of what happened for twenty-four hours. After the *Queen*'s captain, George Orr, the clerk, and the wounded Haines were moved to the *Parsons*, Beall lashed the *Queen* to the *Parsons* and departed. A few miles out he stripped the *Queen* and scuttled her on the Chickenolee Reef.

Two days before Beall had boarded the *Parsons*, a man claiming to be a Confederate refugee in Canada had stepped into the Detroit office of Lieutenant Colonel Bennett H. Hill, Commander of the Michigan District. The mysterious figure was likely Captain Charles Smith, a former officer in the Confederate army turned Federal spy. The thirty-year-old Smith was operating under cover as a manager of a Windsor hotel that had some 60 to 90 boarders, nearly all of them Confederate refugees, among whom had been Beall and several of his crew.[15] Smith proceeded to inform Hill of Thompson's Johnson's Island plot, warning that some of the men aboard the *Michigan* had been compromised. Hill immediately sent a dispatch to Captain Carter informing him of the plot in which some of his very own men had been bribed into participating. Naturally, Carter was defensive, dismissing the threat entirely and the involvement of any of his staff in treachery. In case there was any doubt as to Smith's claims, the following day he returned with more precise details—that Cole had bribed several officers aboard the *Michigan* and that a group of pirates planned to seize the *Philo Parsons* or another steamer and descend the lake to Johnson's Island and free the prisoners. Needing no further convincing, Carter summoned his ensign, Captain James Hunter, whom he had sent on previous occasions to investigate rumors of imminent rebel attack on the island. This time Carter said, "Hunter, you need not go. For here is a telegraphic dispatch that the rebels are coming on the steamer *Philo Parsons*, from Detroit, and that some of our ship's officers are traitors, that you are to be poisoned ... and that Mr. Cole is a spy!"[16] Fearing Carter suspected him of complicity in the affair, Hunter declared that he was "a thorough Union man," so eager to serve that he had even paid his own fare to New York to enlist in the navy. Evidently satisfied by Hunter's declaration of fealty, Carter asked if he knew of a certain Cole and if he thought there were men aboard who would betray him. Hunter replied that he knew Cole to be an oil executive from Philadelphia who had tried to enlist him to captain the schooner *Frémont* and take a load of oil to Liverpool, England. Hunter also confessed to having been the recipient of his generosity, though not more so than Ensign Pavey, who had once received a case of champagne from Cole. As a precaution, Carter ordered Pavey off the ship, thereby depriving Cole of his most reliable asset in the plot.

On Sunday, Commander Hill arrived to meet with Carter and Hunter. After some discussion it was agreed that the *Michigan* should remain in the harbor and await the arrival of the *Parsons*. In the meantime, Hill would send a regiment to the Sandusky

11. The Johnson's Island Raid

train station to watch for any rebel reinforcements that might come by rail. Returning to his vessel, Hunter ordered his crew to prepare her for action. The *Michigan* was moved closer to Johnson's Island and positioned in such a way as to cover the entrance to the harbor with its massive firepower. Once in position a few rounds of its guns were test-fired to fix their elevation and range. Fourteen guns, including a sixty-eight-pound smooth-bore Paxton mounted forward on a pivot, six twenty-five-pound Dahlgrens mounted aft, and six twelve-pound Howitzers, were now trained on the harbor's entrance. If they entered the channel, Beall and his men would not know what hit them. As a further precaution, the tug *General Burnside* was to go out and patrol the waters each night and inspect every vessel entering the harbor.

Wishing to arrest Cole himself, Hunter armed himself with a revolver and set out for West House. He had not gone far when he was ordered back to the ship and told not to take a sidearm, as Cole might have accomplices and should be arrested quietly. Hunter took several men instead and set out in a barge. Once in Sandusky he instructed the coxswain, Turley, to turn the barge around and for the men to stand ready at the oars, adding that if he sounded his distinctive whistle *Coooo! Weee!* they were to rush to his aid.

Upon reaching Cole's room at West House, Hunter and Turley found it empty. Assuming he had absconded, Hunter went down to the hotel clerk and asked how long it had been since Cole had left. "He is all ready to leave," the clerk replied, "but just now he is in parlor B."[17] Hunter dashed to the parlor, where he found Cole and Annie clad in travel attire standing alongside their trunks and baggage in preparation for a quick departure. Master confidence man that he was, Cole appeared pleased to see him, offering a swig from his bulbous demijohn. At first Hunter declined but when Cole insisted, he took a sip so as not to make him suspicious. Realizing the libation might be poisoned, Hunter began to cough and choke before emptying his mouth in a spittoon. "Take another," Cole urged. "After you," replied Hunter. After Cole took a hearty swig and swallowed, Hunter felt it was safe to take another. Turning to Irish Liz, Cole said he had some business to attend to and beckoned Hunter to follow

John Yates Beall, Son of the South

him to the bank. As they strolled down the street, the coxswain followed close behind, dodging from one lamppost to another so as not to be seen. At the bank Cole withdrew $900 and returned to the hotel, where they had a few more drinks. Seeing Cole warmed by the liquor, Hunter led him on a stroll—toward the barge. As they were nearing the dock Cole invited Hunter to a gala he was throwing that afternoon at the Seven Mile House, a resort out of town where, he assured, there would be girls. Hunter immediately saw this as a ploy to get the officers off the ship to disable it. He replied that he would first need the Commander's permission but that if Cole waited at the dock he would go and seek it. By now the two had reached the barge, and with a stiff push, Hunter sent Cole falling backward into the boat. Turley, who had been right on their heels, rushed to the stern and took the tiller. As they rowed back to the *Michigan*, Cole played innocent to the last, shouting to be released and offering to treat them to a lively afternoon.

It was 3 p.m. At this moment Beall was at Middle Bass Island, refueling.

Once back at the *Michigan*, Cole was taken to Carter's cabin. Removing a revolver from Cole's hip pocket, Hunter handed it to Carter, asking him to cover Cole while they strip-searched him. In his pockets were found several documents, $600 in cash, and several certified checks for $5,000 each drawn on the Bank of Montreal. After being allowed to dress, Cole was placed in irons and locked in the wardroom.*

Cole's papers revealed a trove of information about the plot—and the mysterious Cole. One document revealed that the confidence man was commissioned a major in the Confederate Army. Another contained the names of seven of his accomplices in Sandusky, as well as a U.S. Army captain in Columbus, Ohio, that he turned. Some were to cut the telegraph wires at the time of the takeover, while others were to spike the guns at Sandusky. Among the other papers was a dispatch that showed to what lengths Cole could take the charade:

---

*Though his accomplices in Sandusky were all acquitted for lack of evidence, Cole would spend the rest of the war in prison.

11. The Johnson's Island Raid

"I am sending you today by messenger the thirty shares of Mt. Hope Oil Wells purchased as you previously advised."[18]

Runners were sent ashore to inform Hill, who arrested all eight of the accomplices Cole had finally named, including a Sandusky clothier named Louis Rosenthal. Carter then ordered that all of Cole's effects at West House be brought to the ship to be searched. As for Cole's wife, Annie, she was also arrested and held for a day but was acquitted on charges of violating the Webster–Ashburton Treaty.* As Carter cried out, "Guns loaded, steam on the engines, and anchor hove short," the *Michigan* readied to welcome the arrival of the Confederates in the *Parsons*.

By this point, darkness had fallen. As Beall eased into Sandusky Bay, he ordered the remaining captives into the hold. Left on deck were the engineer and the wheelsman Campbell. As Campbell steered the ship toward bay, he cautioned Beall that it was too dangerous to enter it at night, for they could run aground. They halted just short of the entrance, unaware the entire plot had been exposed. In the moonlight the rebels could see the menacing contours of the *Michigan*'s guns and its lights reflected on the glassy surface of Lake Erie. Standing on the *Parsons'* forward deck was Beall, gazing intently toward Johnson's Island, expecting any minute to see the rocket from Cole as the signal to attack. Once the signal was launched, he would set fire to the coal tar on board to draw the crew off the *Michigan* to rescue the innocent passengers aboard. When they neared the *Parsons* in their scows, Beall would demand their surrender, failing which they would turn their guns on them and sink them in their boats.

As time passed with no sign from Cole, the crew became anxious, convinced that the plot had been uncovered and that to attack the *Michigan* now would now be suicide. Beall, however, insisted all was well and that any minute Cole's rocket would pierce the sky. Thirty minutes had passed when Beall was suddenly blindsided:

---

*Article 10 of the treaty between the United States and British colonies in North America provided for extradition of individuals found guilty of murder, assault with intent to commit murder, piracy, forgery, and other crimes.

John Yates Beall, Son of the South

Seventeen of the raiders declared that they refused to participate another minute in a plot that they believed had gone awry. Only the reckless Burley and two others stood by him. At first Beall pleaded with the men, arguing they had come so far, and were on the verge of a glorious victory. Whatever befell Cole, he assured them, their presence on the water was entirely unsuspected. Why, the officers of the *Michigan* were most likely in Sandusky, lost in revelry and drunkenness! But the men were resolute and refused to prosecute further a mission they believed was doomed. Beall became unhinged, berating them as "strangers to him" unworthy of the name Confederates, just as he had while a prisoner on the Chesapeake seeking to escape.[19] Seeing they were adamant, he ordered the mutineers into the cabin and ordered them to write down their decision as both evidence of their perfidy and vindication of his own willingness to stay the course. Written on the back of a bill of lading, it read:

On board the *Philo Parsons*:

> September 20, 1864
>
> We, the undersigned, crew of the boat aforesaid, take pleasure in expressing our admiration for the gentlemanly bearing, skill, and courage of Captain John Y. Beall as a commanding officer and a gentleman but believing and being well convinced that the enemy is already apprised of our approach and is so well prepared that we cannot by possibility make it a success, and having already captured two boats, we respectfully decline to prosecute it any further.[20]

It must have been one of the most civil mutinies in the history of naval warfare, demonstrating, despite their mutiny, the affection and admiration Beall invariably inspired as a leader. Reluctantly, he ordered the *Parsons* back to Canada post-haste. As it raced passed Middle Bass Island, black smoke billowing from its stacks, one of the female captives who had been put ashore saw it fly by, "making for the Detroit River like a scared pickerel."[21] In the morning they arrived at Amherstburg, where Beall stripped the *Parsons* and sent her valuables ashore in a small boat. Around 8 a.m. he reached Fighting Island, where he put Captain Orr, Nichols, Campbell, and Denison ashore, unharmed. Upon entering the Detroit River an angry Beall prepared to attack every ship he passed until he learned he was in Canadian waters but saw nothing. Further up, at Sandwich, he

11. The Johnson's Island Raid

had everything of value removed—a piano, chairs, trunks, and bedclothes—then ordered the engineer to cut the steam pipes so the boat would sink. A comical interlude followed when Canadian customs authorities arrested two of the rebels for importing goods without a permit. Despite the evidence against them, a judge released them the next day. Beall then discharged his men, none of whom would subsequently be prosecuted for mutiny. Although Campbell and Denison later recovered the *Parsons*, Beall had done an estimated $6,000 in damage; that to the *Queen* was put at $3,000.*

The *Michigan* had waited all night at Sandusky for the *Parsons* to appear. At dawn it steamed out of the harbor to Kelley's Island, where the men learned that the mail frigate had indeed been captured by the rebels and was last seen heading northward at breakneck speed. Just beyond South Bass Island, Carter came across Ashley in a rowboat hastening to Sandusky with, by now, old news of the rebel takeover. As the *Michigan* passed Middle Bass, the men were loudly cheered by the passengers put ashore by Beall. A little further on they encountered another solitary man in a rowboat— it was none other than John Brown, Jr., son of the notorious abolitionist. From his vineyard at Put-in Bay on South Bass, Brown had noticed a lot of activity across the strait on Middle Bass and was rowing across to report to Colonel Hill what the rebels had done after capturing the *Parsons*.

At the mouth of the Detroit River Carter encountered a schooner and shouted to the owner, asking whether he had seen the *Parsons*. "No!" came the reply. Further up they hailed a tugboat, but it had not seen the ship either. Concerned that Beall might have gone to attack one of the lake cities or another steamer, Carter consulted with his staff and decided to return to Sandusky. With Beall still at large—so they believed—Johnson's Island was vulnerable.

---

*To his dying day, Beall believed that but for the cowardice of his crew, he would have succeeded in seizing the *Michigan* and freeing the prisoners. He insisted the plot had not been uncovered until *after* he seized the *Parsons*. The officers of the *Michigan* had attempted to cover up their dereliction of duty by claiming that Cole had been arrested one day prior—as the Sandusky papers had erroneously reported—and not hours before his arrival in Sandusky Bay.

John Yates Beall, Son of the South

Thus far, even though he had expended a great deal of money, none of Thompson's wild schemes had borne fruit.

Yet, neither he nor Beall would concede defeat.

12

Last Stop at Dunkirk

In the days following the aborted raid, Burley returned to the house of a cousin in Guelph where he had previously been staying. It wasn't long before he resumed tinkering with ordnance experiments in his yard. His pyrotechnics came to the attention of Canadian authorities, who arrested him for involvement in the Johnson's Island plot. At first the Canadians took him for the notorious pirate John Beall, a mistake which Burley did nothing to correct.

Beall was distressed by Burley's arrest, feeling responsible for having recruited him for Johnson's Island in the first place. He consulted his friends in Toronto about turning himself in to Canadian authorities, but they advised that nothing practical could be gained by it. In the meantime, Burley was released on a technicality only to be re-arrested on charges of piracy, robbery, and intent to commit murder in connection with the Johnson's Island plot. This time Canadians knew who they had, for Burley had carelessly given his real name to the captain of the *Philo Parsons*, who identified him. When the U.S. government learned of Burley's capture, it demanded his extradition. Since Britain was unlikely to recognize a piracy charge against its own subject, the United States charged him with armed robbery, for just before Burley put the clerk of the *Parsons* ashore, the Scotsman had relieved him of his wallet.*

Burley's arrest had larger repercussions. With each new attempt by Thompson to stir up trouble in the North, Canadian sympathy for

---

*After a long legal battle, Burley was extradited to the United States. On September 17, 1865, just days before his trial, he escaped. The indomitable Burley eventually returned to Scotland, where he changed his name to Burleigh and became a celebrated war correspondent for the *London Daily Telegraph*.

John Yates Beall, Son of the South

the Confederate cause was waning. An editorial in the *Toronto Globe* roundly denounced Burley for the *Parsons* raid as a blatant violation of Canadian law. In defense of their actions Beall responded with a letter to the editor:

> Mr. Editor: You condemn the conduct of those who captured the two steamers on Lake Erie as infringing the laws of Canada.... The United States is carrying on war on Lake Erie against the Confederate States (either by virtue of right or sufferance from you), by transportation of men and supplies on its waters; by confining Confederate prisoners on its islands, and lastly, by the presence of a 14-gun steamer patrolling its waters. The Confederates clearly have the right to retaliate, provided they can do so without infringing your laws. They did not infringe those laws; for, first, the plan for this attack was matured, and sought to be carried out in the United States, and not in Canada; there was not a Canadian, or any man enlisted in Canada.
>
> Secondly, no act of hostility was committed on Canadian water or soil.... These men embarked on an American vessel from Detroit, or sprang onto it while in motion, from Canadian wharves. The boat did not properly stop at Sandwich, or Amherstburg at all, as the Customs will show....
>
> Thirdly. What is this *Michigan* that she cannot be attacked? Is the fact that she carries thirteen more guns than the treaty stipulation between the United States and England allows, a sufficient reason why she should not be subject to attack?* England allows this boat to remain guarding Confederate prisoners, though she carries an armament in violation of the treaty.
>
> Before these men are condemned, judge if they have broken your laws. No "murder" was committed, indeed not a life lost. There was no searching of prisoners, no "robbing." It is true the boats were abused; but, sir, they were captured by Confederates, enemies of the United States and however questionable the taste, the right is clear. These men were not "burglars" or "pirates," enemies of mankind unless hatred and hostility to the Yankees be taken as a crime against humanity, or a crime against civilization.[1]

This was as much as a defense of his men as legitimate combatants as it was an exposition of his creed on how to wage war honorably and with a minimum loss of life. As a defense of his violation of Canada's neutrality, however, it rested on a slender legal reed indeed. For how could Canada maintain a truly neutral position in the war, so long as Confederates operated from its soil?

Canada could, at least, take some solace in the fact that virtually

---

*This is a reference to the Rush–Bagot Treaty of 1818 between the United States and Britain that limited armaments on the Upper Great Lakes to one ship and one eighteen-pound cannon.

12. Last Stop at Dunkirk

all of Thompson's attempts to wage war against the North had come to naught. Indeed, Johnson's Island marked yet another embarrassing failure the commissioner was determined to rectify. If a ship could not be commandeered to establish dominance on the lakes, then he would simply purchase one. In due course he bought a propeller-driven steamship, the *Georgian*, from an old sea captain, James P. Bates, for the princely sum of $17,000—about twice what it was worth—and anchored it off the Canadian shore at Port Colburn.

News of the ship's purchase by Confederates spread like a prairie fire. Not only did the Union army get wind of it, so, too, did the wider public. On November 7, the *Buffalo Commercial Advertiser* ran a front-page article suggesting the true nefarious intent behind the purchase.

> Whether Mr. Bates bought the *Georgian* for the purpose, as is supposed in Buffalo, of converting her into a privateer, to encounter and destroy the *Michigan*, and liberate the rebel prisoners on Johnson's Island—or whether, as he asserted here, he made the purchase for the purpose of using the vessel in the lumber trade—we shall not pretend to decide. A day or two more will no doubt clear up the whole mystery.[2]

The *Georgian* wasn't exactly a battle-hardened warship. Recently built, its only activities had consisted of towing rafts of square timber to sawmills at Collingwood. To prepare her for raiding, Thompson planned to upgrade her engines, strengthen the hull in the bow for a ram, and add a sail mast to supplement the steam engines. But all that would have to wait, as time was running out to turn the war around. Since she was seaworthy, he gave command of the vessel to Beall, who set about to assemble a crew and procure supplies.

Two crew members were seasoned fighters who had just arrived in Toronto courtesy of James Seddon: Kentuckian John W. Headley had served as a spy for General Braxton Bragg and ridden with General John Hunt Morgan; Colonel Robert Martin was another Morgan veteran who walked hunched over from a chest wound he sustained in Tennessee. A third, George S. Anderson, was merely a boy who had served for a fortnight as a courier for Colonel Martin during Morgan's last raid into his native state of Kentucky. Anderson had been captured near Greenville, Tennessee, and was on his way to prison when he escaped from the train. Like so many escapees, he made his way to Toronto, where he had attached himself to his old commander in the hope of returning to combat.

In late September Thompson called a meeting at his sumptuous suite in the Queen's Hotel to lay out his plan. In attendance were Beall, Colonels Martin and Headley, George Anderson, Colonel Thomas Hines, Thompson's secretary Walter Cleary, and his erstwhile confidant Godfrey Joseph Hyams. Thompson planned to send the *Georgian* east and bombard Buffalo in a bid to exact a hefty ransom from her. While the city was reeling from the heavy shelling, Beall was to seize three steamers at the wharf and destroy the rest. With his small fleet he would then proceed to seize all the towns along the shore as far as Cleveland, where more rebels would come aboard to man the vessels. Led by the *Georgian* they would then make straight for the Canadian shore—destroying every Union vessel in their path. Meanwhile, another ship would descend to Sandusky to scout their old nemesis, the *Michigan*. If it were found that the warship had gone to rescue Buffalo, Beall would circle around to Johnson's Island and release the prisoners before hunting down the *Michigan*. Once again, Thompson's scheme was long on grandiosity and woefully short on contingencies should things go awry.

And awry they went. The next day, Martin, Headley, and Anderson proceeded to Port Colburn on Lake Erie's north shore to board the *Georgian*. For two days they waited, but Beall failed to show. Returning to Toronto, they learned that within days of Thompson's purchase of the *Georgian*, U.S. authorities had been tipped off. All points along the lake had been alerted and tugboats were armed to destroy her. "The panic could not have been greater if we had captured a city," Headley observed.[3] When the Union steamer *Pacific* stopped to inspect her, finding nothing on board save eight men, six of whom were drunk, she was released. Heading north the *Georgian* stopped at Sarnia, Canada, where this time Canadian authorities searched the ship. Once again, nothing threatening was found and she was released. Continued propeller problems forced Bates to disembark in search of a new propeller. Meanwhile, the *Georgian* was to proceed to the shipyard in Collinwood, where it would be repaired.

12. Last Stop at Dunkirk

By this point, winter was setting in and lake ice forced the ship to dock at Collinwood until spring, when it would be seized by Canadian authorities.

Once again, Thompson's ambitious plan had fizzled out even before it ever got off the ground. Despite yet another intelligence leak, he made little effort to root out the problem, and remained blithely unaware the mole was not only in his very midst, but was his confidant, Godfrey Joseph Hyams.

A native of Little Rock, Arkansas, Hyams had been expelled from the state by Union soldiers in 1863. With his wife he had made his way to Toronto, where he lived in desperate poverty, eking out a living by repairing shoes and running occasional errands for Thompson. But when his newborn son became a tragic casualty of his poverty in February of 1865, Hyams showed up at the U.S. Consulate in Toronto offering his services as a spy.

Ironically, one of the few successes that fall was an expedition Thompson had known nothing about, which had been authorized by his erstwhile rival Clement Clay in Montreal. In October, twenty-one-year-old Lieutenant Bennett H. Young had led two dozen Confederates, mostly escaped prisoners, from Canada into St. Albans, Vermont. There they held terrified villagers at gunpoint while they robbed three banks of more than $150,000. During the holdup five of the villagers were shot, one of whom later died. Before fleeing, the Confederates attempted to set fire to the town. Although the fires were quickly extinguished, they created a panic in the city. Fears that another attack was in the offing only heightened public anxiety. Extra guards were placed at all government buildings and large public buildings in the city and even those in Washington. An enraged General Dix had immediately issued orders to the commanding officer at Burlington to pursue the marauders into Canada if necessary, but by then the rebels were long gone. To further infuriate Dix, when they were finally arrested by Canadian authorities, a Canadian court ruled that because they were Confederate soldiers acting under military orders, they could not be extradited by a neutral country.

The audacious raid on St. Albans was followed by an even more

John Yates Beall, Son of the South

brazen attack a month later with the attempted burning of New York City. The possible brainchild of Colonel Martin, the plot was intended to be a diversion in order to seize Federal and municipal buildings, free the prisoners at Fort Lafayette, and throw General Dix into a dungeon.[4] Although the plot was scheduled to coincide with the presidential election on November 8, it was postponed after General Dix, acting on an intelligence tip—possibly from Hyams—beefed up security with 10,000 troops under General Butler.

As weeks passed waiting for Butler to depart, the Confederates debated whether it was now too risky to pull off. But any doubts they had were soon brushed aside after news reached them of Sherman's burning of Atlanta and Sheridan's wanton destruction of the Shenandoah Valley. Over a thirteen-day period between September and October, Sheridan's men had ruthlessly torched thousands of barns and houses in the valley and destroyed hundreds of thousands of bushels of wheat and corn. Beall's beloved Walnut Farm had been reduced to a barren waste by Union soldiers. So too had the Zion Episcopal Church in Charles Town. Butler or no Butler, they were now determined to burn New York City to "let the Government at Washington understand that burning homes in the South might find a counterpart in the North."[5]

On November 24 Colonel Headley went to a chemist on Washington Place, where he picked up a valise containing 144 small bottles of "Greek fire," a highly combustible mix of phosphorus and carbon that ignited spontaneously on contact with air. The next evening he rendezvoused with the members of his party—Colonels Martin and Headley and a new arrival, Robert Cobb Kennedy, who had recently escaped from the Johnson's Island prison by digging a tunnel under the prison fence. Despite being hampered by a pronounced limp from a wound sustained at Shiloh, Kennedy had walked from Sandusky to Windsor, Canada, a distance of over one hundred miles. Arriving by train in Toronto, he went straight to Jacob Thompson's suite at the Queen's to offer his services. Precisely where Beall was is unclear, though it is likely he chose not to participate in a mission in which innocent civilians might be killed.

The following night the rebels simultaneously set fire to thirteen

12. Last Stop at Dunkirk

hotels, as well as P.T. Barnum's popular museum. A terrified crowd poured into the streets during the attacks, but the panic faded when the fires were quickly extinguished. Once again the attack was a flop. The next day an article in the *Evening Post* claimed the plot to burn New York had been divulged to the authorities a month earlier by a man from Canada but no precautions had been taken because it seemed too far-fetched.[6] Detectives had even tracked Headley and his co-conspirators for several days but gave up after concluding they were up to nothing more than a good time. Headley concluded that Hyams was behind the leak, but when he returned to Toronto to confront Hyams, the snitch had disappeared. "There appeared nothing to do now," said Headley, "since all our attempts everywhere had failed."[7]

For his part, however, Thompson refused to admit defeat, though a more sensible person might have. Shortly after the New York City fires, he received information from spies in Sandusky that on December 15 seven Confederate generals being held at Johnson's Island were to be transferred to Fort Warren in Boston. He summoned Hadley and Martin and expressed a desire for them and Beall—who was out of town—to undertake the rescue. Freeing the generals, it was hoped, would replenish the dwindling senior officer ranks in the Confederacy and revitalize the war effort—so the desperate argument went. Because of the short time frame and hazardous nature of the mission, Thompson said he would not order them, but if they wished to accept the mission, he would be grateful. Without the slightest hesitation they formed a crew of ten men that included Beall, Headley, Anderson, and Robert Cobb Kennedy. Colonel Martin would be head of the operation.

On Saturday December 13, the men crossed the Niagara Falls suspension bridge into the United States and boarded a train for Buffalo. Headley and Martin went to Hamilton to connect with Beall. Though they had been together in meetings at the Queen's Hotel, Martin and Headley had never met Beall but had heard of his raids on the Chesapeake and Lake Erie. When they finally met, they were taken with him at once. In his memoir, Headley recalled his impression of the serious yet likable Beall:

John Yates Beall, Son of the South

We had never met Beall before, but fell in love with him at once. He was a modest, unassuming gentleman. I soon observed that he did not talk to entertain but was a thinking man and was resourceful and self-possessed. He did not get excited in relating an exciting episode and only smiled at amusing stories when others laughed aloud. And yet he was an interesting companion.[8]

After going over the details of the plan, the three rode the train to the suspension bridge and crossed over into New York. Once in Buffalo, Headley picked up George Anderson at the Genesee House and briefed him on the mission. Beall and the others would board the train at Dunkirk and overtake the guards a few miles outside Buffalo. Once in control of the train, Beall would break open the safe so that the officers would have money. The generals would change clothing with passengers of the same size, with Martin reimbursing them for their loss. (Thompson had directed that none of the passengers should be robbed or harmed unless they interfered, in which case they should be shot.) After decoupling the passenger coaches, they would then run the engine and express car to within two miles of the city, where they would derail them. Walking in pairs into Buffalo they would board any train heading west or south before circling back to Canada. The fanciful plan clearly had all the rosy optimism of Thompson on it, with virtually no backup plan should it fail.

On the morning of the planned attack, the rebels picked up the papers to see to their great dismay that, once again, General Dix was a step ahead of them. Having been tipped off that something was afoot, Dix had issued General Order #97 alerting all military commanders that rebel marauders were preparing further attacks. "IN CASE FURTHER ACTS OF DEPREDATION AND MURDER ARE ATTEMPTED, WHETHER BY MARAUDERS OR PERSONS ACTNG UNDER COMMISSIONS FROM THE REBEL AUTHORITIES AT RICHMOND, TO SHOOT DOWN THE DEPRADATORS IF POSSIBLE WHILE IN THE COMMISSION OF THEIR CRIMES."[9]

This time Dix had gone a step further. If the rebels attempted to escape across the border, Federal forces were now authorized to pursue them into Canada. This, of course, was a blatant violation of British sovereignty, which Lincoln rescinded three days later.

12. Last Stop at Dunkirk

Nevertheless, the likelihood of being shot dead succeeded in frightening off some of Headley's men.[10] An early winter storm prevented others from reaching their destination, thereby trimming the composition of the expedition to just five: Beall, Headley, Martin, Anderson, and Kennedy. With virtually every garrison in the lake region on alert, this had now become a suicide mission and they knew it.

So as not to raise suspicion, they proceeded in pairs via the Lake Shore Railroad to Dunkirk, save Martin, who rode to Erie to board the train that would convey the prisoners. At the depot Beall and the others positioned themselves to see each train heading north so they would not miss Martin. On the second train, they spotted Martin at the window frantically waving them aboard. Alas, the generals were not on the train; in fact, they had not even departed Sandusky. As they rode to Buffalo, Martin and Beall decided that if the generals did not arrive in the morning, they would ride some distance out and halt the very next train, even though they had no idea whether the generals would be on it. Expecting a curious crowd would gather, they would then mix in and inquire whether the generals were on board, in which case Martin was to lead an attack on the guards. Once they were in control of the train, the engineer would be ordered to proceed to the suburbs of Buffalo, where Martin would descend with the generals and they would make their way back to Canada. Beall and the others would return to the city in time to board the Niagara train to the Canadian border. With each setback their plan was becoming more desperate ... and riskier.

In the morning they rode out in sleighs—it had snowed heavily overnight—to identify a strategic place to disrupt the train. Four miles out they came to an isolated place where the road crossed the railroad tracks. That evening they returned. After hiding their sleighs in the woods, Martin found an iron rail lying nearby. Laying it across the track, he hurriedly covered it with snow just as a train was approaching. The rebels scurried into the bushes, preparing to attack as soon as the train stopped. But when the train struck the loose rail with a loud clank, its momentum merely pushed it to the side and the train continued down the tracks. Two hundred yards on, the train suddenly halted and two guards started back with lanterns.

John Yates Beall, Son of the South

The rebels scattered into the woods and took the next train back to the Niagara Falls suspension bridge, having accomplished nothing.

At the Niagara Falls station, the four stopped at a restaurant for a quick bite. Looking around, Beall could see that in the wake of the New York City fires the depot was crawling with Federal detectives in plain clothes. He advised his companions not to wait there for the Great Western connection to Hamilton—not due for hours—but instead to cross over the bridge on foot and take the connection from the safety of Clifton, Canada. Heeding Beall's advice, Martin and Headley were to first to go, expecting Beall and Anderson to do the same. But when they arrived at Clifton station, Beall and Anderson were nowhere to be seen. Thinking the two had boarded an early train, they stepped off and waited for another. But when the others failed to appear on the next train, Martin and Headley approached the conductor, who said that the next train to Hamilton would not be until the morning. Perplexed, Martin and Headley went to a hotel for the night. In the morning they boarded the Hamilton train, but there still was no sign of Beall and the boy. When they finally reached Toronto, they found that Kennedy had made it safely back, but Beall and the boy were still missing.

Thompson immediately sent a runner to the suspension bridge, where he learned that Beall had inexplicably failed to heed his own advice. After leaving the restaurant, Beall and Anderson had bought two tickets to Canada. Beall had boarded the train but after settling in he discovered that Anderson was nowhere to be seen. He returned to the depot to find the boy fast asleep on a settee. Just then the station master announced, "*All aboard going east!*" The two started for the gate when out of nowhere two detectives, acting on a tip from Canadian authorities, rushed up and arrested them. Beall had been set upon so quickly that he had no chance of escaping. With a Colt revolver in his coat, however, he could easily have neutralized the detectives. Yet Beall's concern for human life suggested it was not in his nature to shoot two policemen who were doing their job. Also, he was protecting the boy who was in his charge. If that was the case, Anderson would soon repay Beall with betrayal.

The detectives presumed the two to be escaped prisoners

12. Last Stop at Dunkirk

heading to Canada, a notion Beall did not attempt to disabuse them of, saying his name was W.W. Baker of the Second Virginia Infantry. He added that he had escaped from Point Lookout prison in Maryland and had made his way to Baltimore, where friends had given him money to get to Canada. Any hope Beall had of getting by with this story was dashed after the police found the loaded revolver under his heavy coat. More incriminating was the carpet bag lying on the bench between Beall and Anderson. Opening the bag, the police were surprised to see five or six unused tallow candles, some matches wrapped in paper, some dirty shirts, a pair of socks, and a box partly full of paper collars. The contents of the bag suggested strongly they had been involved in the recent hotel fires, so the police brought them in for further questioning.

At the downtown precinct, Detective James Kelso began to interrogate Beall—whose identity he still did not know—to determine whether he had been involved in the attempt to burn the city. Thus far, police still had no break in the case and were under pressure to come up with a suspect. Several times Beall was paraded in a lineup in a blatant attempt to frame him. He would be taken, "roughly clad, dirty, and bearing the marks of confinement," before the city's aggrieved citizens and placed, not next to other inmates, but next to well-dressed and groomed detectives.[11] Small wonder that someone did not finger him out of confusion or simply to claim the reward. When the ploy failed, Kelso approached the turnkey, Edward Hays, who moonlighted as a saloonkeeper, to win Beall's confidence to trick him into confessing his involvement in the fires.

During his interrogation, Anderson was asked who owned the carpet bag. He blurted out that it was Beall's, even though it had been Anderson who had carried the bag into the office. Then the terrified boy panicked and revealed his identity. Pointing to Beall, in a blatant act of betrayal the boy said, "That is Captain Beall." Suspecting him to be the notorious mastermind of the Lake Erie raid, the police summoned the owner of the *Philo*, Walter Ashley, who identified him as the leader of that raid. The two were taken by train to a jail in New York City.

No sooner had Hays positioned himself outside Beall's cell than

John Yates Beall, Son of the South

Beall offered to bribe him with $1,000 for his release. Hays asked, "You must be in big trouble to pay a thousand. Do you have anything to do with these fires?" "I didn't have a hand in them, but I know who did—they're all up in Canada," Beall said. Hoping to learn their location, Hays offered to carry a message to them. Taking the bait, Beall pushed a handful of letters through the iron bars with a coin, asking Hays to mail them. Instead, Hays marched straight to Kelso's office with the letters, one of which was addressed to Jacob Thompson asking for documentation proving he had a military commission.

With the Dunkirk train rescue having failed and Beall in jail, Jacob Thompson finally conceded defeat. After a year of dreaming and cockeyed scheming, neither he nor the other commissioners had been able to pull off anything close to the kind of spectacular attack they hoped would bring a favorable end to the war for the South. Hundreds of thousands of dollars had been squandered and many of Thompson's men were now in prison. Burley was on trial in a Toronto court for extradition and Lieutenant Young was about to be tried on charges of robbery. There remained little to do but wrap up business in Canada and help with the defense of those now in prison or awaiting trial. The rest of the raiders were advised to depart for the South and were given an expense allowance from what little remained of the million dollars Davis had advanced to Thompson.*

Meanwhile, in New York, detectives had finally uncovered Beall's identity by happenstance. While he was standing with a group of prisoners it so happened that the woman with the sick baby who had been a passenger on the *Philo Parsons* recognized him and went over to thank him for the courtesy he had shown when he seized the ship. Beall insisted she was mistaken, but she was so effusive in her expression of gratitude that he finally relented by inquiring as to the health of her child. Little did the grateful woman know that she had inadvertently contributed to her benefactor's doom.

For the next two weeks Beall's home was a tiny, five by eight-foot cell in the notorious New York City jail at 300 Mulberry Street. At

---

*Thompson and Clay eventually fled to Europe.

12. Last Stop at Dunkirk

least he had a blanket and mattress (for which he paid) and a sink with a supply of water and three meals a day. A small window opening to a small outside courtyard afforded enough light for him to resume entries in his diary. His only reading material was the New Testament, so he handed one dollar to a guard to procure a Book of Common Prayer.

During the long hours of solitary confinement, he wondered at the strange turn of events which had pitted the North and South against each other such that he was now a pariah—indeed, a prisoner—in his own country. "Had I, four years ago, stood in New York, and proclaimed myself a citizen of Virginia, I would have been welcomed," he mused, "now I am immured (*sic*) because I am a Virginian, *tempura mutantur, et cum illis mutamus.*" ("The times change, and we change with it.")

The first week, several criminals—men, women, and children— were brought in for various offenses. Initially, their cases interested Beall, but their predatory nature and the hostility they showed toward him as a Southerner quickly cured him of his empathy. "Nearly everyone I have met with," he observed, "seems to regard society as his enemy and a just prey.... Profane, lying, and thieving. What a people!"[12] Most of them encouraged him to desert and join the Union army, a suggestion which the loyal Virginian found unthinkable.

In late December, his Book of Common Prayer arrived. He took comfort in reciting hymns from his boyhood, "Rock of Ages" and "Sinner Turn, Why Will Ye Die?"

> Since I have been placed in this cell I have read the Scripture, and have found such relief In its blessed words, especially where it speaks of God's love for man; how He loved him, an enemy, a sinner, and sent His Son into the world to save His enemy; how He compels the wretched from the hedges and highways to come into the feast; how any may come, and how He bids them, entreats them. Though it may seem unmanly to accept offers in our adversity which we neglected in prosperity, yet it is even so that with His assistance I will go up and beg forgiveness and put my trust in the saving blood of Him who died for man. Aye, I pray Him to grant His grace to my mother and sisters and my loved one.[13]

On New Year's Eve, as a gloomy rain fell in the small courtyard outside, Beall contemplated the tumultuous events of the past year

John Yates Beall, Son of the South

and his grim future. "The year went out in rain—drizzling rain!" he wrote. "Will I see the year 1865 go out?" The next day he turned thirty, "half-way down life's stream," he noted with existential sarcasm. Thinking he would not live to fifty-six, he felt his life had nevertheless been satisfactory.

> Has my life been so crowded with pleasure or good deeds, that I need desire to prolong it? Alas! no. Though well reared, and surrounded with very many advantages, I have not done anything to give me particular pleasure; nor, on the other hand, have I been remarkable for the opposite. I am truly thankful that I always stayed with mother and the girls and tried to do my duty by them; that is one consolation at least, and also that I never voluntarily left them.[14]

On the evening of January 2, two guards entered and handed Beall some newspapers. To his dismay the latest articles revealed a Confederacy teetering on the verge of collapse. "Savannah, indeed, is fallen," he lamented, "but its garrison was saved, so that Hardee and Beauregard have an army. And Butler did not take Wilmington, though the fleet did storm long and heavy. Poor Bragg has some laurels at last. Oh, that General Lee had 50,000 good fresh veteran reinforcements! But what are these things to me here! I do most earnestly wish that I was in Richmond. Oh, for the wings to fly to the uttermost part of the earth!"[15]

It must have been a relief of sorts when, the next day, he was transferred to Fort Lafayette, a military prison in New York Harbor. There he shared a large, dark cell with a half dozen of Thompson's men who had been picked up in connection with the New York City fires. One, a Confederate named John D. Allison, had been pulled from his bed at midnight in the St. Nicholas Hotel as the prime suspect in the fires.* His other cellmate was a rough-looking Irishman named Henry Mulrennon who had been running blockades out of Havana until his capture. The inmates had facetiously dubbed the place "The Hotel Burke," after the warden, Lieutenant Colonel Martin Burke, a veteran of the regular army who had been cited three times for gallantry during the Mexican War.[16] Friendly and

---

*Allison would later be found innocent and was released in a prisoner exchange.

12. Last Stop at Dunkirk

Aerial view of Fort Columbus, where Beall was imprisoned before his execution (courtesy of Library of Congress).

garrulous, Burke liked to sit on his porch while smoking his pipe and converse with the prisoners.

As a jail, Burke's Hotel wasn't all that bad. At one end of the cell were two portholes, though so little of the gray winter light entered that that a candle had to be used at midday. A coal fire at one end of the long room provided warmth and the food was decent, consisting of boiled beef soup with a slice of bread for breakfast, beef and a cup of rice or bean soup, followed by bread for dinner, which Allison prepared. Allison even managed to get them a quart of molasses a week after complaints of "piles."

Two days after Beall arrived, the guards burst into the room to conduct a surprise search. Beds were upturned, books and boxes rifled, and shoes inspected. All that was found were two tiny saw blades tucked in the upper of Beall's left shoe, a possible gift from Dan Lucas, who had given up hope of getting his friend out by legal means.[17] Judging from their threats and the intensity of the search,

John Yates Beall, Son of the South

Fort Columbus, Governors Island (courtesy of Library of Congress).

the guards were expecting to find something significant but did not. "A great failure and fizzle out," Allison mocked.[18]

In late January Beall was transferred to Fort Columbus on the northern neck of Governors Island in preparation for his trial. Prior to departing, Beall gave a lock of his hair to another inmate, Admiral Franklin Buchanan, former commander of the ironclad popularly known as the *Merrimack*, who due for parole in February. Perhaps the hair was destined for his mother, but Buchanan instead passed it back to Allison. Later that day, Rob Kennedy, who had been arrested at the Detroit depot while trying to flee south, would be placed in Beall's old cell. Even though Dix believed Kennedy, not Beall, was one of the arsonists, Dix intended to make an example of both.

13

Dix's Show Trial

With his grim demeanor and thin white whiskers hanging from his chin, Major General John Adams Dix looked like a stern Old Testament patriarch bent on righteous retribution. Over a long and distinguished career, he had acquired a reputation as a no-nonsense man fiercely devoted to his country. Born in New Hampshire, Dix joined the army at fourteen years of age to fight in the War of 1812. He resigned fifteen years later and moved to New York, where he served two terms as Senator. After a stint as Postmaster of New York, he was appointed Secretary of the Treasury by President Buchanan. At the outbreak of the war, when a federal revenue cutter was threatened by secessionists, Dix sent a message to New Orleans famously threating, "If anyone attempts to haul down the American flag shoot him on the spot!"[1]

In July 1863, Dix became Head of the Department of the East, which covered the Canadian border, New England, and the North Atlantic states. Ever since he had taken the job, Beall had been a thorn in his side. After wreaking havoc on the Chesapeake Bay, Beall had turned up in Canada, where he continued to raid, pillage, and plunder on Lake Erie, all the while eluding capture. Dix was doubly frustrated for he did not have enough men to protect New York City, let alone police the Canadian border.

The burning of New York City had been the last straw. Because Dix had evidence that rebel operatives were planning a far more destructive operation to strike New York and other major Northern cities, he intended to make an example of both Beall and Kennedy. By hanging the two miscreants, Dix intended to serve notice to would-be saboteurs operating out of Canada whom he was powerless to control. To ensure a favorable outcome to the trial, Dix would operate as an *éminence grise* during the entire judicial proceeding.

On January 20 Beall was arraigned at Fort Lafayette before a military commission consisting of six officers (the usual size was three), all appointed by Dix. Seated at the bench were Brigadier-Generals Fitz Henry Warren and W.H. Morris, Colonels M.S. Howe and H. Day, Lieutenant Colonel R.F. O'Bierne, and Major G.W. Wallace. Major John A. Bolles served as Judge Advocate. Bolles, who was Massachusetts Secretary of State, was also Dix's brother-in-law. Asked if he objected to any member of the commission, Beall replied that he did not. What he did object to—and strenuously—was trial by a military commission, which he argued was illegal.

After swearing in the officers of the court, Judge Bolles then read the charges against Beall. For seizing and sinking the *Philo Parsons* and the *Island Queen*, John Yates Beall, "a citizen of the insurgent state of Virginia," was charged with two counts of "violation of the laws of war." Less substantive—though no less serious—charges were three counts of spying, one on Kelley's Island, another on Bass Island, and a third "at or near" the Niagara Falls suspension bridge. Finally, for his attempt to derail the Dunkirk–Buffalo train he was charged with irregular and unlawful warfare as a guerrilla.[2] None of Beall's activities on Chesapeake Bay were mentioned in the charges. To all the charges Beall pleaded not guilty.

Bolles then asked whether Beall was ready to proceed to trial. Thus far, Beall had been drawing on his own legal training to prepare his defense. This, however, had carried him only so far and he now realized the need for professional counsel. But Dix had refused him a lawyer. "I am a stranger in a strange land," he pleaded to the court, "alone and among my enemies; no counsel has been assigned me, nor has any opportunity been allowed me either to obtain counsel or procure evidence necessary for my defense." Referring obliquely to his friend Dan Lucas, he added, "I would request that such counsel as I may select in the South be assigned me, and that permission be granted him to appear, and bring forward the documentary evidence necessary for my defense. If this cannot be granted, I ask further time for preparation."[3] Once again, Dix denied his request for

13. Dix's Show Trial

Sketch of Beall's communal cell #2 at Fort Lafayette (from *Harper's Weekly*, April 15, 1865).

outside counsel but granted him four additional days to prepare. In the intervening time, the court took up the case of Harris Hoyt on charges of supplying weapons to the Confederacy in exchange for cotton.

In challenging the legality of the military court, Beall raised an issue that had been frequently debated within legal circles in the North. Although military commissions had occasionally tried both Confederates and Northerners for violating the laws of war, they were more commonly used for *civilians* accused of irregular crimes such as spying, smuggling weapons, or sabotage of railroads and telegraph lines—in other words, guerrilla activities.[4] The brainchild of Judge Advocate of the Union Army Joseph Holt, the military commission's jurisdiction over time expanded to encompass a wide range of behavior, from ordinary crimes unrelated to the war to merely expressing sympathy for the Southern cause. So broad had its jurisdiction become that one Senator was moved to remark that

John Yates Beall, Son of the South

Secretary of War Stanton was "prone to bring every person and every act within military law and military courts."[5] Stanton offered various rationales to justify the use of these courts. While they amounted to little more than sleight-of-hand arguments, they did demonstrate the government's preference for these courts in obtaining convictions. In the case of Beall, Judge Joseph Holt stated that "Beall's last enterprise was a crime of fiendish enormity which cries loudly for the vengeance of the outraged law."

In charging Beall with violating the laws of war, the commission drew directly from the Lieber Code that had been signed into law by Lincoln the previous year as General Code #100. A German American legal scholar, Franz Lieber had been tasked by General Henry Halleck to revise the woefully outdated U.S. Articles of War written in 1806. The result was a thirty-six-page set of guidelines on how war should be conducted by combatants.[6] Lieber, who had fought for Prussia in the Napoleonic Wars and seen its horrors, attempted to lay out principles to make war as humane as possible and to punish those guilty of violating them, particularly as regarded treatment of civilian populations. In citing Code #100, however, the commission failed to specify which article of that code Beall had violated. This was not unusual. Over the course of the war the violation charge had been used with increasing frequency as a catch-all for virtually anything that was considered to undermine the war effort, whether committed by a soldier or—quite illogically and in more cases—civilians.

Halleck had also tasked Lieber to conduct a study of how to treat those charged with guerrilla activities. Lieber found that these were a new subject in the laws of war with little precedent. He therefore concluded that such individuals do not receive the benefits of the law of war but are "answerable for the commission of those acts to which the law of war grants no protection."[7] That Lieber regarded such individuals as *rogues acting independently* [my emphasis] and not sanctioned as "authorized forces" he made explicit in Article 82 of the Code:

> [Individuals] who commit hostilities, whether by fighting, or inroads for destruction or plunder, or by raids of any kind, without commission, *without being part and portion of the organized hostile army*, and without

13. Dix's Show Trial

sharing continuously in the war, but who do so with intermitting returns to their homes and avocations, or with the occasional assumption of the semblance of peaceful pursuits, divesting themselves of the character or appearance of soldiers ... are not public enemies, and therefore, if captured, are not entitled to the privileges of prisoners of war.[8]

For Lieber such individuals were decidedly not soldiers but what he called "armed prowlers" who act without military authorization. Halleck himself agreed with Lieber, for elsewhere he had written:

> Partisans and guerrilla troops are bands of men, self-organized and self-controlled, who carry on war against the public enemy without being under the direct authority of the state. *They have no commissions* [my emphasis] or enlistments, nor are they enrolled as any part of the military force of the State.... If authorized and employed by the State, they become a portion of its troops, and the State is as much responsible for their acts as any part of the military force of the State.[9]

On the other hand, the state recognized that commissioned soldiers could also conduct guerrilla activities. In fact, Lieber went so far as to concede that war justified sabotage:

> Military necessity allows of all destruction of property, and obstruction of the ways and channels of traffic, travel, or communication, and of all withholding of sustenance or means of life from the enemy; of the appropriation of whatever an enemy's country affords necessary for the subsistence and safety of the army, and of such deception as does not involve the breaking of good faith either positively pledged, regarding agreements entered into during the war, or supposed by the modern law of war to exist.[10]

Beall, of course, was an officer, not an armed prowler. He had been officially authorized by Jacob Thompson, President Davis's Secret Service Commissioner in Canada. As for the civilians caught up in Beall's sabotage, Lieber conceded that they could not be fully protected from the conflict. In Article 22 he stated, "The principle has been more and more acknowledged that the unarmed citizen is to be spared in person, property, and honor *as much as the exigencies of war will admit*" [my emphasis].[11]

The charges against Beall regarding espionage, though flimsy, were far more serious, and in all instances they carried the death penalty. Spying had first become an offense in the United States during the Revolutionary War. Those suspected of spying were to be tried by court-martial. If convicted, they could be put to death or given a lesser sentence as directed by the court. It was assumed that spies had no allegiance to the United States and were therefore by definition not U.S. citizens. In 1806 a new statutory provision mandated both a military court-martial and the death penalty for any alien found guilty of spying.[12]

This law remained unchanged until the Civil War, when a new provision enacted in 1862 sought to accommodate the fact that Americans were now at war with each other.

> *That, in time of war or rebellion against the supreme authority of the United States, all persons who shall be found lurking as spies, or acting as such, in or about the fortifications, encampments, posts, quarters, or headquarters of the armies of the United States, or any of them, within any part of the United States which has been or may be declared to be in a state of insurrection by proclamation of the President of the United States, shall suffer death by sentence of a general court-martial.*[13]

Henceforth, Americans on both sides could now be charged and convicted of spying by U.S. military courts. That the legislation was written expressly to deal with spying by Confederates is clear from the clause "the class which would naturally furnish the greatest number of offenders, viz, officers and soldiers of the Confederate army and civilians in sympathy therewith."[14] Two years later, when the law was amended by the Lieber Code, it required that an accused be tried by military commission while keeping the mandatory death penalty in effect.

Lieber defined the nature of a spy as one dressed in civilian clothes conducting land-based warfare.

> *Scouts or single soldiers,* if disguised in the dress of the country, or in the uniform of the army hostile to their own, employed in obtaining information, if found within or lurking about the lines of the captor, are treated as spies, and suffer death. A spy is a person who secretly, in disguise or under false pretense, seeks information with the intention of communicating it to the enemy. The spy is punishable with death by hanging by the neck, whether or not he succeeded in obtaining the information or in conveying it to the enemy.[15]

Lieber's definition of a spy clearly did not encompass Beall's activities, for at no time did he seek "information with the intention of communicating it to the enemy."[16] Since Beall was not involved in

13. Dix's Show Trial

gathering intelligence but in sabotaging Federal infrastructure, the spy charges were baseless and could easily be argued before an objective panel of judges. Dix, however, had no intention of giving Beall a fair trial.

One loophole in the law—one which Dix had effectively closed—concerned the different penalties for spying on land versus maritime espionage. While those convicted of spying against the navy also faced court-martial, the death penalty was not mandated; rather, it was left to the court to decide the appropriate sentence. This appeared to have been the reason Beall was not charged with espionage in the case of the Chesapeake Bay raids.* In charging Beall with spying on land, Dix was attempting to fasten the noose around his nemesis tightly. In the likely event the commission found Beall guilty, the death penalty was virtually guaranteed.

The day after the arraignment, a report of the hearing appeared in several New York papers which caught the eye of Dan Lucas. Lucas immediately wrote to Dix requesting permission to travel to New York to defend his friend, citing a precedent in which both governments had given a Northern father permission to attend his son's court-martial in Abingdon, Virginia. Dix did not reply, determined to try Beall without professional legal counsel. Indeed, Dix had gone so far as to intercept a letter Beall sent to Lucas months earlier informing him of his arrest. His letters to Judge Alexander Boteler, Jacob Thompson, and Holliday had similarly been intercepted with a view to using them against Beall at his trial.

In his letter to Lucas, Beall showed how naively unaware he was of Dix's malign intent:

Fort Lafayette, N. Y., Jan. 22, 1865

Mr. D.B. Lucas,
173 Main St., Richmond, Va.

Dear Dan:—I have taken up board and lodging at this famous establishment. I was captured in Dec. last and spent Xmas in the Metropolitan Hd. Qrs. Police Station.

---

*This contradiction in the law would not be addressed until 1950 with the passage of the Uniform Code of Military Justice, which mandated the death penalty for espionage against both the army and the navy.

John Yates Beall, Son of the South

I am now being tried for irregular warfare, by a Military Commission, a species of court. The acts are said to have been committed on Lake Erie and the Canada frontier. You know that I am not a "guerrillero" or "spy." I desire you to get the necessary evidence that I am in the Confederate service, regularly, and forward it to me at once. I shall write to Cols. Boteler and Holliday in regard to this matter. I must have this evidence. As the Commission so far have acted fairly, I am confident of an acquittal. Has Will been exchanged? I saw that Steadman had been killed in Kentucky. Alas! how they fall! Please let my family know if possible of my whereabouts. Where is my Georgia friend? Have you heard anything from her since I left? May God bless her. I should like so much to hear from her, from home, Will, and yourself. Be so kind, therefore, as to attend at once to this business for me. Remember me to any and all of my friends that you may see. Send me some postage stamps for my correspondence.
Hoping soon to hear from you,
  I remain your friend,
  J.Y. Beall, C.S.N

The letters to Alex Botelier and Jacob Thompson were written the same day to inform them of his situation and to request documents showing that he was in the regular service. Knowing that he was neither spy nor guerrilla, Beall was confident that once he could prove he was acting under orders, he would get a lesser charge as a prisoner of war. In his letter to Thompson, he reiterated he would get a fair trial, saying that the commission "had evidenced a disposition to treat me fairly and equitably."[17]

Eventually, Beall's letter to Thompson got through. The latter responded by sending Dix a statement from Colonel Martin, the commander, that the purpose of the attack on the Dunkirk train had been to free the Confederate officers in route to Fort Warren. Dix, however, would not allow the letter admitted as evidence during the trial.

On Wednesday January 25, the military commission reconvened. Asked by Judge Bolles whether he was ready to proceed to trial, Beall replied that he had sent a written request for legal counsel to James Brady but had received no answer. Brady had in fact replied but to Judge Bolles, saying that although busy arguing a case in Superior Court, he would represent Beall *pro bono* if the commission postponed the trial for an additional week.

13. Dix's Show Trial

Dix could not have imagined a greater adversary than James Topham Brady. With his churlish grin and drooping mustache, Brady looked more like an Irish bartender than the most brilliant barrister of his day. The son of Irish immigrants, he had been groomed so early by his father to become a lawyer that he passed the New York Bar at the age of 21. Steeped in the study of literature and history and possessing a gift for dazzling verbal eloquence, he often quoted poets and thinkers in legal arguments so logically sound as to leave jurors speechless. Though he lost his first case, he drew public attention for "his eloquence, his clear-sightedness, and his legal knowledge."[18] He was soon called on to litigate the most important cases of his time, from large corporate patents to divorce.

James T. Brady, "the finest lawyer of his day," who defended Beall in court (courtesy of Library of Congress).

But it was as a criminal lawyer that Brady was primarily known, having won virtually every capital case he defended. He won an astonishing fifty-one out of fifty-two murder trials, four of which were in the same week. In his most high-profile case, Brady had successfully defended Union General Daniel E. Sickles, who was charged with the assassination of Philip Barton Key, district attorney for the District of Columbia and son of Francis Scott Key. Sickles, who had discovered Key was having an affair with his wife, brutally gunned him down in broad daylight in Lafayette Square across from

John Yates Beall, Son of the South

the White House. Even though Sickles confessed to the murder, Brady had won an acquittal by pleading temporary insanity—the first time the defense was used in the United States.[19]

Once a staunch Democrat, when the Civil War broke out Brady denounced rebellious Southern leaders and rallied to Lincoln's side. Despite his support for the Union, Brady was known to seek cases where he could throw the full weight of his massive talent and energy regardless of politics. In agreeing to represent John Yates Beall, he was taking on the most challenging case of his career.

The trial of *John Yates Beall v the United States of America* began on February 1, 1865. At 10:50 a.m. Beall and Brady were led into the courtroom and took a seat at a table opposite the judges' bench. At precisely 11 a.m. the commissioners filed in and all those present in the courtroom rose to their feet. General Warren motioned for everyone to take their seat and for Judge Bolles to read the charges.

The prosecution's first witness was Walter O. Ashley, part owner of the *Philo Parsons*. Under questioning, Ashley described how Burley had approached him the night before and asked whether, on his way to Sandusky, he would make an unscheduled stop at Sandwich to pick up three of his friends. When the men boarded the next day, Ashley noted they were "roughly" dressed, not in military uniform but civilian clothes. Among the three Ashley pointed to was the accused.

As the ship sailed southward everything transpired in a routine manner—the *Parsons* picking up and discharging passengers, mail, and cargo as she went. Then at 4 p.m. the rebels suddenly seized the ship and all hell broke loose. Ashley calmly proceeded to describe everything that transpired on deck: the hauling up of the chest, the distribution of hatchets and arms, Burley's crazed smashing of the saloon door and baggage compartment. Notably for the prosecution, Ashley said that while some of the other raiders identified themselves as Confederates, Beall had not. Ashley further stated that before being put ashore Beall and Burley shook him down for the fares he had collected that day—a total of $110.

Brady then cross-examined the witness, seeking to portray Beall's actions in a charitable light vis-à-vis those of Burley. He was

13. Dix's Show Trial

able to establish that at no time had Beall threatened to shoot Ashley; rather, it had been the aggressive Burley who had pointed his revolver at him. On the two occasions when Burley threatened to shoot Ashley, Beall was not present. Brady also showed that all the money taken from Ashley had been passenger fares and thus "the property of the boat," which was a registered U.S. vessel, and thus not personal property.

Bolles then questioned Ashley, attempting to portray Beall as little more than a pirate and a spy.

> BOLLES: *State whether there was any military or naval mark or badge on the accused while he was on board the Philo Parsons.*
> ASHLEY: *There was not; they were dressed as citizens, in citizens' dress, and paid their fare as passengers, and were treated as passengers.*
> BOLLES: *Did Burley and Beall divide the money in any way, which you took and laid in a roll of bills on the desk?*
> ASHLEY: *They were taking the money when I left; I laid it on the desk, and they were taking the money; they both made the demand and were both taking the money between them. I saw them taking the money between them and dividing it. I don't know anything about how much either one of them took; there was an actual division of the money, and I saw it.*[20]

The prosecution next called to the stand one of the ship's passengers, William Weston, a fireman from Sandusky. Weston testified that when Beall seized the vessel, he had reassured the passengers that none of them would be harmed and that they had seized the ship expressly to free the prisoners on Johnson's Island. When cross-examined by the defense, Brady tried to get Weston to state that Beall had identified himself as a Confederate naval officer and that his cap bore the gold tassel common to a Confederate officer's dress hat, but Weston could not confirm seeing anything more than a low-crowned hat.

Satisfied with the progress of the trial thus far, Judge Bolles then turned to Beall's attempted attack on the Dunkirk–Buffalo railway. Called to the stand was David H. Thomas, the police officer who, with his partner Saule, had arrested Beall and Anderson in the rail station at Niagara City. During questioning the prosecution once again established that Beall was in civilian clothes when he was arrested, with no sign of being a Confederate officer. A search of his person had turned up a loaded Colt revolver, a few gold pieces, and some Canadian notes. When asked his name, he had first said it was Beall but then claimed it was W.W. Baker.

Brady then cross-examined the witness to show Beall was an officer in the Confederate army.

> BRADY: *Was Beall alone when you arrested him?*
> THOMAS: *No, sir; they were together sitting on a settee, he and Anderson, in the depot of the Central Railroad at that place.*
> BRADY: *Was it day or night?*
> THOMAS: *Night, somewhere between 9 and 10 o'clock—about 10 o'clock.*
> BRADY: *Was any person with you?*
> THOMAS: *Mr. Saule, another policeman.*
> BRADY: *Did he take any part in making the arrest?*
> THOMAS: *He put his hand on Anderson, and I mine on Beall.*
> BRADY: *How large was this vial of laudanum that he had?*
> THOMAS: *I believe what they call a two-ounce vial.*
> BRADY: *Was it full?*
> THOMAS: *There was very little out of it.*
> BRADY: *In this conversation that he had with you did he tell you anything about his being a Confederate officer?*
> THOMAS: *He said that he belonged to the Second Virginia Infantry, was a sergeant in the ranks. I asked him if he held any other position, and he said, No.*
> BRADY: *Did he tell you when he escaped from Point Lookout?*
> THOMAS: *He did not give me the dates, but it was several days previous to his arrival at Buffalo.*
> BRADY: *What kind of a cap was he in?*
> THOMAS: *It was a cloth cap—a citizen's cap.*

At one point Brady submitted into evidence a copy of Beall's warrant as acting master in the navy, which had been certified by Mallory the previous December.

The trial then adjourned until the following day.

When the trial resumed the next morning, the prosecution called Edward Hays, the guard at the Mulberry Precinct where Beall and Anderson had been arraigned. Hays testified that in the beginning the authorities did not know Beall's identity, nor what crimes, if any, he had committed. In the hope of gleaning more information, Hays's superiors had tasked him to win the prisoner's confidence. Hays testified that Beall had asked him for some paper so he

13. Dix's Show Trial

could send word of his arrest to Canada. Hays returned to the office but instead of getting the paper, he relayed to his superior, detective Kelso, what Beall had requested. When he returned to the cell, he told Beall that at the moment there were too many detectives in the office for him to obtain the paper without raising eyebrows. It was at that point that Beall fell into Kelso's trap. Leaning over conspiratorially, Beall whispered, "Hays, I tell you what you can do for me ... you can let me go.... If you do, I will give you $1,000 in gold."[21] Pretending he would assist, Hays went back inside and informed Kelso of Beall's desire to escape, a sign he was guilty of *something*. When Hays returned, he began to bait Beall for information. Since Beall had no money in his possession, Hays asked if he could be paid by two friends Beall had mentioned who were living on 30th Street. After being asked what route he would take Beall incautiously explained that he should first go to a friend on 30th Street after which he should go to a contact near Jersey City. Discreetly, Hays had asked for names and addresses, but Beall refused to divulge them. At one point, Hays came flat out and asked Beall what his name was and what he was charged with. "I think you are a very smart man," Hays said, "and you must have done a good deal of harm to our government since this war commenced." "Yes," Beall replied proudly, "I have taken hundreds and hundreds of prisoners; I have done Lincoln's Government a good deal of harm, and they know it." Beall boasted that he knew many secrets "that would be worth millions of dollars to the government," the inference, if not the implication, being that he was a spy bearing a treasure trove of intelligence. Coming as it did from a police officer, Hays's testimony was damaging in the extreme.

In his cross-examination Brady tried to establish a link between Beall's need for secrecy and his obligation to the Confederate government.

> BRADY: *Did you during any part of this conversation ask him what he was charged with?*
> HAYS: *Yes, sir.*
> BRADY: *What did he say?*
> HAYS: *He said that was his secret.*
> BRADY: *Do you mean to say that he stated that what he was charged with by our Government was his secret?*

John Yates Beall, Son of the South

HAYS: *What he was charged with—the charge he was arrested on? Yes, sir.*
BRADY: *Did he state that as the reason why he could not tell you what he was charged with?*
HAYS: *He did not state what was the reason; he would not tell me.*[22]

The most incriminating testimony was yet to come, and from the very person Beall had tried to protect, George Anderson, who had turned state's evidence in return for his freedom. Anderson recounted how he had reunited in Toronto with his former commander, Colonel Martin, who indicated they had a plan in view in which he could participate. With little knowledge of the plot's details, the boy had followed Colonels Martin and Headley down the tracks, on foot, toward Buffalo. Three miles on, they linked up with Beall and together proceeded toward town. A few miles from the city they halted, Beall with a sledgehammer and Martin with a chisel. They had tried to extract a piece of the rail from the track. Having had no success, they returned to Port Colburn. After scouting a new place to derail the train, the five returned at dusk. It was then that Martin was able to pry up an iron rail and lay it across the tracks, only to watch as the train roared through, throwing the rail to one side.

In his cross-examination of Anderson, Brady established that it had been Colonel Martin who had been in command of the operation and that Beall was merely acting under his orders. But when asked if Beall was, at any time, addressed either by Colonel Headley or Colonel Martin as "Captain," the boy could not recall. Although Brady attempted to sway the boy's testimony by repeatedly referring to Beall as "Captain," Anderson said he could not recall how the others had addressed Beall.

At one point in the day's proceedings, Judge Bolles read and entered into evidence the three letters Beall had sent by flag of truce from Fort Lafayette seeking help in his defense. One had been to Jacob Thompson, another to Dan Lucas, and a third to his old friend Alexander Botelier. Bolles also entered into evidence the diary Beall had been keeping since December 29, which had been taken from him at Fort Lafayette. At this juncture Brady said he was unprepared to proceed further and requested an adjournment until Monday.

13. Dix's Show Trial

An important aspect of Beall's defense for which evidence had not yet been produced was Beall's status as a Confederate officer. When the trial resumed on February 7, Brady introduced into evidence a copy of Beall's warrant as acting master in the Confederate Navy signed by Navy Secretary Stephen P. Mallory. Brady hoped to show that—despite the severity of the charges—as a commissioned officer, he was decidedly not a guerrilla fighter as the prosecution had tried to portray, but a soldier acting under orders and therefore entitled to trial as a prisoner of war. Also submitted was a three-page statement from President Jefferson Davis stating that he had authorized the expedition against the *Michigan* on Lake Erie, which had been prepared for Burley's trial in December.

In his closing argument Brady now summoned his immense oral talents, demonstrating once again his reputation as the greatest lawyer of his day. He began by urging commissioners to avoid being caught up in the anger of the moment. As a New Yorker he was well aware that the recent attempt to burn the city of New York had so infuriated its residents that the blood of any rebel involved in subterfuge was demanded. That Beall had been associated with some of the St. Alban's attackers made him a ripe target. Yet, any suggestion that Beall was involved in the incendiary attempt was, Brady said, without foundation. Brady went on to cite Beall's social pedigree, his "highly respectable origins," and his considerable wealth:

> The accused has been, as the gentlemen of this Court have learned from his diary, I think, intelligently educated; and whether it makes for him or against him, he has received sound moral culture. The mother and the sister to whom he so affectionately refers in that diary, have exercised over him—the mother first, and the sister afterwards—those ennobling influences which in the homestead exercise their great power over all of us in childhood and after life. And being a gentleman of education, a graduate of the University of Virginia, he has his own views about this case, and has communicated them to me, and I will present them to you.[23]

Slowly, persuasively, Brady moved into high gear. He argued that his client was being treated in two contradictory respects: On the one hand he was being treated as a civilian engaged in an offense at society at large; on the other, as a military man in violation of the laws of war. If the first were the case, Beall was constitutionally entitled to a trial by jury. (On September 15, 1863, Lincoln had suspended habeas corpus for Union soldiers in cases related to prisoners of war, spies, and traitors. Ironically, the law was introduced by Thaddeus Stevens, who would become one of Beall's most prominent supporters against his execution.) If in the case of the Lake Erie expedition Beall was being charged with murder as a civilian, then neither the military commission nor a martial court had the authority to try him. "His offense belongs to the ordinary courts and not this," Brady argued.[24] As for "'violating the laws of war, what precisely did this mean?" he asked, for it was a vague legal term and failed to specify the charges against him. In fact, the only accusations that had been levelled against Beall were that he was a *spy* and a *guerrillero*.

Quoting lines from Alexander Pope, Brady then took the judges on a tour of the etymology of the word spy from the French original to Bouvier's Law Dictionary, finally alighting on General Halleck's ("an excellent authority") definition: "the *disguise* or *false pretense*, which constitutes the perfidy, and forms the essential element of the crime, which by the laws of war, is punishable with an ignominious death."[25] Furthermore, according to the law of 1863, to be a spy, persons had to be found "lurking, or acting as spies in or about any of the fortifications, posts, quarters, or encampments of any of the armies of the United States," in which case trial by military commission or martial court was authorized. Importantly, the law stipulated that a spy had to be taken *in flagrante delicto*, which Beall had not been. In any case, he had not come to spy but to free the prisoners on Johnson's Island and to derail the Dunkirk train, acts which Judge Bolles himself recognized when he admitted Beall's diary into evidence. With characteristic eloquence Brady concluded,

> He did not come as a spy; he did not lurk as a spy; he sought no information; he obtained none; he communicated none. He was arrested at Niagara on his way to Canada, having, according to his declaration to Mr. Thomas, a witness of the Government, and whose statement the Government must act upon, reached Baltimore after the failure of the expedition on Lake Erie, been provided there with funds, and was making his way to Canada. Under those circumstances he was not a spy—he was anything and everything but a spy. He was acting under a commission; he was in the service of the rebel

13. Dix's Show Trial

Government; he was engaged in carrying on warfare; he was not endeavoring to perpetrate any offence against society.[26]

As to the accusation of being a guerrilla, Brady framed this as a moral question about war, in language and logic that demonstrated his unmatched skills as an orator. "Where," he asked,

> do you make the distinction between the march of Major-General Sherman through the enemy's country, carrying ravage and desolation everywhere, destroying the most peaceable and lawful industry, mills and machinery, and everything of that nature,—where do you draw the line between his march through Georgia and an expedition of twenty men acting under commission who get into any of the States we claim to be in the Union, and commit depredations there? And what difference does it make if they act under commission, if they kill the innocent or the guilty? There are no distinctions of that kind in war. You kill your enemy; you put him *hors de combat* in any way, with some few qualifications that civilization has introduced. You may say it is not allowed to use poisoned weapons, and yet we use Greek fire. You may not poison wells, but you may destroy your enemy's property. Even Cicero, in his oration against Verres, when the question arose whether the sacred things were to be preserved in warfare, said: "No, even sacred things become profane when they belong to an enemy."[27]

For thirty minutes more Brady continued his verbal pyrotechnics before the defense rested. So stunned was the court by the New Yorker's oral virtuosity that when Judge Bolles rose to address the commission, he began by apologizing for his lack of eloquence. He refuted Brady's suggestion that the court had connected Beall to the recent attempt to burn New York or any other crime that was not mentioned in the charges against him. As to Beall's wealth, family, and character, "these are matters quite outside of the case, and have nothing to do with the real inquiry before this tribunal."[28]

Far less eloquent—or logical—than Brady's, Judge Bolles's argument was essentially that Beall had "violated the acts of war." What this meant finally became clear when he referred to the Chief Justice Sir John Hawkins Haggerty's findings in the case of Bennett Burley, who had been tried in a Canadian court. In reviewing Burley's role in the attempted capture of the *Michigan*, Hawkins had found that "all the prisoner's conduct, while within our jurisdiction during this affair, repels the idea of legitimate warfare."[29] In other words, by staging their operations from neutral Canada, where they were safe from retaliation, the Confederates had simply played foul. That essentially was what the prosecution meant by violating the rules of war. The Confederates were simply not fighting by the rules. According to Bolles, for any man, soldier or otherwise, entering the Union from neutral Canada in the guise of a peaceful citizen, the law pronounces him to be a spy. This, even though Beall had never sought information with the intent of communicating to the enemy as defined in the Lieber Code. Bolles was even willing to admit that Beall was an officer acting under authorization by President Davis. However—with a sleight of hand he leapfrogged to a convenient conclusion—"His superior [Davis] cannot compel any soldier to act as a spy, or as an assassin,..." for that, he argued, "no commission, command, or manifesto could justify."[30] In other words, even though acting under orders, the actions were so morally reprehensible that Beall should have refused to follow them.

One week to the day after the trial began, the commission reached a decision. Two-thirds of the judges found Beall guilty on nine of the ten charges against him. The one charge of which he was found innocent—spying near the suspension bridge—had been nonsense to begin with. His sentence: hanging at Fort Columbus on Governors Island.

Now only one person could reverse that decision—President Abraham Lincoln.

14

Lincoln's Anguish

IN HIS CRUSADE TO MAKE AN EXAMPLE of Beall, Dix had not only improperly orchestrated the entire judicial process, he had also imposed a news blackout of the trial. Had Richmond learned of Beall's wrongful conviction and sentence, it would almost certainly have protested and demanded his release in a prisoner exchange. Failing this, the Confederacy would then have retaliated with a show trial of its own, followed by conviction and execution of one or more Union prisoners. In a similar incident that had occurred in 1861, thirteen rebels captured on the *Savannah* were charged with piracy. The charges drew outrage from the Confederacy, which angrily threatened commensurate retaliation—a life for a life. Eventually, the Federal government dropped the charges, and the men were exchanged as prisoners of war.

Dix had also withheld the date of Beall's execution as long as possible to forestall any attempt to appeal or otherwise derail the execution. As a result, Beall himself did not know of the commission's findings, nor the sentence it had imposed, let alone the execution date. On the evening of February 13, Dix's aide, Captain Wright Rives, finally came to his cell to inform him that he was to be executed in five days at Fort Columbus (now Fort Jay) on Governors Island between the hours of 12 and 2 in the afternoon. The order was to be carried out by the commanding officer at the Fort. In what must have been an awkward task for the kindly Rives, after breaking the grim news he handed Beall a pen and paper with which to draw up his will. He also assured him that his friends could claim his body.

Beall now realized the entire trial had been a sham. "I was

doomed before I was tried and nothing tending to prove my innocence was ever allowed."[1]

After a tortured sleepless night Beall rose the next day and began writing letters. One went to his old college pal, James McClure, informing him of his execution. Of the charges he said, "Some of the evidence is true, some false. I am not a spy or a guerrillero. The charges were not proven. The execution will be murder." Having lost all hope for a reprieve of some sort, he promised to send McClure a transcript of the trial and asked that he share it with his friends to clear his name after his death. "For my family's sake," he added, "please get my body from Fort Columbus after the execution, and have it plainly buried, not to be removed to my native State till this unhappy war is over, and my friends can bury as prudence, and their wishes may dictate."[2]

In a letter to Will he defended the correctness of his actions and asked his younger brother not to be bitter over his unjust execution.

Dear Will:

Ere this reaches you, you will most probably have heard of my death through the newspapers, that I was tried by a military commission, and hung by the enemy, and hung, I assert, unjustly. It is both useless and wrong to repine over the past. Hanging, it was asserted, was ignominious, but crime only can make dishonor. "Vengeance is mine, saith the Lord, and I will repay," therefore do not show unkindness to the prisoners—they are helpless. Remember me kindly to my friends. Say to them I am not aware of committing any crime against society. I die for my country. No thirst for blood or lucre animated me in my course. For I had refused when solicited to engage in enterprises which I deemed destructive but illegitimate, and but a few months ago I had but to have spoken, and I would have been red with the blood, and rich with the plunder of the foe. But my hands are clear of blood unless it be spilt in conflict and not a cent enriches my pocket. Should you be spared through this strife stay with mother and be a comfort to her old age. Endure the hardships of the campaign as a man. In my trunk and box you can get plenty of clothes. Give my love to mother, the girls, too. May God bless you all now and evermore, is my prayer and wish for you.

John Y. Beall[3]

Meanwhile, following protocol, General Dix had asked Holt in Washington to notify President Lincoln of the execution. "In view of the transactions which Beall bore so important a past," Dix wrote, "as well as in consideration of the intelligence daily reaching me that new outrages on our frontier are meditated by rebel emissaries in

14. Lincoln's Anguish

Canada, I deemed it my duty to order the sentence pronounced upon him to be promptly executed. I am sure you will agree with me in the opinion that the execution of Beall was not only due to the cause of civilization and humanity, but that such an example is necessary to the safety of our unprotected habitants on our frontier." Despite wanting very much to see Beall hang, Dix was well aware of the intense pressure Lincoln would face to commute his sentence. For this reason, he included the transcript of the trial "in case an application should be made to you, as has been intimated, to suspend the execution of the sentence."[4]

Lincoln was Dix's final hurdle. He was likely far less concerned with "applications" for clemency than he was with Lincoln himself. Time and again during his administration, Old Abe had demonstrated great empathy toward his fellow human beings in his approaches to poverty, slavery, and the welfare of prisoners. It was a creed he lived by, one enshrined in the final lines of his Second Inaugural Address, "With malice toward none; With charity for all."

Over the course of the war Lincoln had demonstrated an abiding concern for the fate of prisoners, personally reviewing hundreds, if not thousands, of cases, large and small. When trader Abraham Samuels was caught passing into Union territory on a suspicious errand, he appealed to Lincoln, explaining he was not trying to obtain medical supplies for rebels but was simply seeking to escape from the South. After giving Samuels an opportunity to prove his case, Lincoln ordered him released. And when three influential New Yorkers wrote Lincoln to pardon New York merchant Louis A. Welton, who was imprisoned for trading with the rebels, Lincoln consented even though he believed Welton was guilty.[5]

More pressing and anguishing were cases involving the death penalty. He and Judge Advocate Joseph Holt would often spend hours arguing the merits of a death penalty case. Where Lincoln often sought any excuse to commute the sentence, Holt, a rigid letter-of-the law man, was disinclined to exercise mercy. As he saw it, when it came to men destroying the nation, he invariably advocated execution.

Many times the two were at odds over the fate of prisoners.

John Yates Beall, Son of the South

When Charles Clifford was arrested in Springfield, Missouri, in civilian clothes, he claimed he was a Confederate major visiting his wife. But his inability to produce a wife led to a sentence by hanging until Lincoln—over Holt's recommendation—commuted his sentence to life. Lincoln had also commuted the death sentence of one David F. Siegler, who, after taking the Oath of Allegiance, was later captured as a Confederate officer. Although the turncoat was sentenced to be shot, Lincoln commuted this to hard labor.[6] Other Union men who had gotten the death penalty for switching sides had also been pardoned by Lincoln. "He was only merciless in cases where meanness or cruelty were shown," observed Secretary John M. Hay, who juggled his massive correspondence.[7]

Lincoln could also be swayed by pleas from the influential or distraught relatives. Upon hearing that Francis Musgrave was to be shot for violating his oath and serving in Pickett's Regiment, his wife wrote to Lincoln begging him to spare her "misguided husband." After reading her letter, Lincoln commuted his sentence to prison. According to the pardon clerk Edmund Stedman, "there was nothing harder for him to do than to put aside a prisoner's application [for clemency], and he could not resist it when it was urged by a pleading wife and a weeping child."[8]

Lincoln's propensity for compassion no doubt rankled Holt, who wanted the law applied consistently as an incentive to would-be malefactors. Once, after a spate of pardons, an exasperated Holt brought an airtight case of guilt before the President. In the heat of battle a soldier had demoralized his company by throwing down his gun and hiding behind a tree stump. "Here is a case," said Holt to the President triumphantly, "exactly within your requirements. He does not deny his guilt; he will serve his country better dead than living ... no relations to mourn for him ... not fit to be in the ranks of patriots." Expecting to have finally checkmated his bleeding-hearted boss, Holt was dumbfounded when Lincoln replied in all seriousness, "If Almighty God gives a man a cowardly pair of legs how can he help their running away with him?"[9] Cases of cowardice in battle—and they were legion—Lincoln placed in a special file sympathetically dubbed "leg cases."

14. Lincoln's Anguish

While most cases that came before him involved Union soldiers convicted of desertion, robbery, or murder, Lincoln also reviewed cases of Confederates convicted of serious offenses such as spying, smuggling, guerrilla warfare, and recruiting in Union territory. Even with the enemy he had shown his capacity for forgiveness, commuting death sentences in sixty percent of cases involving spies, guerrillas, and civilian criminals.

But there were two things the President had little compassion for. One was those who operated behind enemy lines. The other was recruiting in the North for the Confederate army. Indeed, in his review of Confederates sentenced to death for recruiting in the North, Lincoln had not commuted a single case, demonstrating his thoroughgoing dislike of those who operated behind enemy lines. For Lincoln, in going behind enemy lines, Beall had committed the ultimate sin. But surely, Beall's friends reasoned, that once the "President of Compassion" learned of the true details of his case, and the rushed, biased nature of the trial, he would commute Beall's sentence.

The first to approach Lincoln was James Brady, who was not only a friend, but one to whom Lincoln owed a big favor. Early in the war Lincoln had summoned the Irishman to the White House to inform him that, as a staunch Unionist, he had a duty to raise a company of Irishmen in New York City. After protesting that he did not know a "a major from a colonel," Brady returned to New York and raised an entire brigade of three thousand fellow Irish who, bedecked in blue and with drums rolling, marched down Broadway to the battlefront.

But Brady wasn't just calling in an old chit. He had solid legal ground to stand on. In his letter to Lincoln, Brady called the former prairie lawyer's attention to the biased way the court had been run. "It seems to me that there are questions of law in the case which should be carefully examined before the sentence is approved," he wrote. "They are presented in the argument which I addressed to the court.... I respectfully refer you to it and earnestly advise that it may be submitted to the Judge Advocate General." He accused Judge Bolles of moving too quickly to carry out the sentence. "The day appointed for Beall's execution seems to be very early and under the circumstances I submit that no haste should be exhibited." As for the verdict, Brady concluded that Beall did not deserve death but "some other punishment."[10] Brady's missive was not that of an emotional mother or wife pleading to spare her loved one, but an alarm raised by one of the country's most respected trial lawyers essentially accusing the court of malfeasance.

One might have expected that, as a lawyer himself, Lincoln would have been moved to investigate further. Instead, he instead referred the case to Holt. Holt, who claimed to have reviewed the case, told Lincoln that Beall had been convicted upon "indubitable proof as a spy, guerilla, outlaw, and would-be murderer of hundreds of innocent persons travelling in supposed security upon one of our great thoroughfares, Beall fully deserves to die a felon's death, and the summary enforcement of that penalty is a duty government owes to society."[11] Unlike similar cases, Lincoln did not personally review this one, in part because he had a high degree of respect for Dix. He was also reluctant to go against Dix, who felt strongly that the execution of Beall was indispensable to the security of Northern cities. Dix, it appeared, suspected Beall had been involved in the burning of New York hotels.

Against Holt's recommendation marched an army of Beall petitioners to the White House. The previous day, Congressman Robert Mallory of Kentucky and Senator Thomas A. Hendricks of Missouri paid a call on Lincoln, accompanied by a party of civic-minded ladies. While Lincoln had made no commitment, the party had left with the impression that since victory for the North was in sight, Lincoln saw no need to make an example of Beall by his execution. For the moment, however, he said he would defer to Dix and not interfere in the case. With the threat of more rebel attacks lingering over New York—indeed the entire Northeast—he did not wish to contradict him.

Meanwhile, James McClure had received Beall's letter on Wednesday the 16th at his home in Baltimore. With the execution two days away, he immediately hired a local lawyer, Andrew Sterrett Ridgely, to lay a formal appeal before the President requesting a stay of execution until the sentence could be commuted. Ridgely and

14. Lincoln's Anguish

his associate Albert Ritchie, another friend of Beall's from the University of Virginia, and Dan Lucas worked late into the night preparing their argument. In the morning, however, Lucas thought that in lieu of an official appeal, showing the President Beall's letter to McClure would be more convincing in demonstrating his "polished character and manly tone."[12] But Ridgely had already left for Washington armed with the appeal. In the hope of catching Ridgely before he reached the White House, Ritchie hastened after him, but by the time he arrived Ridgely was already back in Baltimore, having failed to so much as get an audience with Lincoln.

The three lawyers quickly realized that neither legal arguments nor eloquent letters were going to change Lincoln's mind. What they needed was political muscle, someone with deep ties to Old Abe. Late Thursday night Ritchie and Ridgely roused Francis L. Wheatly from bed at his Baltimore home and asked that he go to Washington on Beall's behalf. Influential in Washington circles, Wheatly agreed to help in any way he could. The next day he and Ritchie traveled to Washington, where they met with several New York humanitarians who had come with the same aim in mind.

On the 16th a tug came up to Fort Lafayette to transfer Beall to Governors Island for the execution. As he was being led from his cell, Beall paused to salute Allison and his other cellmates who were exercising in the yard. At Fort Columbus, irons were placed on Beall's wrists and ankles for attempting to bribe the previous turnkey to free him. His final days would be spent alone in a dark, dank cell, deep within the prison bowels. A small pine table was brought in and some paper for him to write his final words. The federal officer in charge, Captain Tallman, sent down his best reading lamp to Beall's cell and some books, including *Enoch Arden*.

At Fort Columbus, Beall's new cellmates included fellow Virginians Brigadier General Richard Lucian Page from Clarke County, and General Roger A. Pryor, who had been recently captured in Virginia. While holding down Fort Morgan in Alabama, fifty-eight-year-old Page had withstood a Union siege of five months. In the final weeks of it he had endured massive bombardment, surrendering only after

John Yates Beall, Son of the South

he ran out of gunpowder. Pryor, who had served as a scout for the 3rd Virginian Cavalry under General Fitzhugh Lee, was, like Beall, charged with spying. Beall took an instant liking to Pryor. As he had a law degree from the University of Virginia, Beall had initially asked that he serve as his counsel. Dix had referred the request to Stanton with a recommendation that he approve, if only, perhaps, to prevent Beall's seeking more experienced professional legal counsel in New York.[13] Stanton, however, denied the request on the grounds that a prisoner of war could not act as counsel for a person accused of espionage. In hindsight the rejection had been a blessing in disguise, for it had opened the way for Brady to serve as Beall's defense.

With just two days remaining until the execution, Beall was visited by Mrs. Algernon Sydney Sullivan (née Mary Hammond). When Mary had first heard that that the "notorious pirate" John Yates Beall had been captured she failed to connect him with the congenial boy who had been her sister's schoolmate. It wasn't until Beall was arrested a second time on Lake Erie that she heard through relatives in Virginia that he was one of the Bealls of Jefferson County.

Like John, Mary was of Scots Irish ancestry, and like him she was well born. Coincidentally, her husband, Algernon Sydney Sullivan, had agreed to represent the prisoners of the Confederate brig *Savannah* who had been charged with piracy but were later exchanged after the Confederacy threatened to retaliate. Before the case could go to trial, Sullivan was arrested on charges of disloyalty to the government and confined for a time in Fort Lafayette prison.

During the war Mary had been something of a Florence Nightingale for the Confederacy. To ease the suffering of Confederate prisoners she set up soup kitchens at David's Prison in Long Island Sound. After General Edward Canby closed the kitchens, claiming she was "a dangerous woman," she turned to corresponding with Confederate prisoners and sending them small sums of money.[14] So active was she in the Southern cause that she soon came under surveillance by Union authorities. On one occasion a man appeared at her home in Confederate uniform claiming to be a destitute Texan trying to return to his unit through Union lines. Suspecting a Union

14. Lincoln's Anguish

ruse, she told the man she could only work through official channels. She never saw him again.

Mary was living in New York when she read of Beall's trial and sentence. She immediately went to Fort Lafayette to see him. She waited for hours for an interview. When Dix finally appeared, he refused to issue her a pass unless Beall himself requested to see her. Undaunted, Mary returned home and wrote a letter requesting to visit Beall, who responded on February 14:

> My Dear Madam:
> Your note has just been handed me. I reply at once. If you can come to see me, it certainly would be my wish to see you. I am truly obliged to you for your sympathy.
> Truly and respectfully yrs,
> John Y. Beall

Dix finally issued her a pass for the 16th. But by the time she arrived she was told Beall had been transferred to Governors Island, a fact likely known to Dix when the pass was issued. Again she returned to Dix's office to obtain a new pass, which was granted. When she finally arrived at Fort Columbus, she found Beall sitting alone in a tiny cell. The meeting with a friend from childhood came as a great comfort to him. They reminisced about the days of their youth and the bucolic life in the Valley before the war. "It called me back to good old times," Beall would later say.[15] Because the interview was supervised by the guards, Beall conveyed in hushed tones personal messages to his mother, his brother Will, and Martha.

Noticing his sickly pallor, Mary asked if he was ill. Beall said he was suffering from a severe toothache. Although he had asked the guards for some laudanum, they refused to give it to him, fearing he would commit suicide. He scoffed at the notion, saying that under no circumstances, as a Christian man, would he take his own life. In any case, if he wished to, his shoe concealed a tiny saw made from a steel watch spring which could serve the purpose.[16] Beall had intended to use it to escape, but the waters around Fort Lafayette were thinly frozen over. Wishing to leave some mementos for his family, Mary, and friends, he arranged to send her a locket containing a few locks of his

John Yates Beall, Son of the South

hair and a photo of himself. In the ensuing days, Mary lobbied for Beall's mother to visit, a humane courtesy that Dix denied.

The day before Beall's execution, Dix prolonged his agony by suspending the sentence until the Military Commission could reconvene and revise its findings. For the record, Dix wanted to clarify which averment contained the date and place for which he was judged to be spying. The Commission quickly reconvened and determined Beall had been spying near the Suspension Bridge in New York on or about December 16, 1864. Dix's concern for the technicality was deeply ironic given that all along it had been a sham trial. The new date for the trial was set for February 24th.

On the 18th, the original date of his execution, John's mother came to see him, thanks to Mary Sullivan's efforts in getting her a pass. In one sense, Beall confessed he *had* been glad for the delay in execution for it gave his heartstricken mother a chance to visit. "The instant she entered the door," he said, "I saw she could bear it, and that it made no difference with her whether I died on the scaffold or fell upon the field."[17] Seeing that she could bear the outcome, John refused to indulge her grief. As the guards looked on intrusively, she asked, "A pardon, my son—is there no hope?" He replied stoically, "No mother, they are thirsting for my blood. There will be no pardon."[18] Beall then wrote to friends in Richmond expressing the hope that if they could not protect his life, they would at least vindicate his memory.

Not until the morning of the 18th did Dr. S.H. Weston of St John's Church, who had prepared to conduct a service for Beall, learn that that the execution had been postponed. Nevertheless, he hastened to Governors Island to see how Beall was doing and to administer Holy Communion. When he entered, he was surprised to see that while the Bible was on the table, the Book of Common Prayer the doorman at the New York City jail had given him was missing. (Beall had gifted it to Martha shortly after receiving it.) Dr. Weston stressed the importance for John to be chaste and to exhibit nothing but charity for all and to forgive all his transgressors, to which John agreed. Not knowing how long his reprieve would be, Beall asked Dr. Weston if he might bring some books the next time he came.

14. Lincoln's Anguish

With the execution delayed, more supplicants now descended on the White House: Librarian of Congress Richard S. Spofford, John W. Garrett, President of the Baltimore and Ohio Railroad, Hanson A. Risley from the U.S. Treasury, Rep. Thaddeus Stevens of Pennsylvania, Massachusetts Governor John Andrew, as well as George W. Grafflin and Edward Stabler, both prominent Maryland Quakers. At the final hour, Beall's distraught mother and sister came to see Lincoln. Surely the great man's heart would be softened by their pleas. But the war years had sapped his deep well of compassion. He told them, "I've had more questions of life and death to settle in four years than all the other men who sat in this chair put together. No man knows the distress of my mind. The case of Beall on the lakes has to be an example."

Back in Washington, with just a day remaining before the execution, Dan Lucas had found the political heavyweight they had been seeking—Orville H. Browning. During the early 1830s both he and Lincoln had worked as prairie lawyers on the demanding Illinois circuit. As fellow members of the Whig Party in the state legislature, the two shared similar points of view and often deliberated on legislation.[19] Both had assiduously opposed Stephen Douglas's Kansas–Nebraska Bill to block the extension of slavery in the western territories. And when Lincoln was revising his Presidential inaugural address, it was Browning to whom he turned for criticism. If anyone could sway Lincoln, it was his old friend Browning.

Now fifty-nine, Browning was practicing law in Washington. After being briefed on Beall's case, Browning agreed to prepare an appeal which he would read to the President. In the meantime, Lucas and Ritchie were on Capitol Hill lobbying with a Baltimore Presbyterian, the Rev. John J. Bullock, for a commutation of Beall's sentence. By late afternoon they had gotten a petition requesting a commutation of the sentence. Astonishingly, the petition was signed by eighty-five Congressmen and six Senators, including House Speaker Schuyler Colfax. Armed with the Congressional appeal and the Browning letter, Ritchie, Lucas, and Browning hastened to the White House to present their case. When they arrived, Lucas and Ritchie were made to wait outside while Browning met privately with Lincoln. Aware that Lincoln was inundated with petitions requesting mercy for prisoners, Browning made his concise:

THE PRESIDENT:

Capt. John Y. Beall has been tried by a court martial at New York, found guilty and sentenced to be hung (*sic*) as a spy and guerrilla. The sentence was approved by Major General Dix on the 14th Feb'y and directed to be carried into execution tomorrow the 18th. This is brief time for preparation for so solemn and appalling an event. The friends of Capt. Beall desire to appeal to your clemency for a commutation of the sentence from death to imprisonment and that they may have the opportunity to prepare and present to your consideration the reasons which they hope may induce to a commutation. They now beseech you to grant the unhappy man such respite as you may deem reasonable and just under the circumstances. As a short respite is all that is asked for now and as that can in no event harm, I forbear at present to make any other suggestion.

Most respectfully your friend,

O.H. Browning

After an hour, Browning emerged with good news: Lincoln had said he would send a letter to General Dix requesting a delay, though for how long Browning could not say.*[20] In the evening Ridgely came in from Baltimore with several others and they all repaired to Browning's office to map out next steps.

On Saturday, good news—a delay in the execution had been granted, though why and for how long no one knew. Browning naturally attributed it to his meeting with Lincoln. In fact, the delay was due to an error in the trial record. The law required the court to affirm or deny every averment under the Specification of Charges. The specification under Charge 2—accusing Beall of spying near the suspension bridge—had no response, requiring the commission to reconvene. Browning hastened to the White House to obtain more information on the delay, but Lincoln refused to meet with him. Knowing Lincoln as he did, Browning took this as a bad sign, telling Ritchie that unless they could prevail upon Dix, a delay in the sentence was likely the best they could hope for.[21] Wheatly and Ritchie

---

*As there is no record of such a letter, it is likely that Lincoln said this merely to appease his old friend and terminate the meeting amicably.

14. Lincoln's Anguish

returned to Baltimore to draft letters to Dix, leaving Browning and Ridgely in Washington to keep the pressure on.

When Beall learned the date of his execution had been reset to Friday the 24th, he wrote to inform Mary Sullivan. While saying he had no doubt as to Dix's intentions, he was nonetheless afraid, confiding, "I do not pretend to possess a mind so evenly balanced as to be indifferent to life and death. While desiring one, I will not fail, I hope to meet the other manfully—I know it will be cruelly felt by my family."[22]

Concerned that he would be executed with the opprobrium of a robber and a spy, on the 21st, Beall wrote to Jacob Thompson asking that he clear his name so that in the eyes of his friends and history, he would be seen as having honorably fought for his country in the way he saw fit. "Vindicate me, at least to my countrymen," he wrote. He also wrote to Colonel Robert Ould, asking him to do his utmost to spare him from execution, failing which Ould should vindicate his reputation as being neither spy nor guerrilla but "a true Confederate."

By Monday his friends and supporters were still in the dark as to the reason for the delay in Beall's sentence. Ritchie decided he needed to go to New York to obtain an update on the disposition of the case. Had Ritchie read the transcript of the trial he might have spared himself the effort. Ritchie arrived in the city on Wednesday evening. In the morning he picked up the morning paper to read that Beall's sentence would be carried out the very next day. He hastened to Dix's headquarters to be told that the report was in fact true. Surprisingly, Dix agreed to meet with Ritchie, who presented the letters he had prepared several days earlier. As far as he was concerned, Dix said, "there was not a gleam of hope" that Beall's sentence would be commuted. In any case, he said, any hope ultimately lay with President Lincoln.[23] At once Ritchie telegraphed Baltimore instructing McClure to send Ridgeley and Wheatly back to Washington. He asked McClure to hasten to New York so that, if nothing more could be done to avert disaster, together they could at least be with Beall and offer comfort in his final hours.

Around noon on Thursday Ritchie's boat reached Governors Island, where he was met by Captain Rives. As the two were approaching Beall's cell, they were joined by a Catholic priest who also wished to see Beall. Inside the cell Ritchie saw another priest who asked that he and the Catholic priest have an uninterrupted moment with Beall, who had earlier agreed to meet with them if they came "through sympathy and not curiosity." The other minister was struck by Beall's calm demeanor "as much at ease as if he were in his own parlour.... There was no bravado, no strained heroism, no excitement in his words or manner, but a quiet trust in God, and a composure in view of death, such as I had read of, but never beheld to the same degree before."[24]

When the two departed Ritchie entered, shook hands, and took a seat on Beall's mattress. He was surprised to find the condemned Virginian full of "cheerful self-possession."[25] After the usual pleasantries, Beall said, "Yes, I never slept more soundly than I did last night; and I expect to sleep just as soundly tonight. I had such sweet dreams!"[26] He had dreamed of his boyhood, something, by his own admission, he hadn't done in years. He and his sister were hunting eggs together in the straw. Beall had found some and called out in delight, "Annie, here are some!" Clearly now that death was imminent Beall had begun to let go, to accept his fate, and unconsciously to survey the life he had enjoyed, however briefly.

To be encouraging, Ritchie described to Beall the vast number of those who had gone to the White House to appeal to Lincoln and other efforts on his behalf. While Ritchie was speaking of the petition by the Congress to get his sentence commuted, Beall interrupted, "Stop for a moment—what do you mean by a commutation? Because if you mean some indefinite and prolonged imprisonment, I'd rather be hung (*sic*)."[27] Ritchie explained that if the commutation was obtained, they were confident of being able to accomplish more. When Ritchie finished Beall asked him to write to his mother and tell her all that he had just told him. Captain Rives then asked John about his will. Beall said that when he learned Dan Lucas was in nearby Hamilton, he had changed the executor of his estate to Dan, and essentially bequeathed all his Jefferson County property to his mother. Beall then asked Ritchie to send a photographer so that his photograph could be taken for the lockets. Ritchie promised to send

14. Lincoln's Anguish

an artist who would do him proud. "Well," said Beall lightheartedly, "if I am to have my photograph taken, you must get me a shirt and a collar."

Looking at his suit laid out, Ritchie asked, "This, I suppose is your uniform, John?"

"The only uniform I have ever had since I have been in the service," he replied, "except for a little while when I served in the infantry. And this is another reason I am glad you have come. I have been a little annoyed about some slight pecuniary obligations. The guards have been very kind, and several times have given me newspapers, and postage stamps, and little things of that sort. I suppose they paid for themselves. I would like them to be reimbursed."

By now it was late afternoon. In departing, Ritchie said that he would request from Dix permission to pass the last night with Beall in his cell. Beall smiled and said that while he would like to see Ritchie again, he would not think of letting Ritchie share "such accommodations as his cell afforded." Ritchie then took leave to perform errands for Beall. Perhaps in a final gesture of compassion, Dix gave Ritchie permission for him to spend the night with John, subject to the supervision of the commanding officer on the island.

Shortly after, Brady stopped by. In parting, his lawyer took Beall's hand in his warmly and bid a sad and final farewell. As he exited the cell, Brady turned back to ask if John might provide the address of his mother so that he could communicate with her. As Beall wrote out the address, Brady was struck to see that while he himself was shaken, Beall's hand was even and steady, no tremulousness of the fingers, or twitching of the nerves, or emotion. It was born of the confidence of knowing he had done the right thing in the war. "I care nothing for the judgment of mankind, and nothing for the punishment I have to suffer, because I know my mother thinks her son is right, and my sister will honor my memory."[28]

After Brady's departure, Beall spent his final hours writing letters to his friends. He first wrote James McClure, with whom he had arranged a transcript of his trial to be sent to Lincoln with the attached note: "Some of the evidence is true, some false. I am not a spy or guerrillero. The execution of the sentence will be murder."

John Yates Beall, Son of the South

He reiterated to McClure that while some of the evidence presented at the trial was indeed factual, he was neither a spy nor a guerrilla and that his punishment amounted to murder. Beall asked that his body be "plainly buried" on Governors Island until after the war, when it could be returned to his church in the Shenandoah Valley.

In the evening Beall again wrote to his brother, a letter that read like a codex of his actions during the war: "Remember me kindly to my friends, say to them that I am not aware of committing any crime against society. I die for my country. No thirst for blood or lucre animated me in my course.... My hands are clean of blood, unless spilled in conflict, and not a cent enriched my pocket... 'Vengeance is mine' saith the Lord, and I will repay.' Therefore, do not show unkindness toward the prisoners; they are helpless."[29]

Around dinner time two unexpected visitors showed up at the Fort. "If they come through sympathy," shouted Beall, "admit them, if through curiosity I do not care to see them."[30] Among those drawn to Beall's case was the Rev. Stuart Robinson, pastor of the Second Presbyterian Church in Louisville, Kentucky. Born in Ireland and raised in Virginia, a prolific pro-slavery preacher who undertook many initiatives in support of the Southern cause, Robinson thought better than to travel North to visit Beall in prison and in his stead sent the Rev. Henry J. Van Dyke of the First Presbyterian Church in Brooklyn. A Northern Copperhead, the forty-three-year-old minister was all too willing to offer some spiritual solace. When he arrived, he found Beall alone in his cell, a lamp burning forlornly at midday. In his letter to Robinson he described his encounter with the condemned man:

> He received me with as much ease as if he were in his own parlors; and his conversation at every turn revealed the gentleman, the scholar and the Christian. There was no bravado, no strained heroism, no excitement in his word or manner; but a quiet trust in God, and a composure in view of death, such as I have read of but never beheld to the same degree before. He introduced the subject of his approaching end himself, saying, that while he did not pretend to be indifferent to life, the mode in which he was to leave it had no terror or ignominy for him; he could go to heaven through the cross of Jesus Christ as well from the gallows, or from the battlefield, as from his

14. Lincoln's Anguish

own bed. He died in defense of what he believed to be right, and so far as the particular things for which he was to be executed are concerned, he had no confession to make, no repentance to exercise. He did not use one angry or bitter expression towards his enemies, but calmly declared his conviction that he was to be executed contrary to the rules of civilized warfare. He accepted his doom as the will of God.[31]

When Van Dyke began to quote the latter part of the eighth passage from the Epistle to the Romans, John, in a half whisper, immediately took up the recitation and completed it. Looking up at Van Dyke he said the passage had been very much on his mind of late. During their conversation, Beall quoted several Biblical hymns. Van Dyke left the cell so bowled over by the soldier's stoic composure that he would later remark, "If this is a specimen of the people it is proposed to subjugate, it will require more gallows than can be erected in fifty years to accomplish the object.... I have read the history of heroes, but I never met one before"[32]

On the eve of the execution, Browning went back to the White House, this time to persuade Lincoln to commute Beall's sentence to life. Browning was struck by Old Abe's appearance. "He looked badly and felt badly—apparently more depressed than I have seen him since he became President," Browning wrote. Beall's case had clearly taken its toll on the war weary President. An hour-long discussion followed during which Lincoln confessed that had it been his decision from the start he would not have sentenced Beall to die. The fact was that the President had listened to appeals for clemency for Beall and he had expressed deep compassion for his plight. But he was reluctant to go against Dix, who believed strongly that the execution of Beall was indispensable to guarantee the security of Northern cities. No sooner had the President made this admission when he again wavered, saying there was "a possibility" he would intervene, but that it was not probable.[33]

Shortly after Browning left, Francis Blair showed up with Ridgely and the wife of John S. Giddings, President of the B&O Railroad. The Giddingses were no strangers to the President. Mrs. Lincoln and her two younger sons had enjoyed the hospitality of their home on Mount Vernon when the President-elect made the secret night journey to Washington four years earlier. Before receiving them, Lincoln sent a message to Blair telling him that if the purpose of his visit concerned Beall, he was not available.

Throughout the night still more visitors arrived—a joint call by Washington McLean, editor of the *Cincinnati Enquirer*, and General Roger A. Pryor from Fort Lafayette, where he had met Beall. McLean had already prevailed upon Lincoln to release Pryor, reminding the President of Pryor's generous treatment of Union prisoners, paroling an entire camp of Federal wounded and surgeons. There were two purposes to this call—to secure Pryor's parole and to plead for clemency in Beall's case. Like Beall, Pryor, having been one of the first secessionists to shell Fort Sumter, had been sentenced to hang. Over the express wishes of Secretary Stanton and General Grant, McLean went to Lincoln with Horace Greeley. Citing Pryor's record of favorable treatment of Union prisoners in his custody, McLean convinced Lincoln to parole him in the temporary custody of Colonel John Forney.

Next the party raised the subject of Beall. Pryor described the Virginian's fine character he had observed while his cellmate at Fort Lafayette. Lincoln was deeply interested in all Pryor had to say about Beall. Yet when he finished, Lincoln showed a telegram from Dix arguing that Beall's execution was necessary "for the security of the northern cities." Yes, said Lincoln, the sentence was harsh but necessary, adding he had personally read the record of the trial and concluded that Beall was a spy and a privateer.[34] Pryor inferred this to mean "that Captain Beall was also implicated in the burning of the New York Hotels," though later events would show this wasn't the case.[35] Finding the President impervious to further arguments, the three withdrew. Pryor had with him Beall's diary, which he handed to McLean. A copy of this he kept, and another copy he gave to Brigadier General W.N.R. Beall (unrelated).

Despite Lincoln's intransigence, they refused to give up. The day before the execution, Brady, Francis Blair, and Stabler appeared only to be informed by the President's private secretary that "the case of Captain Beall was closed, and that he could not be seen any further in reference to it." Henceforth, for the President the doors of the executive mansion were shut against all supplicants, male or female,

14. Lincoln's Anguish

and his ears against all appeals. "General Dix may dispose of the case as he pleases," he thundered. "I will not interfere!" That same morning in New York Mrs. McClure was meeting with Dix to lodge a final appeal but was told by Dix, "All action now rests with the President—as far as my action rests there is not a gleam of hope."[36]

At half past eight in the evening Ritchie returned to the island and presented Dix's permit to the commanding officer, Major Cogswell. Cogswell made Ritchie promise that he would not give Beall any weapons or poison. Ritchie gave his word, adding, "John Beall was the last man in the world to act upon such a suggestion even if it were made." To which Cogswell replied, "I believe so myself."[37]

During Ritchie's brief absence, Beall had prepared several letters of instruction for him to transmit, indicating his wishes with regard to his remains, his debts, to whom the lockets should be distributed, and expressions of gratitude for all his friends who rallied to his aid in his final weeks. As he handed them to Ritchie he made a startling admission: "And here, too, is a letter for my mother, and one for my sweetheart. This will surprise mother for she doesn't know that I am engaged."[38] Beall said there were a few additional people he would like to send his lockets to, but because the simple fact of being acquainted with Beall might cause trouble for them, he wrote them down on a separate piece of paper.

Beall then began to talk at length about his trial. At a loss at what to say at such a time, Ritchie remarked on the wide interest his case had attracted and the great number of individuals, friends and strangers alike, who had attempted to intervene on his behalf. Efforts, he said, were still being made in Washington, which Ritchie said was cause for some hope, however slight, for a last-minute reprieve. "I do not," Beall replied. "I have been satisfied from the beginning what the end would be," adding gloomily, "I am perfectly convinced that when tomorrow's sun rises, I shall never see it set. In fact, I was sorry when the respite was granted, because I knew it would be only for a brief time." The reality of his imminent death caused him to pause momentarily, and then he continued, "I do not pretend to be indifferent to life, I would rather live than die, but if I had to die, I think I can do it."[39]

John Yates Beall, Son of the South

Just then Ritchie noticed a few current newspapers lying on the table and asked how Beall managed to get them into his cell. Usually when he asked, the guards brought them in, paid for out of their own pockets, and, knowing the guards were of little means, he rarely asked for them. Ritchie then showed him an article from a New York paper containing a remark by Brady regarding the courage and fortitude Beall had displayed the last time he saw his client. "I didn't know," Beall said with a smile, "that he was watching me so keenly." He asked that Ritchie send such articles to his mother, adding, "She is a true woman. It may be because she is my mother, but I don't think there is any other woman like her."

A messenger from Major Cogswell arrived saying that Ritchie could remain with Beall until midnight, with an invitation to stay the rest of the night at Cogswell's. In a moment of levity, Ritchie remarked on how, upon entering, he was required to promise he would give Beall neither poison nor a weapon with which to prematurely end his life. Beall scoffed at the idea of suicide, saying that just before his execution he planned to tell Major Cogswell he had been aware of his fear in that regard and intended to reveal the little steel saw hidden in the toe of his left shoe. Cogswell had in fact been quite solicitous toward Beall, bring in a reading lamp from home and several books for Beall to pass the time. On several occasions Cogswell had been so sensitive to Beall's feelings that he shielded Beall from the prying of newspaper reporters, acts for which Beall was deeply grateful. Little did he know that it was Beall's own character that had inspired such respect in the first place.

At this point Ritchie asked Beall if he wasn't detaining him from his final devotional prayers. "Don't be uneasy about that," Beall said, "there is nothing to be arranged between me and my God. I feel that it is all clear and safe there." Referring to the years following the death of his grandfather and father when he became religious, he added, "I have not postponed the consideration of those matters for the last moment. They have been the subject of reflection and consideration for years. You cannot, of course, appreciate the support it is to a man, in an hour like this, to be clear and firm in his faith."[40] He was

14. Lincoln's Anguish

referring to the respect for innocent civilians and private property he had scrupulously observed during the raids on the Chesapeake and Lake Erie. "No indeed!" he blurted out, "There is no innocent blood on my hands, there is no blood on my hands unless it be that shed in battle."[41] Beall then made a remarkable admission that had not come up at the trial. Referring to the attempt to recapture the Confederate officers on the Dunkirk train, he had told Colonel Martin, his superior, that he refused to lay obstructions on the track for it would put innocent civilians on the train at risk. He would never have been captured that night had the hapless boy Anderson not fallen asleep on the train, a reality that, in the final analysis, must have been anguishing to contemplate. As midnight approached, Ritchie rose to leave. Beall rose too and swept a handful of cigars from the table, passing them out to the guards to express his gratitude for the kindness they had shown. After Ritchie left, Beall sat at his tiny table and wrote some letters. He then warmed his feet by the stove before going to bed, his last night on earth.

Just hours earlier, in Washington, Ridgely, Mrs. Giddings, and Montgomery Blair had gone to the White House. By his messenger, Lincoln inquired as to the purpose of their visit, adding that if it concerned Captain Beall, he "could not give an interview."[42]

Early the next morning in Washington, Wheatly and Duncan called on Browning at home with a carriage to take him to the Willard Hotel to meet with Brady, who had just arrived. Over breakfast, Browning advised him to go to the President, as the previous night he had assured Browning he would receive the distinguished lawyer from New York. But when Brady appeared a few hours later he was told by the President's secretary that it was useless for them to meet as "the case was closed" and Lincoln could not be seen.

Later Browning met with Ridgely and a Maryland Quaker, Ed Stabler, and urged them to get Frank Blair to push for a commutation of the sentence. A few hours later Brady, Blair, and Stabler descended on the White House, but Lincoln refused to meet with them, declaring that further entreaties were useless, his mind was made up. Alas, this visit of Forney, McLean, and Pryor to the White House would be

John Yates Beall, Son of the South

the last direct appeal on behalf of Beall.* The President had henceforth closed the doors of the executive office to all supplicants. That did not stop Thaddeus Stevens from sending a last hour plea to Lincoln. Alerting Lincoln to the fact that he was but hours from the execution, Stevens wrote that "from all I can hear of the case he deserves mercy, and if nothing better can be done let the execution be postponed for a month. That being accomplished you can let public opinion be exercised on the subject. I wish this of you as a personal friend."[43]

Lincoln did not respond.

---

*On his arrival in Richmond three weeks later, Pryor met with a distraught President Davis to relate his meeting with Lincoln. He then went to his old home in Petersburg, which was shortly afterward occupied by General Grant. The President at this time made a flying visit to that town. While there he expressed a wish to have Pryor call and see him. Pryor, fearing that his people at this peculiar juncture might misconstrue his motive and resent his intercourse with the "Yankee President," deemed it best to decline the invitation.

15

The Hanging

THE MORNING OF FEBRUARY 24 BROKE fair and springlike. On his final day on earth, John Beall had dressed himself with unusual care and neatness, in a crisp white linen shirt with a black silk cravat gracefully tied beneath a rolling collar. He wore a new pair of saffron-colored, dog-skin gloves.

Dix had ordered the execution to take place between noon and 2 p.m.

Around 9 a.m., an anxious Ritchie returned to Beall's cell to find Dr. Weston reading scripture with him. Together they accompanied Beall to have his formal photograph taken in a little gallery on the island. After several were taken, Beall reviewed the negatives, comparing his position in the chair, the angle of his posture, and the light in his eyes, finally selecting what he thought was the best one. As they were returning to his cell, Ritchie reminded Beall, as he had requested, to tell Cogswell of the tiny saw in his shoe. Preoccupied with far more momentous matters now, Beall replied that he had decided not to say anything but asked Ritchie to inform him after the execution. His last wish was that his diary, love letters, pictures, and Prayer Book be sent to Martha.

Once back in the cell, Ritchie joined Dr. Weston and Beall in prayer and in the taking of communion. Ritchie then stepped outside to allow Beall to complete the service in private with the doctor. Around 11, McClure arrived. Seizing the opportunity to challenge Dix's low assessment of Beall, McClure assaulted Dix with a long-winded diatribe, extolling his friend as a man of high mindedness and moral principles. When McClure finished, Dix made an astonishing remark. "I believe him, sir, to be all you have stated and something more—he is a Christian," Dix confessed. "And how did you learn this," McClure asked, astonished. "I have his diary," Dix replied, seemingly unfazed that he was sending a good man to his death.[1]

As McClure and Ritchie were walking to the cell, one of the guards approached them to ask Beall, since his breakfast had been early, whether he would like someone sent to the guard's home to prepare anything he might wish to eat. Beall replied that he would be pleased to have a cup of coffee and some toast.

Alone with his childhood friends Ritchie and McClure, John now began to reminisce about

Photograph of John Yates Beall taken three hours before his execution (Courtesy of Library of Congress).

his youth, thinking of happier, simpler times, inquiring after old school mates. He then recounted his raids on the Chesapeake and Lake Erie, and the attack on the Dunkirk railway, perhaps seeking in it some satisfaction for the high price he was about to pay. In a way, knowing his end was near was a relief. He began to rub his hands together in his habitual manner, and for a moment he seemed cheerful.

Then he once again began to speak of his wishes after his death. "Bury me," he said in a calm voice, "somewhere near here; I do not wish to be taken to Virginia until I can have on my tombstone the

15. The Hanging

epitaph I want, and that is the noblest epitaph any man can have: 'Died in the Defense of His Country.'"[2] Beall confessed he was suffering from a toothache that had kept him awake most of the night. He wanted very much to take some laudanum to relieve the pain but feared that if he did it would be misinterpreted as an attempt to anesthetize himself from the horror of the execution.

As the hour approached, McClure glanced nervously at his watch. Beall asked what time it was. It was noon.

His last meal was brought in, though he hardly touched it. Major Milton Cogswell entered to say goodbye to John, who received him with the courtesy he would have extended to a dear friend. Cogswell could easily sympathize, having himself been a prisoner in Richmond. Thinking Cogswell had come to lead him to the gallows, John said, "Well, Major, I am at your service."[3] Cogswell quickly corrected him, saying he had come only to say farewell. With that, Beall gathered up all the books the Major had lent him, commenting on the merits of each that he had read.

When Dr. Weston entered, John offered him some coffee. Groping to fill the awful void of the moment, Ritchie glanced at the table and remarked banally that instead of the toast, some warm rolls had been prepared. "You know, Doctor," Beall said, "we Virginians are fond of warm bread."[4] Turning to McClure, he told him to inform the Major that he was ready at any time and that, when the moment arrived, there should be no unnecessary delay. Holding back tears, Ritchie and McClure then stepped outside so that Dr. Weston could administer last rites. For several minutes the two read passages from the Bible, prompting John to recall that when he was first captured in New York he came into the possession of a Bible. Upon opening it then, the first passage that caught his eye was the final verse from Chapter Four, 2nd Corinthians, which he now recalled:

> *For our light and momentary troubles are achieving for us an eternal glory that far outweighs them all.*
> *So we fix our eyes not on what is seen, but what is unseen. For what is seen in temporary, but what is unseen is eternal.*

John Yates Beall, Son of the South

At 12:30 Provost Marshall Tallman and Marshal Robert Murray came in with the guards. As Tallman placed the manacles on his wrists, John said, "All I ask is that there be no unnecessary consumption of time in the execution; for after all it will be to me but a mere muscular effort."[5] As he was being led away, he turned one last time to his friends as McClure extended his hand in farewell. Feigning a cheerful tone, John said, "Goodbye, boys. I can't shake hands with you. You see my arms are fastened." At that moment, Ritchie noticed something strange—John's eyes shined with "an unusual and unearthly splendor."[6] Suddenly recalling one final detail, Ritchie said he need a clarification from John regarding his epitaph—was it "Died in the Defense or in the Service of His Country?" John replied firmly, "I die *for* my country, both in its service and in its defense."[7] The cell door then opened, and McClure called after, "Goodbye, God Bless You, John." As he stepped forward John turned and said, "Ah, no doubt of that.... Well, goodbye boys, I die in the hope of a resurrection and in the service and defense of my country. ... Tell my friends in [probably Canada] that every secret of which I have been the depositary dies with me!"[8] A black execution cap was then drawn over his head, its tassel falling to one side. The blackness of the cap contrasted sharply with the paleness his face had acquired from months of confinement. A blue-black military cape was thrown over his shoulders, concealing his manacled wrists.

As he passed, one of the guards whose eyes had welled up with tears remarked, "Ah, he's a brave man!"

Shortly after 1 p.m., the other prisoners were ordered into their cells as Lieutenant Tallman began the somber march through the arched sallyport to the gallows. Behind Tallman was John, followed by Dr. Weston, Marshall Murray, and several aides, with the entire cortège flanked by two companies of guards. Ritchie and McClure trailed solemnly far behind. As the garrison sounded a mournful death march, John strode with the same sure, unfaltering step as he had as a private under Stonewall Jackson. As they walked, John could see on the brow of a hill south of the fort the dark outline of the gibbet with its weights and pulleys, a noose dangling ominously from the beam above. There was no trap door. Instead,

15. The Hanging

a secondary rope supporting heavy weights would be cut, causing the weights to fall and jerk Beall's body violently upward. Dan Lucas thought the gruesome contraption "a specimen of Yankee ingenuity."[9] Not by accident, it was the same gallows used three years earlier to hang the notorious slave trader Nathaniel Gordon, whom Lincoln had also refused to pardon, and which was intended to raise the profile of the execution. In doing so, it further shamed Beall. As Lucas later observed, "Just as the Jews imagined the contemporaneous execution of thieves would add to the shame of the Crucifixion."[10] The executioner had been a prisoner on the island for desertion, and for the discharge of this lurid duty had been promised release.

Suddenly a signal was sent to Tallman to halt the procession, the very delay John had asked to be spared. "Oh, this is cruel, and cowardly!" Ritchie exclaimed, unaware there was a last-minute glitch.[11] Even the callous crowd was appalled at the delay. During the wait, however, John stood erect, his eyes taking in his surroundings one final time. It was a cloudless day and he remarked to Dr. Weston, "How beautiful the sun is! I look upon it for the last time!"[12] Noticing the hills of Staten Island in the distance, he asked Dr. Weston what their name was, remarking that he had some "friends" there, Confederates he had served with. "After all is over," he said, "write to my mother that I died without bravado and without craven fear."[13]

After nine minutes had passed, Tallman received a signal to resume the procession. As they neared the scaffold, a wry smile went across John's face when he saw the large number of spectators that had come out to witness the hanging. In striking contrast to Dix's tight control of visitors had been the liberalness with which he distributed passes for Beall's execution to the nearly five hundred spectators who surrounded the scaffold.

John then uttered to Dr. Weston something he had retained from his reading, "That we might be as near God on the scaffold, as elsewhere."[14] Once on the platform he took a seat in the chair beneath the noose. On the ground in front of the scaffold he could see a simple pine coffin that would be his final resting place. Post

John Yates Beall, Son of the South

Adjutant Lieutenant Keiser then read aloud the charges and orders against him, the findings and sentence of the court, and the order of General Dix approving the sentence and directing the execution. Respectfully, Beall stood for the reading staring into the distance. But when he saw that Dix, for dramatic effect, had written an unnecessarily long-winded declamation, he indignantly drew up the chair with his leg and sat down in disgust. A *New York Times* reporter noticed that when John sat down, he turned his back on the adjutant and faced South. He continued to gaze in that direction. Perhaps in those final moments he was moved to recall his beloved Shenandoah Valley, reliving moments of frolicking innocently in the grassy fields and rivers of his youth, a time so strange and distant from the current moment as to seem another life altogether.

As Keiser rambled on, John shook his head three times disapprovingly and smiled in derision, once when he heard "the insurgent state of Virginia," his beloved native land now contemptuously referred to as "a rogue entity." Again, he smirked when his attempt to rescue prisoners on Johnson's Island was referred to as "piracy," and lastly at the accusation that he was a "guerrillero" who had imperiled the lives of innocent passengers on the Buffalo train by placing an obstruction on the tracks. Keiser concluded with a damning pronouncement from Dix:

> The Government of the United States, from a desire to mitigate the asperities of war, has given to the insurgents of the South the benefit of rules which govern sovereign States in the conduct of hostilities with each other; and, any violation of those rules should, for the sake of good order here, and the cause of humanity throughout the world, be visited with the severest penalty.[15]

Keiser droned on and on. At one point, when Dix announced that a failure to execute Beall today would constitute nothing less than "an offense against the outraged civilization and humanity of the age," it became too much, and Beall burst out loud in scornful laughter. Failing to grasp the moment, reporters thought he was reminiscing about some humorous incident in his past. But it was the Union's own hypocrisy John mocked as he reflected on Sheridan's wanton burning of the Shenandoah Valley, the ransacking and

15. The Hanging

plundering of his farm before his helpless mother, and the soldiers' shameless taunting and mocking of his sisters.

By now the long ordeal of Dix's speech had become too much even for the executioner, who shouted crudely, "Cut it short! Cut it short! The captain wishes to be swung off quick!"[16]

At last, the insufferable sermonizing was over. John stood up and positioned himself under the rope, announcing he was ready. He inclined his head reverently toward Dr. Weston, who proceeded to read the commendatory prayer from the Episcopal liturgy. Anguished tears of sympathy appeared on the faces of the guards. After Weston pronounced the benediction, Lieutenant Tallman asked if there was anything he wished to say. John replied, "I protest against the execution of this sentence. Its execution will be absolute murder, brutal murder. I die in the service and defense of my country." Asked if he had anything more to say, John replied, "No, I beg you to make haste."[17]

At quarter past 1 p.m., Tallman stepped to the rear allowing the executioner to step forward and adjust the knot around Beall's neck before placing a black hood over his head. As he lifted the saber, sunlight caught the shiny metal blade, shooting a glint of light across the scaffold onto the crowd of onlookers. Tallman gave the signal, and with a swipe, the executioner slashed the rope, causing the weights to fall as Beall's body was jerked violently into the air. His neck snapped instantly. As his body dangled above the platform, his right leg twitched briefly, and his shoulders shrugged. Then all went quiet as his body swayed silently in the breeze. Around the scaffold Federal soldiers were weeping out of both pity and admiration for the brave rebel.

After twenty minutes, John's body was cut down and taken inside the fort, where Dr. Conner of the U.S. Army pronounced him dead. "Thus they [Lincoln and Dix] stood as the pillars of the gallows," Daniel Lucas angrily wrote, "on which Beall's fate was suspended, and between them he died."[18]* When Beall's old cellmate

---

*John Beall was the last person to be executed on Governors Island.

John Yates Beall's final resting place in Zion Episcopal Church graveyard, Charleston. On the headstone was inscribed, according to Beall's wishes, "Died in the Service and Defense of His Country" (courtesy of Bradley Owen, HMdb.org).

15. The Hanging

Allison heard what happened, he cried, "God what a lamentable death, and for one [far] from home and friends, a prisoner in the hands of his bitter, bitter enemies."[19]*

In stunned silence, Ritchie and McClure returned to John's cell to gather his personal effects to send to his mother. On Sunday, the two returned to Governors Island to collect John's body for burial. In accordance with John's wishes, only a handful of friends were invited to the service, which took place on Fern Hill at Greenwood Cemetery in Brooklyn, overlooking the Hudson River. Dr. Weston was on hand to read the Episcopal burial service. As they laid him in the coffin, a button dropped from his coat, which Ritchie added to John's personal effects. His gravestone was a plain marble slab on which was written "John Y. Beall, died February 24th, 1865." During the time his body was interred at Greenwood, visitors came regularly to lay fresh flowers at his grave.

Two years after the war, Beall's body was exhumed and buried in Zion Episcopal Church in Charles Town, West Virginia.

---

*Dix had imposed a news blackout on the trial so that Richmond would not learn of Beall's wrongful conviction on charges of being a spy. Otherwise, the Confederacy would almost certainly have retaliated with similar treatment of one or more of its Union prisoners.

Postscript

IN THE HISTORY OF MILITARY JUSTICE during the Civil War, never had so many and from such high places appealed on behalf of a prisoner most did not even know. While it seemed that all pleas on Beall's behalf had only hardened Lincoln's resolve that he be executed, they had also deepened his anguish. The Beall affair had, in fact, exhausted him. A few weeks after his execution, in a meeting with Representative Henry Bromwell of Illinois and Secretary of State William Seward, Lincoln explained the reason for the difficult decision and the toll it had taken on him: "I've had more questions of life and death to settle in four years than all the other men who sat in this chair put together. No man knows the distress of my mind. Some of them I couldn't save. There are cases where the law must be executed. The case of Beall on the Lakes—there had to be an example. They tried me every way. They wouldn't give up. But I had to stand firm. I even had to turn away his poor sister when she came and begged for his life, and let him be executed, and he was executed, and I can't get the distress out of my mind yet."[1] At this, tears welled up in Lincoln's eyes and in the eyes of those listening. Perhaps, it was the agony of that decision that led Lincoln to issue a proclamation three weeks after Beall's execution, stating that any deserter, whatever might have been his reason for deserting, would be fully pardoned on return to his regiment or company.

In March, after much sobbing and protests over his sentence, Robert Cobb Kennedy was hanged at Fort Lafayette for the burning of New York City.

Postscript

It was not until a month after Beall's execution that Commissioner of Prisoner Exchange Robert Ould learned of Beall's case, when he happened to read about it in the newspaper. In a letter to President Davis he complained that the U.S. Military Commission never brought the case to his attention, nor did the trial proceedings become public until February 15, three days before his originally scheduled execution. This was because, anticipating retaliation, Dix did not mail Beall's letter to Ould until after his execution. The entire affair was quietly done to prevent the Confederacy from making any effort to intervene on Beall's behalf.

After the war, Martha returned to Nashville with her sister and opened the Nashville Select School for Young Ladies. She never married. To her dying day, she wore around her neck the locket John had sent containing a tuft of his hair and a photo of him on the back. In her later years she retired from teaching to undertake charitable work for the underprivileged. When she died in 1910, a nonprofit organization was created in her name, which still operates today.

After Beall's death Daniel Lucas remained in Montreal, unable to return to his native state. When the war ended a few months later he honored his promise to vindicate his friend's memory for posterity. Gathering Beall's diary and other papers, he published them in the form of an annotated memoir. Soon after, he returned to Jefferson County, though under the oath test he was prohibited from practicing law until 1870. He married in 1869, fathering an only daughter he named Virginia—after his beloved state. Years later he served as state legislator and judge on the appellate court, eventually becoming its president. Despite his busy legal career, he found time to pen three dramatic plays and as many volumes of poems, which would mark him as a major Southern writer. His most celebrated poem, "The Land Where We Were Dreaming," written in Canada in the gloomy days shortly after Beall's execution, was both a paean to the halcyon days of their youth and a eulogy to a lost South. The closing verses reveal that, like so many sons of the South, he continued to cling to a lost dream—and a lost cause—that the South would one day rise again.

Postscript

Woe! Woe! is us, the startled mothers cried,
While we have slept, our noble sons have died!
Woe! Woe! is us, how strange and sad,
That all our glorious visions fled,
Have left us nothing real but our dead,
In the land where we were dreaming!

And are they really dead, our martyred slain?
No, Dreamers! Morn shall bid them rise again,
From every plain,—from every height,—
On which they seemed to die for right,
Their gallant spirits shall renew the fight,
In the land where we were dreaming![2]

Fully a half century after the death of John Yates Beall, soldiers stationed at Governors Island regularly reported seeing his ghost haunting the fort's earthen ramparts.[3]

Chapter Notes

Chapter 1

1. Thomas Jefferson, *Notes on the State of Virginia* (Richmond: Randolph, 1853), 17.
2. M.M. Beall, *Colonial Families of the United States Descended from the Immigrants Who Arrived Before 1700* (Washington, D.C.: C.H. Potter, 1929), 30.
3. J.W. McIlvain, "Ninian Beall: An American Elder of the Seventeenth Century," *The Presbyterian Review* (New York: Scribner's, 1888): 382.
4. Cameron Moseley, *John Yates Beall, Confederate Commando* (Great Falls, Va.: Bell Family Association, 1980), 3.
5. Franklin Ellis, *History of Fayetteville County, Pennsylvania* (Philadelphia: L.H. Everts, 1882), 467.
6. Michael Graham, S.J., "Popish Plots: Protestant Fears in Early Colonial Maryland, 1676–1689," *The Catholic Historical Review*, 79.2 (1993): 197–216.
7. C.C. Magruder, "Colonel Ninian Beall," *Records of the Columbia Historical Society, Washington, DC* (1937): 17–29.
8. Macgruder, "Colonel Ninian Beall," 26.
9. Lois Carr and David Jordan, *Maryland's Revolution of Government, 1689–1692*. Ithaca, N.Y.: Cornell University Press, 1974), 234–235.
10. Elizabeth Daniel, *John Yates of England and Virginia: His Family and Descendants* (n.p., 1936), 3.
11. *Ibid.*, 4.
12. A.E. Terrill, ed. *Memorials of a Family in England and America, 1771–1851* (n.p., 1887), 198.
13. *Ibid.*, 338.
14. Benjamin S. Morgan and Jacob F. Cork, *Columbian History of Education in West Virginia* (Charlestown: Moses Donnally, 1893), 12.
15. Terrill, *Memorials of a Family in England and America*, 332.
16. Maurie D. McInnis and Louis P. Nelson, eds., *Educated in Tyranny: Slavery and Thomas Jefferson's University* (Charlottesville: University of Virginia, 2019), 5.
17. *Ibid.*, 13.
18. Stephen Puelo, *The Caning Assault that Drove America to Civil War* (Yardley, Pa.: Westholme Publishing, 2012), 102, 114–115.
19. Rex Bowman and Carlos Santos, *Rot, Riot, and Rebellion. Mr. Jefferson's Struggle to Save the University that Changed America* (Charlottesville: University of Virginia Press, 2013), 1–2.
20. Maurie D. McInnis, "The Liberty and Tyranny of Jefferson's Academical Village," in *The Founding of Thomas Jefferson's University*, John Ragosta et al., eds. (Charlottesville: University of Virginia, 2019), 135.
21. Phillip Bruce, *History of the University* of Virginia, 1818–1919, 3 (New York: Macmillan, 1921), 111–118.
22. Daniel B. Lucas, *Memoir of John Yates Beall* (Montreal: John Lovell, 1865), 4–5, 15.
23. Lucas, *Memoir*, 9.
24. Cameron Moseley, *Confederate Commando*, 7.
25. Lucas, *Memoir*, 8.
26. State of West Virginia, County of Jefferson, *Register of Deaths*, 1855, 8.

Chapter Notes

Chapter 2

1. In his autobiography Frederick Douglass wrote that John Brown had confided the plan to him in 1847 without specifically mentioning Harpers Ferry. See Frederick Douglass, *Life and Times of Frederick Douglass* (Hartford, Conn.: n.p., 1882), 309–314.
2. James M. McPherson, *Battle Cry of Freedom, The Civil War Era* (New York: Oxford University Press, 2003), 205.
3. Thomas Gold, *History of Clarke County* (Berryville, VA: Chesapeake Book Co., 1962), 150–151.
4. Benjamin Beall, "Jefferson Guards," *Spirit of Jefferson*, October 27, 1860.
5. "Letter of Col. Gibson to Governor Wise, October 18, 1859," *Governor's Message and Reports of the Public Officers of the State, of the Boards of Directors, and of the Visitors, Superintendents, and other Agents of Public Institutions or Interests of Virginia* (Richmond: William F. Ritchie, 1859), 61–67.
6. Alexander Boteler, "Recollections of the John Brown Raid by a Virginia Who Witness the Fight," *Century Magazine* (July 1883): 399–411.
7. "Letter of Robert Baylor to Governor Wise," Charleston, October 22, 1859.
8. Israel Green, "The Capture of John Brown," *The North American Review*, 141, no. 349 (December 1885): 564–569.
9. Lucy J. Ambler, *When Tidewater Invaded the Valley* (Charleston: n.p., 1934), 8.

Chapter 3

1. Jim Surkamp, "A Dozen Set Fires a Sign of Slave Resistance," June 16, 2011, http://www.Civilwarscholars.com, accessed July 7, 2019.
2. Edmund Ruffin, *The Diary of Edmund Ruffin, 1* (Baton Rouge: Louisiana State University Press, 1972), 373.
3. Dennis E, Frye, *The 2nd Virginia Infantry* (Lynchburg: H.E. Howard, 1984), 2.
4. "Let the Dis-unionists Pause," *Virginia Free Press*, December 6, 1860.
5. *Ibid.*, 854.

6. Quoted in John Walter Wayland, *History of Shenandoah County, 2* (Strasburg, Va.: Shenandoah Publishing House, 1927), 855.
7. Claude E. Fuller and Richard D. Steuart, *Firearms of the Confederacy* (Huntington, W.V.: Standard Publications, 1944), 2, 11, 23.
8. Captain William Maynadier, *The War of the Rebellion: A Compilation of the Official Records of the Union and Confederate Armies* (Washington, D.C.: Government Printing Office, 1880–1901), 51, 308.
9. U.S. Senate, "Destruction of the Harpers Ferry Armory," *Extracts from Senate Rep. Com. No. 37*, 37th Congress, 2d Session.
10. Dennis Frye, *Harpers Ferry Under Fire: A Border Town in the American Civil War* (Brookfield, Mo.: Donning Publishing, 1980), 1.
11. Daniel B. Lucas, *Memoir of John Yates Beall* (Montreal: John Lovell, 1865), 6.
12. James M. McPherson and William J. Cooper, *Writing the Civil War: The Quest to Understand* (Columbia: University of South Carolina Press, 1998), 137.
13. Lucas, *Memoir*, 52–53.
14. A.L. Long, *Memoirs of Robert E. Lee: His Military and Personal History* (Secaucus, N.J.: Blue and Grey Press, 1983), 92.
15. *Ibid.*, 93.
16. *Ibid.*, 95.
17. George Francis Robert Henderson, *Stonewall Jackson and the American Civil War, I* (Secaucus, N.J.: Blue and Grey Press), 99.
18. David Strother, "Personal Recollections of the War by a Virginian," *Harper's New Monthly Magazine*, 33 (June 1866): 1–25.
19. U.S. Senate, "Destruction of the Harpers Ferry Armory," No. 37, 37th Cong., 2d Session.
20. *Ibid.*
21. "The Late Invasion at Harper's Ferry," *Harper's Weekly*, 3 (November 5, 1859): 10.
22. *Ibid.*, 11.
23. *The War of the Rebellion: A Compi-*

Chapter Notes

lation of *Official Records of the Union and Confederate Armies*, Series 1, 2 (Washington, D.C.: Govt. Printing Office, 1880–1901), 1.
  24. Strother, "Personal Recollections," 12.
  25. Joseph Barry, *The Strange Story of Harper's Ferry* (Martinsburg, W.V.: Thompson Brothers, 1903), 99.
  26. *Ibid.*
  27. James M. Garnett, "Extracts from the Diary of Captain James M. Garnett," *Southern Historical Society Papers*, 2 (1900): 59.
  28. Robert Underwood Johnson and Clarence Clough Buel, eds. *Battles and Leaders of the Civil War* 1 (New York: Century Company, 1887), 118.
  29. Henry Kyd Douglas, *I Rode with Stonewall* (Chapel Hill: University of North Carolina Press, 1940), 6.

Chapter 4

  1. S.C. Gwynne, *Rebel Yell: The Violence, Passion, and Redemption of Stonewall Jackson* (New York: Scribner, 2014), 38.
  2. Joseph Barry, *Annals of Harper's Ferry* (Hagerstown, Md.: Dechert & Co., 1869), 64.
  3. Dennis Frye, *2nd Virginia Infantry* (Lynchburg, Va.: H.E. Howard, 1984), 7.
  4. D.B. Conrad, "History of the First Battle of Manassas," *Southern Historical Society Papers*, 18 (1890), 83.
  5. *Ibid.*
  6. *Ibid.*, 84.
  7. Barry, *Annals of Harper's Ferry*, 64.
  8. John Esten Cooke, *Stonewall Jackson: A Military Biography* (New York: D. Appleton, 1876), 103.
  9. Douglas, *I Rode with Stonewall*, 6–7.
  10. *Ibid.*, 7.
  11. *Ibid.*, 8.

Chapter 5

  1. John O. Casler, *Four Years in the Stonewall Brigade* (Girard, Kans.: Appeal Publishing, 1906), 57.
  2. *Ibid.*, 57–58.
  3. Daniel B. Lucas, *Memoir of John Yates Beall* (Montreal: John Lovell, 1865), 13.
  4. *Ibid.*
  5. James B. Avirett, *The Memoirs of Turner Ashby and His Compeers* (Baltimore: Selby and Delany, 1867), 127.
  6. "Report of John W. Geary, 28th Pennsylvania Regiment," *Official Records of the War of the Rebellion*, Series 1, 5, 239–244.
  7. *Ibid.*
  8. "Report of Lt. Col. Turner Ashby, C.S. Army," *Official Records of the War of the Rebellion;* Series 1, 5 (1882): 246–247.

Chapter 6

  1. Daniel B. Lucas, *Memoir of John Yates Beall* (Montreal: John Lovell, 1865), 219.
  2. *Ibid.*, 17.
  3. *Ibid.*, 252.
  4. *Ibid.*, 17.
  5. *Ibid.*, 221.
  6. Barry Sheehy, *Montreal, City of Secrets: Confederate Operations in Montreal during the American Civil War* (Montreal: Baraka Books, 2017), 32.
  7. *Ibid.*, 239.
  8. *Ibid.*, 18.
  9. Robert J. Driver, *The Confederate Soldiers of Rockbridge County, Virginia: A Roster* (Jefferson, N.C.: McFarland and Co., 2016), 167.
  10. Ralph Lindeman, *Confederates from Canada: John Yates Beall and the Rebel Raids on the Great Lakes* (Jefferson, N.C.: McFarland and Co., 2023), 42.

Chapter 7

  1. Daniel B. Lucas, *Memoir of John Yates Beall* (Montreal: John Lovell, 1865), 289.
  2. *The War of the Rebellion: A Compilation of the Official Records of the Union and Confederate Armies* (Washington, D.C.: 1880–1901), Series 1, 5, 581.
  3. Peggy Robbins, "The Confederacy's

Chapter Notes

Bomb Brothers," *Journal of Mine Action*, 6 (April 2002): 1–7.

4. W.W. Baker, *Memoirs of Service with John Yates Beall*, edited by Douglas S. Freeman (Richmond: The Richmond Press, 1910), 18.

5. Alexandra Lee Levin, *This Awful Drama: General Edwin Gray Lee, C.S.A. and his Family* (New York: Vantage, 1987), 64.

6. Cameron Moseley, *John Yates Beall, Confederate Commando* (Great Falls, VA: Bell Family Association, 1980), 22–23.

7. Daniel B. Lucas, *Memoir of John Yates Beall* (Montreal: John Lovell, 1865), 25.

8. Baker, *Memoirs of Service*, 19.
9. *Ibid.*, 22–23.
10. *Ibid.*, 20.
11. *Ibid.*, 205.
12. *Ibid.*
13. *Ibid.*, 26.
14. *Ibid.*
15. *Richmond Enquirer*, October 10, 1863.
16. Baker, *Memoirs of Service*, 27.
17. Isaac J. Wister, *The Autobiography of Isaac Jones Wistar, 1827–1905*, 2 (Philadelphia: Wister Institute, 1914), 83.

Chapter 8

1. W.W. Baker, *Memoirs of Service with John Yates Beall*, edited by Douglas S. Freeman (Richmond: The Richmond Press, 1910), 31.

2. *Official Records of the Union and Confederate Navies in the War of the Rebellion* (Washington, D.C.: GPO, 1899), Series 1, 29, Part 1, 639–640.

3. *Official Records of the Union and Confederate Navies in the War of the Rebellion* (Washington, D.C.: GPO, 1899), Series 1, 9, 306–307.

4. Baker, *Memoirs of Service*, 32.
5. *Ibid.*, 33.
6. *Ibid.*, 35.
7. *Ibid.*, 29.
8. *Ibid.*, 37.
9. *Baltimore Sun*, December 20, 1863.
10. Baker, *Memoirs of Service*, 40.
11. *Ibid.*, 43–44.

Chapter 9

1. Daniel B. Lucas, *Memoir of John Yates Beall* (Montreal: John Lovell, 1865), 30.

2. *The Wartime Papers of Robert E. Lee*, edited by Clifford Dowdy and Louis Manarin (Boston: Little, Brown, 1961), 507–509.

3. Jefferson Davis, *The Rise and Fall of the Confederate Government*, 1 (New York: D. Appleton, 1881), 611–612.

4. Francis Trevelyan Miller, *The Photographic History of the Civil War in Ten Volumes: Soldier Life, Secret Service*, 8 (New York: The Review of Reviews, 1911), 294.

5. Thomas, H. Hines, "The Northwestern Conspiracy," *The Southern Bivouac*, 2 (December 1886): 437–445.

6. John Breckenridge Castleman, *Active Service* (Louisville, Ky.: Courier-Journal, 1917), 133.

7. James D. Horan, *Confederate Agent: A Discovery in History* (New York: Crown Publishing, 1954), 84.

8. *Ibid.*, 80.
9. *Ibid.*, 88–89.

Chapter 10

1. Edmund H. Cummins, "The Signal Corps in the Confederate States Army," *Southern Historical Society Papers*, 16 (Richmond: Virginia Historical Society, 1888), 93–105.

2. W.W. Baker, *Memoirs of Service with John Yates Beall*, edited by Douglas S. Freeman (Richmond: The Richmond Press, 1910), 47–48.

3. *Ibid.*, 48.

4. Daniel B. Lucas, *Memoir of John Yates Beall* (Montreal: John Lovell, 1865), 31.

5. Quoted in Ralph Lindeman, *Confederates from Canada: John Yates Beall and the Rebel Raids on the Great Lakes* (Jefferson, N.C.: McFarland and Company, 2023), 44.

6. *Ibid.*, 44–45.

7. Quoted in Jennifer L. Weber, *Copperheads: The Rise and Fall of Lincoln's*

Chapter Notes

Opponents in the North (New York: Oxford University Press, 2006), 80.

8. William Dudley Foulke, "Governor Morton and the Sons of Liberty," *The Atlantic* (July 1893): 73–88.

9. John W. Headley, *Confederate Operations in Canada* (New York: Neale Publishing, 1906), 223.

10. Stephen Z. Starr, *Colonel Grenfell's Wars* (Baton Rouge: Louisiana State University Press, 1971), 146.

11. *Ibid.*, 219.

12. Jefferson Davis, *The Rise and Fall of the Confederate Government*, 2 (New York: D. Appleton, 1881), 516–517.

13. James D. Horan, *Confederate Agent: A Discovery in History* (New York: Fairfax Press, 1954), 88.

14. Adam Mayers, *Dixie and The Dominion* (Toronto: Dundurn Press, 2003), 58.

Chapter 11

1. Ralph Lindeman, *Confederates from Canada: John Yates Beall and the Rebel Raids on the Great Lakes* (Jefferson, N.C.: McFarland and Company, 2023), 18.

2. Quoted in Lindeman, *Confederates from Canada*, 25.

3. Christopher Britten, "Cooped Up and Powerless When My Home Is Invaded: Southern Prisoners at Johnson's Island in Their Own Words," *Ohio Valley History*, 10 (Spring 2010): 51–72.

4. http://johnsonsisland.org/history-pows/civil-war-era/union-guard-garrison, accessed July 25, 2020.

5. Fredrick J. Shepard, "The Johnson's Island Plot," *Publications of the Buffalo Historical Society*, 9 (Buffalo, N.Y.: 1924): 1–53.

6. *Ibid.*, 21.

7. *Ibid.*, 10.

8. John W. Headley, *Confederate Operations in Canada* (New York: Neale Publishing, 1906), 234–236.

9. Charles Frohman, *Rebels on Lake Erie* (Columbus: Ohio Historical Society, 1965), 76.

10. Daniel B. Lucas, *Memoir of John Yates Beall* (Montreal: John Lovell, 1865), 100.

11. *Ibid.*

12. Constance F. Woolson, "The Wine Islands of Lake Erie," *Harper's New Monthly Magazine* (June 1873): 27–36.

13. U.S. Military Commission, *Trial of John Y. Beall: As a Spy and Guerrillero* (New York: D. Appleton, 1865), 15–16.

14. *Ibid.*, 11.

15. Edward Adams Sowles, *History of the St. Albans Raid: Annual Address Before the Vermont Historical Society* (Montpelier, Vt.: Messenger Printing: 1876), 36.

16. John Miller, *A Twentieth Century History of Erie Pennsylvania* (Chicago: Lewis Publishing, 1909), 346.

17. *Ibid.*, 348.

18. Frohman, *Rebels on Lake Erie*, 82.

19. Lucas, *Memoir*, 40.

20. John Castleman, *Active Service* (Louisville, Ky.: Courier Journal, 1917), 162.

21. Woolson, "The Wine Islands of Lake Erie," 33.

Chapter 12

1. John W. Headley, *Confederate Operations in Canada* (New York: Neale Publishing, 1906), 252–253.

2. *Buffalo Commercial Advertiser*, November 7, 1864.

3. *Ibid.*, 255.

4. Nat Brandt, *The Man Who Tried to Burn New York* (Syracuse, N.Y.: Syracuse University Press, 1986), 75.

5. Headley, *Confederate Operations*, 272.

6. *Ibid.*, 278.

7. *Ibid.*, 300.

8. *Ibid.*, 302.

9. *Ibid.*, 303.

10. *Ibid.*

11. U.S. Military Commission, *Trial of John Y. Beall: As a Spy and Guerrillero* (New York: D. Appleton, 1865), 45.

12. Daniel B. Lucas, *Memoir of John Yates Beall* (Montreal: John Lovell, 1865), 52.

13. U.S. Military Commission, *Trial of John Y. Beall*, 46.

14. Lucas, *Memoir*, 54.

Chapter Notes

15. U.S. Military Commission, *Trial of John Y. Beall*, 47.
16. Brandt, *The Man Who Tried to Burn New York*, 209.
17. Alexandra Lee, *This Awful Drama: Edwin Gray Lee and His Family* (New York: Vantage Press, 1987), 138–139.
18. John D. Allison, *Diary* (Louisville, Ky.: The Filson Club, n.d.), 5.

Chapter 13

1. Carl Sandburg, *Abraham Lincoln: The War Years*, 1 (New York: Harcourt Brace, 1939), 45.
2. U.S. Military Commission, *Trial of John Y. Beall: As a Spy and Guerrillero* (New York: D. Appleton, 1865), 6–7.
3. Daniel B. Lucas, *Memoir of John Yates Beall* (Montreal: John Lovell, 1865), 57.
4. Martin S. Lederman, "The Law of the Lincoln Assassination," *Columbia Law Review* (March 2018): 355; Thomas P. Lowry, *Don't Shoot That Boy! Abraham Lincoln and Military Justice* (Mason City, Iowa: Savas, 1990), 183.
5. Quoted in Lederman, "The Law of the Lincoln Assassination," 357.
6. Francis Lieber, *Instructions for the Government of the Armies of the United States in the Field* (New York: D. Van Nostrand, 1863).
7. Quoted in Lederman, "The Law of the Lincoln Assassination," 367.
8. Lieber, *Instructions*, 21–22.
9. Lieber, *Instructions*, 2, 6.
10. Lieber, *Instructions*, 6–7.
11. *Ibid.*, 8.
12. Act of April 10, 1806, ch. 20, S 2, 2 Stat. 371 (1806).
13. Act of Feb. 13, 1862, ch. 25, S 4, 12 Stat. 340 (1862).
14. *Ibid.*
15. Lieber, *Instructions*, 22.
16. *Ibid.*, 23.
17. Lucas, *Memoir*, 62.
18. "James T. Brady," *The National Cyclopedia of American Biography*, 3 (New York: J.T. White Co., 1893), 386–387.
19. "Death of James T. Brady," *The New York Times*, February 10, 1869.
20. *Trial*, 19.
21. Lucas, *Memoir*, 121.
22. U.S. Military Commission, *Trial of John Y. Beall: As a Spy and Guerrillero* (New York: D. Appleton, 1865), 31.
23. *Ibid.*, 51.
24. Lucas, *Memoir*, 161.
25. Henry Wagner Halleck, *Halleck's International Law* (London: Kegan Paul, 1893), 31.
26. *Ibid.*, 172–173.
27. *Ibid.*, 175–176.
28. *Ibid.*, 184.
29. *Ibid.*, 187.
30. *Ibid.*, 185.

Chapter 14

1. Louise Davis, "She Kept the Vigil," *Tennessean Magazine*, February 5, 1950.
2. Daniel Lucas, *Biographical Notes of John Yates Beall* (n.p.: n.d.), 13–14.
3. W.W. Baker, *Memoirs of Service with John Yates Beall*, edited by Douglas S. Freeman (Richmond: The Richmond Press, 1910), 50–51.
4. "Telegram from General John Dix to President Abraham Lincoln," February 14, 1865, Library of Congress. Abraham Lincoln Papers: Series 1, General Correspondence, 1833–1916.
5. Carl Sandburg, *Abraham Lincoln: The War Years*, 3 (New York: Harcourt Brace, 1939), 507.
6. Thomas P. Lowry, *Don't Shoot That Boy! Abraham Lincoln and Military Justice* (Mason City, Iowa: Savas, 1990), 18.
7. *Ibid.*
8. *Ibid.*, 13.
9. Sandburg, *Abraham Lincoln*, 3, 523–524.
10. "James T. Brady to Abraham Lincoln, February 15, 1865," Abraham Lincoln Papers, Series 1, General Correspondence 1833–1916 (Library of Congress).
11. *Ibid.*
12. Daniel B. Lucas, *Memoir of John Yates Beall* (Montreal: John Lovell, 1865), 69.
13. Baker, *Memoirs of Service*, Appendix VI.
14. Anne M. Holmes, *Mary Mildred*

Chapter Notes

Sullivan: A Biography (Concord, N.H.: Rumford Press, 1924), 46.
15. "Letter from John Y. Beall to Mrs. Mary Sullivan," "John Yates Beall 1865, Letters by Him to Mrs. A.S. Sullivan," University of North Carolina Archives, February 17, 1865.
16. Matthew Page Andrews, *The Women of the South in War Times* (Baltimore: Norman Remington Co., 1927), 429–448.
17. *Ibid.*, 51.
18. Lucas, *Biographical Notes*, 78.
19. Maurice G. Baxter, "Orville H. Browning: Lincoln's Colleague and Critic," *Journal of the Illinois State Historical Society* (Winter 1955): 431–455.
20. Orville H. Browning, *Diary of Orville H. Browning* (Springfield: Illinois State Historical Society, 1925), 7.
21. Lucas, *Memoir*, 71.
22. "Letter of John Y. Beall to Mrs. A. Sullivan," Ft. Columbus, "John Yates Beall 1865, Letters by Him to Mrs. A.S. Sullivan," University of North Carolina Archives, February 21, 1865.
23. Lucas, *Biographical Notes*, 36–37.
24. Lucas, *Memoir*, 76.
25. *Ibid.*, 42.
26. *Ibid.*, 43.
27. *Ibid.*, 44.
28. Lucas, *Memoir*, 66.
29. Constance Woolson, "The Wine Islands of Lake Erie," *Harper's Magazine* (June 1873): 33–34.
30. Lucas, *Biographical Notes*, 78.
31. John Castleman, *Active Service* (Louisville, Ky.: Courier Journal, 1917), 164.
32. Lucas, *Biographical Notes*, 41.
33. *Ibid.*, 8.
34. Carl Sandburg, *Abraham Lincoln: The War Years*, 3 (New York: Harcourt, Brace and Co., 1939), 131.
35. Mrs. Roger A. Pryor, *Reminiscences of Peace and War* (New York: Macmillan, 1904), 341.
36. Issac Markens, "President Lincoln and the Case of John Y. Beall," *American Historical Magazine* (May 1911): 425–435.
37. Lucas, *Biographical Notes*, 48.
38. *Ibid.*, 48–49.
39. *Ibid.*, 50.
40. *Ibid.*, 54–55.
41. *Ibid.*, 56.
42. *Ibid.*, 38.
43. "Letter of Thaddeus Stevens to Abraham Lincoln," February 24, 1865. Library of Congress. Abraham Lincoln papers: Series 1, General Correspondence. 1833–1916.

Chapter 15

1. Daniel Lucas, *Biographical Notes of John Yates Beall* (n.p.: n.d.), 80.
2. *Ibid.*, 60.
3. *Ibid.*, 61.
4. *Ibid.*, 62.
5. *Ibid.*, 79.
6. *Ibid.*, 80.
7. *Ibid.*, 63.
8. Daniel B. Lucas, *Memoir of John Yates Beall* (Montreal: John Lovell, 1865), 56.
9. *Ibid.*, 81.
10. Lucas, *Biographical Notes*, 81.
11. *Ibid.*, 82.
12. *Ibid.*, 83.
13. *Ibid.*, 73.
14. *Ibid.*, 65.
15. *Ibid.*, 85.
16. *Ibid.*, 86.
17. *Ibid.*, 66.
18. *Ibid.*, 74.
19. John D. Allison, *Diary* (Louisville, Ky.: The Filson Club, n.d.), 7.
Postscript
1. Carl Sandburg, *Abraham Lincoln: The War Years*, 4 (New York: Harcourt Brace, 1939), 132–133.
2. *The Land Where We Were Dreaming and Other Poems by Daniel Bedinger Lucas*, edited by Charles Kent and Virginia Lucas (Boston: R.G. Badger, 1913), 13–16.
3. Helen Worden, "Army Reception Gay Despite Island Ghost," *New York World-Telegram*, January 3, 1935.

Bibliography

Books

Baker, W.W. *Memoirs of Service with John Yates Beall,* edited by Douglas S. Freeman. Richmond: The Richmond Press, 1910.
Beall, M.M. *Colonial Families of the United States Descended from the Immigrants Who Arrived Before 1700.* Washington, D.C.: C.H. Potter, 1929.
Brandt, Nat. *The Man Who Tried to Burn New York.* Syracuse, N.Y.: Syracuse University Press, 1986.
Browning, Orville H. *Diary of Orville H. Browning.* Springfield: Illinois State Historical Society, 1925.
Daniel, Elizabeth. *John Yates of England and Virginia: His Family and Descendants.* n.p., 1936.
Frohman, Charles. *Rebels, on Lake Erie.* Columbus: Ohio Historical Society, 1965.
Frye, Dennis E. *The 2nd Virginia Infantry.* Lynchburg: H.E. Howard, 1984.
Henderson, George Francis Robert. *Stonewall Jackson and the American Civil War, I.* Secaucus, N.J.: Blue and Grey Press, 2015.
Holmes, Anne M. *Mary Mildred Sullivan: A Biography.* Concord, N.H.: Rumford Press, 1924.
Lindeman, Ralph. *Confederates from Canada: John Yates Beall and the Rebel Raids on the Great Lakes.* Jefferson, N.C.: McFarland & Co., 2023.
Lowry, Thomas P. *Don't Shoot That Boy! Abraham Lincoln and Military Justice.* Mason City, Iowa: Savas, 1990.
Lucas, Daniel B. *Biographical Notes of John Yates Beall.* n.p., n.d.
_____. *Memoir of John Yates Beall.* Montreal: John Lovell, 1865.
Maynadier, Captain William. *The War of the Rebellion: A Compilation of the Official Records of the Union and Confederate Armies.* 70 vols. Washington, D.C.: Government Printing Office, 1880–1901.
McInnis, Maurie D. "The Liberty and Tyranny of Jefferson's Academical Village," in *The Founding of Thomas Jefferson's University,* edited by John Ragosta. Charlottesville: University of Virginia Press, 2019.
McInnis, Maurie D., and Louis P. Nelson, eds. *Educated in Tyranny: Slavery and Thomas Jefferson's University.* Charlottesville: University of Virginia Press, 2019.
Moseley, Cameron. *John Yates Beall, Confederate Commando.* Great Falls, Va.: Bell Family Association, 1980.
Sandburg, Carl. *Abraham Lincoln: The War Years.* 4 vols. New York: Harcourt, Brace and Co., 1939.
Sheehy, Barry. *Montreal, City of Secrets: Confederate Operations in Montreal During the American Civil War.* Montreal: Baraka Books, 2017.
Terrill, A.E., ed. *Memorials of a Family in England and America, 1771–1851.* n.p., 1887.

Bibliography

U.S. Military Commission, *Trial of John Y. Beall: As a Spy and Guerrillero.* New York: D. Appleton, 1865.

Articles

Beall, Benjamin. "Jefferson Guards." *Spirit of Jefferson*, October 27, 1860.

Boteler, Alexander. "Recollections of the John Brown Raid by a Virginia Who Witness the Fight." *Century Magazine* (July 1883): 399–411.

Graham, Michael, S.J. "Popish Plots: Protestant Fears in Early Colonial Maryland, 1676–1689." *The Catholic Historical Review*, 79.2 (1993): 197–216.

Magruder, C.C. "Colonel Ninian Beall." *Records of the Columbia Historical Society, Washington, D.C.* (1937): 17–29.

Markens, Isaac. "President Lincoln and the Case of John Y. Beall." *American Historical Magazine* (May 1911): 425–435.

McIlvain, J.W. "Ninian Beall: An American Elder of the Seventeenth Century." *The Presbyterian Review* (New York: Scribner's, 1888).

Index

Numbers in **_bold italics_** indicate pages with illustrations

Accomack County 83
Aglionby 93
Aglionby, Elizabeth 58
Aglionby, Henry 11
Aglionby, Mrs. 14, 15
Allen, Col. William 36, 37, 40
Anderson, George S. 129–135, 153, 154, 156, 181
Ashby, Capt. Richard 30, 39
Ashby, Capt. Turner 30, 31, **_37_**, 39, 40, 41; and Battle of Bolivar 51–54
Ashley, Walter O. 115, 137, 152, 153; and seizing of *Philo Parsons* 116–119

Baker, William W. 67; privateering on Chesapeake 79–88, 90, 102, 137, 154
Baltimore 5, 15, 35, 60, 82–84, 86, 89, 100, 137, 158, 166, 167, 171–173
Baltimore and Ohio (B&O) Railroad 6, 20, 22, 24, 41, 46, 47, 50, 51, 177
Banks, Gen. Nathanel 50, 56
Barbour, Alfred M. 29–33, 37
Battle of Bolivar 50–54
Baylor, Col. R.W. 24
Baylor, Capt. William S.H. 32
Beall, George Brooke 12
Beall, Col. George Sr. 10
Beall, Hezekiah 10, 12, 18
Beall, Hezekiah (Beall's brother) 18, 57
Beall, John Yates 1, 2, **_8_**, 90, **_183_**; arrest in New York 138–142; and Brown's raid 22–24; capture 82–83; early years 11–18; Johnson's Island raid 112–126; Northwest Conspiracy **_101_**; privateering on Chesapeake 64–80; trial 152–160
Beall, Mary 18
Beall, Ninian 7–10
Beall, William 18, 21, 34, 164

Bee, Gen. Bernard E. 48
Blair, Francis 6, 34, 35, 177, 178, 181
Blair, Montgomery 6, 181
Bolivar Heights 22, 40, 50, 52, 102
Bolles, Maj. John A. J. 144, 150, 152, 153, 158–160, 165
Booth John Wilkes 26
Botelier, Alexander 150, 156
Botts, Capt. Lawson **_21_**, 22, 25–28, 37, 39, 43, 58; see also Botts Greys
Botts Greys 21–24, 27, 28, 43, 48
Brady, James Topham 2, 150, 165, 166, 168, 175, 178, 180, 181; background 151; defense of Beall 152–159
Brooke, Lt. John Mercer 66
Brown, John 12, 28, 30, 39, 46, 47, 51, 57, 68; Harpers Ferry raid 19–25, **_20_**; trial and execution 25–27
Brown, John, Jr. 125
Browning, Orville H. 5; appeal for Beall 171–181; colleague of Lincoln 171
Buffalo, NY 61, 106, 109, 112, 129, 130, 133–135, 144, 153, 154, 156, 188
Burley, Bennett G. 65–67, 80, 114, 127, 128, 138, 152, 153, 157, 159; and Johnson's Island raid 115–125
Butler, Gen. 88, 89, 132, 138, 140

Calvert County, Maryland 8–10; see also Prince Georges County
Charlestown, Virginia 2, 15, 18, 21, 26, 33, 36–38, 40, 42, 46, 49, 50, 51, 53, 54, 71, 93; see also Charles Town, West Virginia
Charlestown, West Virginia 12, 71, 102, 132, 191
Charlottesville, Virginia, 3, 15, 16, 26, 32, 56
Chesapeake Bay 2, 61, 63, 81, 100, 102,

207

Index

114, 124, 133, 143, 144, 149, 181, 184; privateering 64–76
Cincinnati Enquirer 6, 178
Clay, Clement C. 96, 98, 105, 106, 108, 131, 138
Cogswell, Maj. 179, 185
Cole, Charles Henry 109; and Johnson's Island raid 113–125
Coode, John 7–10
Copperheads 95, 99, 107, 108
Cromwell, Sir Oliver 7, 8

Davis, Pres. Jefferson 45, 60, 61, 63, 64, 94, 182, 194; Northwest Conspiracy 100–160; peace party 95–99
Detroit, Michigan 110, 113, 115, 116, 119, 124, 125, 128, 142
District of Columbia 9, 151
Dix, Maj. Gen. John Adams 64, 131, 132, 134, 142; and imprisonment of Beall 161–191, 194; and trial of Beall 145–160
Douglas, Henry Kyd 42, 47
Douglass, Frederick 19
Dumbarton 9, 10
Dunbarton 10; *see also* Dumbarton
Dundas, Canada 58, 59, 60
Dunkirk 134, 135, 138, 144, 150, 153, 154, 158, 181

Fitzgerald 81, 82, 102
Fort Columbus **141, 142**, 162, 167, 169
Fort Lafayette 6, 132, 140, 144, 145, 149, 156, 167, 168, 178, 193
Fort McHenry 84, 88, 90
Fort Monroe 30, 68, 71, 77, 88, 89
Fort Norfolk 88, **89**

Gansevoort, Capt. Geert 72
Geary, Col. John W. 50, 51–54, 57; *see also* Battle of Bolivar
USS *George W. Rodgers* 71
Georgian 129, 130
Gibson, Col. John T. 21, 22
Gillis, Lt. J.H. 76, 77
Gould, Maj. Jacob Parker 49, 50
Governors Island 142, 160, 161, 167, 169, 170, 173, 176, 189*n*, 191, 195
Greeley, Horace 106, 178
Green, Lt. Israel 25

Halleck, Gen. Henry 112, 146, 147, 158
Halltown 20, 21, 28, 37–40, 51, 53, 54
Hamilton, Ontario 133, 136, 174

Harper, Maj. Gen. Kenton 32, 41
Harpers Ferry 7, 19, **23**, 30, 32, 33, 36, 38, 45; Brown's raid 21–25
Hays, Edward 137, 138, 152, 154, 156
Headley, John W. 130, 132–134, 136, 156, 201
Herr, Abraham 49
Hill, Lt. Col., Bennett H. 119, 120, 123, 125
Hines, Col. Thomas H. 105, 107, 108, 130
Holcombe, James, P. 96, 106
Holliday, Col. William Mackay 102, 149, 150
Holt, Joseph J. 145, 146, 162–164, 168
Hunter, Andrew J. 53, 102
Hunter, Capt. James 120–122
Hyams, Godfrey J. 130–133

Imboden, Capt. John 30–33, 42
Ireland, Capt. David 73–75
Island Queen 118, 119, 125, 144

Jackson, Maj. Thomas Jonathan (Stonewall) 1–3, 26, **36**, **43**–46, 48, 49, 87; valley campaign 56–57; *see also* Stonewall's Brigade
Jefferson Guard 21, 36, 38
Jefferson County 7, 10–12, 18, 25, 27; secession 28–29, 39, 42, 51, 57, 60, 71, 111, 168, 174, 194
Jefferson, Pres. Thomas 7; and University of Virginia 15–17
Johnson's Island 59, 94, 99, 105, 129, 130, 132, 133, 153, 158, 198; raid 109–127
Johnston, Gen. Joseph E. 45–47, 49, 50
Jones, Lt. Roger: defense of Harpers Ferry 31–41

Kennedy, Robert Cobb 132, 133, 135, 136, 142, 143, 153
Kernstown 1, 56

Lake Erie 3, 59, 61–63, 94, 109, 111, 115, **116**, 123, 128, 130, 133, 137, 143, 150, 157, 158, 168, 181, 184
Lee, Edwin Gray 13, 19, 60, **61**, 68–70
Lee, Gen. Robert E. 2, 19, 24, 34, 71, 92, 102
Letcher, Governor John 30–32, 34, 37
Lieber, Franz 146–148, 160
Lieber Code 146–148
Lincoln, Pres. Abraham 2, 4, 5, 28, 30, 34–36, 56, 64, 95, 96, 98, 103, 104, 106, 115, 134, 145, 152, 155, 158; attitude

Index

toward pardons 161–165; and upholding Beall's sentence 165–182, 187, 189, 193
Lockwood, Gen. Henry H. 83–85, 87
Loudoun Heights 22, 46, 52, 53
Lucas, Daniel Bedinger 3, *13*, 17*n*, 28, 29*n*, 34, 60, 102, 141, 149, 156; on appeal for Beall 167–171, 174, 187, 189, 194

MacDonald, Roy 68, 71, 73, 74, 76
Mallory, Stephen R. 61–64, 71, 80*n*, 87, 94, 100, 154, 157, 166, 206
Martin, Col. Robert 129, 130–136, 156, 181
Maryland Heights 19, 22, 45, 50–52, 54
Mathews Courthouse 68, 73, 77, 78, 81
Maxwell, John 65, 67
McClure, James A.L. 5, 162; on appeal for Beall, 166–179, 183, 184, 186, 191
McGuire Ed 68, 75, 81, 83, 87, 88
USS *Michigan* 61, 95, 109, 110, *111*; and Johnson's Island conspiracy 112–125, 128–130, 157, 159
Middle Bass Island 116, 118, 122, 124, 125
Montreal, Canada 58, 98, 105, 131, 194
Morgan, Gen. John Hunt 59, 105, 129
Moseby, John Singleton 70

Niagara Falls 99, 106, 133, 136, 144
Norris, Maj. William 100
Northampton County 64, 72, 83
Northwest Conspiracy 103
Nunnery 11, 13, *14*, 15

O'Bryan, Martha 55, 59, 93, 169, 170, 183, 194
Old Dominion 29, 33–35
Osborne, Logan 29, 30, 36
Ould, Col. Robert 88, 173, 193

Patterson, Gen. Robert 46, 49
Philo Parsons 113, *114*, 115, 120, 124, 127, 137, 138, 144, 152, 153
Piankatank River 75, 77–79
Potomac 7, 22, 31, 35, 41, 45, 46, 49–51, 53, 63, 76, 103, 112
Prince Georges County 10
Pryor, Gen. Roger A. 6, 167, 168, 178, 182

Rains, Gen. Gabriel 66
Rappahannock River 68, 77, 78, 114
Richmond 26, 33, 37, 39, 55–58, 60, 63, 65, 67, 70, 72, 75–77, 80, 81, 87, 90, 92, 93, 102, 104, 106–108, 134, 140, 149, 161, 170, 182, 185, 191
Richmond Enquirer 30, 67
Richmond Whig 68, 88
Ridgely, Andrew Sterett 166, 167, 173, 177, 181
Riley's Hotel, 58, 59, 109
Ritchie, Albert 5, 167, 174, 175, 179–187, 191; appeal for Beall 171–173
Rives, Capt. Wright 161, 173, 174

St. Albans, VT 131
Sandusky, Ohio 109–111, 113, 114, 116–118, 120–125, 130, 132, 133, 135, 152, 153
Scott, Gen. Winfield 33, 34, 38
Seddon, James A. 39, 70, 94, 100, 102, 105, 109, 129
Shenandoah River 7, 10, 20, 22, 38, 47, 50, 51
Shenandoah Valley 7, 10, 55, 60, 63, 64, 176, 188, 192; *see also* Shenandoah River
Shepherdstown 12*n*, 13, 21, 22, 45, 46
Smith Sand 76, 78, 79, 81
Sons of Liberty 104, 106, 108
Stanton, Edwin 30, 72, 83, 111, 146, 168, 178
Staunton 26, 30–32, 56
Stedman, George C. 67, 83, 84, 102
Stevens, Thaddeus 6, 171, 158, 182
Stonewall's Brigade 43, 47, 57, 102, 111
Strother, David H. (Porte Crayon) 36, 41
Stuart, Lt. J.E.B. 24, 25, 92
Sullivan, Mary 168–170, 172

Thompson, Jacob 102, 103; and Johnson's Island raid 112–127, 130–133, 138, 140, 147, 150, 156, 173; and Northwest Conspiracy 104
Toronto, Canada 98, 112, 114, 115, 127, 129–133, 136, 138, 158

University of Virginia 5, 15–16, *17*

Vallandigham, Clement L. 103–104
Virginia 1–3, 11–13, 15, 18, 21, 24, 25, 27, 29–32, 34–36, 38, 40, 41, 43, 45, 51; *see also* Old Dominion
Virginia Free Press 29
Virginia Military Institute (VMI) 1, 3, 21, 26, 30, 37, 43

Index

Walnut Grove 11, 12, 18, 26, 53, 55, 93*n*
Washington, D.C. 5, 24, 27, 31, 32, 35, 40, 48, 50, 63, 95, 99, 106, 131, 132, 162, 167, 171, 173, 177–179, 181; *see also* District of Columbia
Washington and Lee University 1, 3
Wells, Gideon 72
West Virginia 12, 57, 70, 114, 191
Weston, Dr. S.H. 170, 183, 185, 187, 189, 191
Wheatly, Francis, L. 167, 172, 173, 181

Winchester 1, 31–33, 39, 40, 47, 49
Wise, Governor Henry 26–28, 30
Wistar, Gen. Issac 76–78, 80, 82, 83, 114

Yates, Charles 11, 15
Yates, Janet 11, 12
Yates, John, Jr. 11, 12, 14
Yates, John Orfeur 11, 14

Zion Episcopal Church 18, 26, 132, 190, 191

www.ingramcontent.com/pod-product-compliance
Lightning Source LLC
Chambersburg PA
CBHW052059300426
44117CB00013B/2209